What Others Are Saying Abo

"Chris Hayward and Ray Beeson are two of the most theologically balanced and spiritually sensitive leaders I know. Their experience and their impact in the body of Christ through their pastoral work and writings, as well as capable conference ministry, is known in many segments of the evangelical community. Their pastoral backgrounds highly qualify them as sensitive and wise communicators. I commend this book as a helpful resource for pastoral and group study, as well as a self-examining read for any church leaders wise enough to open their hearts to learn how to heal the hearts and souls of broken people."

—*Jack W. Hayford*
Chancellor
The King's University
Southlake, TX

"There are multitudes of people from all walks of life suffering from deep wounds and great pain. They are seeking help, hope, healing, and happiness. When they turn to the church for answers they are often hurt worse rather than embraced, understood, and led through a healing process. Most churches are ill prepared to bring wholeness to these hurting individuals. Often the leadership of the church hinders rather than helps by not having been equipped to address the real issues at the source. Deliverance and inner healing are misunderstood by much of the church, and shunned, ignored, or glossed over with holy-sounding answers. *Wounded in the Church* very accurately describes the seriousness of the issue, and pinpoints the existing need with many true-life examples. We are deeply indebted to Chris Hayward and Ray Beeson for exposing these problems, and especially for indicating ways to repair them. I love this book, and I know you will also!"

—*Doris M. Wagner*
Global Spheres, Inc.
Wife of C. Peter Wagner

"This book is long overdue. During my own years in pastoral ministry, I have seen and experienced everything described here. I remember well when my friend and brother in ministry, the author Ray Beeson, first began this project several years ago. Now, with the collaboration of Chris Hayward, they have together described "abusive congregations" at both the pastoral or leadership level and the congregational level. They describe so clearly the demonic culprit guaranteed to wound the Body of Christ—the perfectionistic 'religious spirit' which lies at the heart of all church abuse. The best part, however, is their presentation of biblical solutions. May the healing of the wounded in the church begin as Christ, the Master Healer, is exalted!"

—*Jim Ayars*
Pastor, Ventura Seventh Day Adventist Church
Ventura, CA

"Our churches and ministries are filled with hurting hearts—among them, those who too often have been wounded by the body of Christ itself. These are suffering souls we cannot ignore; problems we cannot sweep under the proverbial rug. We wound Christ when we wound others! *Wounded in the Church* is a powerful resource every church leader urgently needs. Filled with honest and heartbreaking stories, this book will open your eyes to the real emotional pain far too many are experiencing at the hands of those who should be loving them into the kingdom. Don't miss this timely and life-transforming message. It's needed now more than ever."

—*Dr. Dick Eastman*
International President
Every Home for Christ

"'And one will say to him, "What are these wounds between your arms?" Then he will answer, 'Those with which I was wounded in the house of my friends' (Zechariah 13:6). Any real discussion of the various kinds of abuse that have taken place in the church must embrace this allusion to Christ's suffering at the hands of God's people. Chris Hayward and Ray Beeson have combined their many years of ministry to hurting people and produced an impressive discussion of the reality that exists in too many churches. It's informative, instructive, and essential for those who believe that the church ought to be first and foremost a place of healing. Jeremiah 6:14 issues a strong rebuke from God, to those who have 'healed the hurt of My people slightly....' This book is timely and critical to the ministry of healing."
—*Bishop Joseph L. Garlington, Sr.*
Founder and senior pastor, Covenant Church
Pittsburgh, PA

"The word *church* means 'a gathering.' God's people gather to fellowship and to strategize for war. But both of these types of gathering can create woundings. Ray Beeson and Chris Hayward have developed the best book for the 'wounded church.' God's Word tells us not to forsake the assembling of ourselves, but when we end up wounded, the spirit of rejection attempts to force us into isolation. *Wounded in the Church* will not only help you heal, but get you positioned for your future."
—*Dr. Chuck D. Pierce*
President, Global Spheres Inc.
President, Glory of Zion Intl.

"Thank you, Ray and Chris, for writing a book which explores the many areas where God's people may experience hurt and wounds in churches and religious communities. A pastor recently said to me, 'If you as a pastor are not sensitive to the hearts of your people, then you are not in the right calling.' Above all else, the gathering of believers should be a safe place, where people find hope for restoration. As a cancer survivor I know every individual goes through dark seasons, and during those times, gentle love is the greatest treasure to be found in the believing community. God is a God of restoration and healing!"

—*Julie A. Dawson*
Youth With A Mission
Wife of John Dawson, International President of YWAM

"This book pulls the covers off the death-dealing processes in 'Christian' interactions. People are so hungry for this material. I have dwelt in such a dark land for so long, but now I am beginning to sense there is life in life. We have options. What we got isn't all there is that can be gotten. I have a birth certificate into His kingdom. Yes, that's it. No one can take away my experience or citizenship in that kingdom!"

—*Jean DeHaven*
Church hurt survivor

WOUNDED
IN THE
CHURCH

RAY BEESON &
CHRIS HAYWARD

WOUNDED
IN THE
CHURCH

WHITAKER
HOUSE

Note: This book is not intended to provide medical advice or to take the place of medical advice and treatment from your personal physician or counselor. Neither the publisher nor the author nor the author's ministry takes any responsibility for any possible consequences from any action taken by any person reading or following the information in this book. This book is in no way a replacement for any medical, mental, or counseling treatment from a qualified health care professional. Always consult your qualified health care professional before undertaking any change of treatment or regimen.

Wounded in the Church:
Hope Beyond the Pain

ISBN: 978-1-62911-813-0
eBook ISBN: 978-1-62911-814-7
Printed in the United States of America
© 2017 by Ray Beeson and Chris Hayward

Whitaker House
1030 Hunt Valley Circle
New Kensington, PA 15068
www.whitakerhouse.com

Library of Congress Cataloging-in-Publication Data (Pending)

1 2 3 4 5 6 7 8 9 10 11 12 ⨄ 25 24 23 22 21 20 19 18 17

ACKNOWLEDGMENTS

It is quite difficult to write a book without the insights and ideas of other people. This is why many books have a page for acknowledgments. Ours is no different. The following people have helped us to attain something we could not have done on our own. Jean DeHaven has been willing to share the pain that has made her life so difficult. Her ability to communicate hard to talk about subjects is exceptional. Lindsey Hoegger helped edit the material as well as did Rebecca Hayford Bauer and Darrel Faxon. These are the kinds of people that help you think through your material before it's too late. We thank them abundantly.

Ray Beeson

Chris Hayward

CONTENTS

INTRODUCTION

This book is about the pain and heartache that happens in churches. Collectively, the two of us have spent more than seventy years in ministry. During that time we have seen neglect, tactlessness, and blatant insensitivity fostered by some leaders and congregations resulting in the wounding of others. We realize it is not prolific in every church, but the wounding is significant and needs attention.

In this book, we've tried to prevent a broad-stroked, abstract, or overly professional approach to the problem by including specific stories, incidents, and issues that real people have lived through. We want to pinpoint the things that have brought heartache to so many, but at the same time we do not want examine these experiences in a detailed manner like a judge and jury. We simply want to show the pain regardless of who was right or who was wrong.

Sometimes people are abused by a leader and there is no justifiable excuse. It was wicked, harmful, and wrong. There are also times when leaders themselves have been abused by people within the congregation. It was inexcusable and unjustifiable. We will share stories both of those who have been abused by leaders and of those abused by the people they lead. And again, we're going to let the stories speak for themselves. We trust that healing will come when readers see that they are not alone and recognize that their wounds are a part of a vicious war involving all of mankind. We hope all will realize that simple words and small actions can bring about emotional pain and irreparable loss. We hope to bring an increasing awareness that the church belongs to Jesus and to Him alone, and that it is no small thing to mess with His people.

Our challenge is not to the church proper, the church that Jesus started two thousand years ago, but rather to the minority among us: those who have a reputation for abuse, those who preach holiness achieved by extra-biblical behaviors and beliefs, those who use manipulation to keep others in a belief system, and especially those who continue to linger in the Old Testament for their doctrinal expressions, exclusive of the grace that is found in the New Testament. We also want to address the too-common situation of churches that had, for the most part, been healthy, until an incident took place and someone was wounded, which was followed by ungodly responses that eroded the body. And lastly, we want to examine how the kingdom of darkness instigates and perpetrates small-mindedness, petty issues, and self-interest in order to destroy lives.

Numerous times in this book we refer to the fulfillment of the Old Testament law. When we do, we are not suggesting that the righteousness of the law has been done away with. If that were our point, we would further open the door to lawlessness which is the basis of human pain. What we are suggesting is that the fulfillment of the law is only accomplished through the indwelling Holy Spirit, and that a personal walk with Jesus is a walk in wholesomeness. We do not suggest that sin is of little concern to a gracious God. We believe in confession and repentance when necessary, always remembering *"that the goodness of God leads…to repentance"* (Romans 2:4). Furthermore, there needs to be a sharp distinction between what Christ accomplished for us on the cross and the further work of the Holy Spirit in us.

As a courtesy some of the names have been changed of those who, for whatever reason, have suffered in their Christian experience and shared their story in this book.

PART I: THE PAIN

1

I THOUGHT CHURCH WOULD BE DIFFERENT

Never be ashamed of a scar.
It simply means you are stronger than whatever tried to hurt you.
—*Unknown*

I am among those who have a hard time comprehending the love of God. You've no doubt heard the warning given to rambunctious children, "I may not see what you do, but God does." While that's true, it doesn't portray a loving God, but rather a God who keeps score—implying that when all is said and done, the bad will outweigh the good, by far. I was brought up with the image of God as a sternly frowning father figure who was always disappointed with me and the choices I made. That mind-set has built within me an incredibly powerful atmosphere of guilt. I am always waiting for God to say, "Okay, that's enough grace spent on Tom, he's just not panning out. Off to hell with him." That thought is so crushing to me it makes me choke even as I write this. When you said [in your e-mail], "Many people may go on serving God, but secretly do so simply and only because they do not want to go to hell," you hit the nail on the head. And you're right about the next point as well. It is a pretty miserable existence.   —*Tom*

Tom is not an unusual case. He is one of countless people who, for numerous reasons, are wounded in the church.

UNFULFILLED EXPECTATIONS

When they get up on a weekend, get in the car, and drive to Sunday service, most people are expecting to swing open the doors and find someone who is happy to say hi, someone to listen, or someone to help. It's certainly normal and healthy to expect that Christians in church will support and encourage and teach others how to walk out the Christian life.

But too much of the time, just the opposite is true.

One young lady moved several hundred miles to take a new job in another city and then began looking around for a church to attend. After about six months her father noticed she wasn't going to church. He asked why, and she responded, "Every church I attended acted as if I wasn't there. When I entered, nobody came to me offering assistance in finding what to do or where to go."

We can testify by experience that this is not uncommon. Over the years, we have visited far too many churches that were uninviting. But why? Why were they unfriendly? Why did we feel that this was just "church" and not a devoted group of believers? Why did it seem there was no interest in the people walking through their doors?

"A BIG AND PAINFUL BACKGROUND"

I chose the church because I needed a big and living God since I had a big and painful background. Two of the leaders in the church, a husband and wife, became my most trusted friends. But when I began attending small groups, each one said that my needs and questions indicated I was a deficient Christian. They said my pain was "because I was refusing to be healed," that I was a "stubborn sheep who needed its leg broken by the Shepherd." Or, that I was "not ready for this class." Sermons, especially during the last several years I attended there, reinforced my growing personal fear of the people and the pastor. When I told one of the leaders that I found a sermon painful and questionable, she said, "You can take a perfectly good sermon and ruin it!" When I said I felt no love in the church, she replied, "There is love here if you would just take it!"

I began to experience migraines in the Sunday services. The extreme headache, tunnel vision, and unstable walking were accompanied by confusion, fear, and exhaustion which caused me to miss work some Mondays. During the week, I began spending two to three hours a day in the Word to encourage and stabilize myself.

I eventually met with my two trusted friends and told them I was considering leaving the church to preserve my ability to function at my job. When I told them I disagreed with what the pastor said in some sermons, they became upset. In cold voices they said I was "not hearing correctly." Everything I tried to say was more evidence against me. I might as well have had no voice at all. The fact that I got headaches in church was unacceptable: "Why can't you see that every sermon isn't directed at you? You must not be spending time with the Lord during the week! This is because you are not resisting the enemy!"; "What? Aren't you over this yet?"; "We were raised in 'the little house on the prairie,' and you were raised in 'the house from hell.' We can't wrap our heads around what your experience was, and you can't wrap your head around ours." Then they told me they loved me.

A few days later I wrote my letter of church membership resignation. It was not accusatory toward the pastor or church. It did quote some of what my two friends said, using that as evidence that I did not fit into the church because of my culture and painful background, and in it I also apologized for not fitting in. I waited six days before phoning one of my trusted friends and informing her of my membership resignation. She paused, and in a very cold voice, said, "Well, I hope you find everything you are looking for!" I guess I had done the unforgiveable.   —Diane

She thought church would be different.

Diane's story was painful to read, not just for her sake, but also for the sake of all those experiencing similar pain and thinking that it is normal church life.

EMOTIONAL PAIN IS REAL

Regrettably, some leaders believe that emotional pain like Diane's cannot be a part of a true Christian's life. In fact they are quite glad when hurting people leave. Still others find it hard to conceive of the idea that someone can experience emotional pain while inside a church. And it really gets complicated when people are wounded in a church at the hands of those who are supposed to have "new life" in Christ. We expect those who are *outside* the church to do the wounding, but we don't expect those who call themselves Christians, let alone pastors, to wound.

In Christian circles where pain and suffering are not supposed to exist, they are considered to be signs of a lack of faith, and then laid at the doorstep of the hurting person. Some ardently insist that mental and emotional difficulties cannot touch Christians. They maintain that Christ's cross eliminates all suffering and sorrow, and if you do suffer, they say things like, "Just change your ways and everything will be all right"; or "If you just had enough faith, things would be different"; or "God is trying to teach you something." Such clichés provide quick steps to hopelessness.

Let's dispel any myths and face the truth head-on: emotional pain inside churches is real. It happens.

But why?

ARE CHRISTIANS BETTER THAN OTHER PEOPLE?

Misconceptions about emotional pain inside the church come from not having a good biblical understanding of sin. Why are Christians so often charged with being hypocrites? Because many have this notion that they are basically *good*. Their hypocrisy keeps some people from ever attending church, and those who do come are often disappointed to find that churchgoers are no better than the rest of the world.

If the church is going to properly address emotional pain caused by Christians, it needs to teach the biblical view of human sinfulness as found in Romans 3:9–18 and Jeremiah 17:9, instead of assuming that Christians are indeed "good people." Only when we have a proper understanding of sin can we understand the tremendous need for and the magnificent application of grace. Only then can the church extend grace to others.

Briefly consider these things about sin:

+ All of us have it and God wants us delivered from it through Jesus. (See John 3:16.)

+ All people, including Christians, deal with it throughout life. (See 1 John 1:10.)

+ The reality isn't that Christians are better than other people, it is that God has offered His Holy Spirit to help them live better, and they accepted the offer. (See Acts 4:31.)

Let's say that again. Christians are no better than anyone else. We trip over our feet and spill our coffee and have the capacity to intensely, terribly wound and be wounded by one another. Yet God has broken into our broken lives—and that has made all the difference.

THE REAL GOSPEL

Something in human thinking finds it hard to fathom that God *wants* to strengthen us in His righteousness, He *wants* to do something in us to bring about total transformation, and He *will* do that something through the indwelling of the Holy Spirit. Instead, our natural way of thinking is that the solution is to simply do more and be better on our own. But, as most of us have learned through personal experience, the harder we try, the worse we get.

It is here that God wishes to insert the gospel, to tell us that not only does the blood of Jesus cleanse from sin, but that the Holy Spirit is sent to help us to live for God and not to condemn us when we have trouble doing so. It is here that we learn God's love and begin to love Him in return.

The Holy Spirit's indwelling is an amazing grace that can transform unrighteous people into people with the ability for right living. In a religious sense, our human condition has us hardwired to believe that reaching up to God is the only way to please Him. But the message of hope, the gospel, is God reaching down to us. It's amazing that He wants us to know that *He truly loves us* and that it's safe for us to love Him, too. In this book we put great emphasis on the inner work of the Holy Spirit, which is based upon the work of Christ already accomplished on the cross.

Throughout history, not one of God's men or women arrived at a place even remotely close to perfection before God showed them His love. Abraham was a liar. Moses was a murderer. Jacob was a deceiver. King David confessed that it was God's gentleness that made him a great man. (See 2 Samuel 22:36.) Paul the apostle recognized that only by God working in us could we be the people He desired. (See Philippians 2:13.) All of God's great people were approached by God while in sin, deep sin. It is God's grace that brought them to a place of relationship and fellowship with Himself. Christians don't achieve a place in heaven as a result of hard work and good deeds; righteousness is a free gift from a loving God. (See Ephesians 2:8–9.)

And let's take it one step further. Many are told that Jesus died for their sins. However, what they are not often told is that Jesus also died to destroy the *effects* of sin—not only the sins they committed personally, but also the sins others have done to them. Christians (not just unbelievers) suffer from overwhelming amounts of guilt, shame, condemnation, rejection, and a host of other devastating emotional pressures that transform life into raging pain. But Jesus died for the severe pain we suffer, and He wants us free of it. And that means that He is not interested in adding more to our current heartache—it is neither biblical nor godly to keep trying to "atone" for our sins or "prove" that we are truly sorry. To all who truly repent, God forgives. (See 1 John 1:9.)

So yes, it is true that emotional pain is real—but so is God's help. What person, even a Christian, has the ability to reach into the inner recesses of his or her mind and put it to rest? That's why the gospel, the message that recognizes the need for God's help to solve problems, is so important. He promises to work in us both to will and to do of His good pleasure. (See Philippians 2:13.) The gospel includes His good intent to heal the soul (will, mind, emotions) and bring it to rest. (See Psalm 23:3; Matthew 11:28–30.)

We know emotional pain includes not only rejection and guilt, but also anxiety, depression, abandonment, condemnation, and shame, just to name a few. This book is for people who want to live an abundant life, but who seem to find so little of it no matter how hard they try. It is also a book about severe emotional difficulties arising from events that have happened in churches. It is our hope that as you read through these chapters you will find tangible help for the pain you have experienced. The reason we believe that is possible is because God is a God of hope—and He has a proven record as attested by millions of people.

Jesus will never disappoint. People do, but He doesn't and He won't. He is infallible, and He is incorruptible. He's not saying we have to accept the lie that all Christians and churches are safe and cozy. He would never whitewash a lie. But Jesus is our place of safety when people are not.

Whether you have been wounded in the church, or whether you have wounded others, the starting place is the same: empty hands before God who, because of the work of Christ, sends His Spirit of healing to fill the hands, protect the heart, and transform the life.

A PROVERB

The Lord's blessing brings wealth, and no sorrow comes with it.
                                                      (Proverbs 10:22 NCV)

PSALMS FOR THE WOUNDED

Be merciful to me, God; be merciful to me because I come to you for protection. Let me hide under the shadow of your wings until the trouble has passed.   (Psalm 57:1 NCV)

My God loves me, and he goes in front of me. He will help me defeat my enemies.   (Psalm 59:10 NCV)

God, my strength, I will sing praises to you. God, my defender, you are the God who loves me.   (Psalm 59:17 NCV)

2

THE PAIN GOES SO DEEP

What God says is best, indeed is best, though all men in the
world are against it. Seeing, then, that God prefers his religion;
seeing God prefers a tender conscience; seeing they that make
themselves fools for the kingdom of heaven are wisest;
and that the poor man that loveth Christ is richer than the
greatest man in the world that hates him: Shame, depart,
thou art an enemy to my salvation.
—*John Bunyan*

There was a pastor's assistant who served faithfully for many years, but eventually felt that the extra time she was putting in at church was a major strain on her marriage. She cut back her hours. And although she was still keeping up with her responsibilities, she was no longer able to do all the little extras she used to do. The pastor was so domineering that this assistant's "little extras" had included scheduling and taking his kids to doctor's appointments, sports events, and whatever else was on the calendar, along with running errands and many other things that were not in her job description. As the assistant began setting up boundaries at church, the pastor started telling the woman that her husband was a problem and needed deliverance.

The pastor conveyed he had no concern for his assistant's marriage or her work/life balance. In fact, her boundaries infuriated him. This tension went on for close to a year, until finally the assistant quit the job in frustration and anxiety. Her husband eventually left the church feeling rejected and abandoned by the pastor.

THE POWER OF EMOTIONAL PAIN

A physical body that is marked with wounds and bruises eventually heals and, although it always bears the scars, the pain is mostly gone. That person's body shows the evidence of physical pain. Emotional pain, however, leaves no visible mark. But that makes it no less agonizing: "When people feel emotional pain, the same areas of the brain get activated as when people feel physical pain."[1] The scars, however, are difficult to see and understand. We may perceive that a person has suffered from it, but we cannot tell how deep it goes.

As time goes on, emotional pain can become, in some ways worse than physical pain. The memory of physical pain does not cause you to re-experience the intensity of the actual pain. Emotional pain, on the other hand, can be re-experienced simply by recalling it. Tor Wagner, associate professor of neuroscience at the University of Colorado in Boulder, wrote in her research, "That may be why social pain is so painful: every time you remember it, you feel it all over again."[2]

Deep emotional pain usually has many layers, like a house that is been repainted time and again. Over the years, the many layers of emotional pain result in pessimism, resentment, criticism, skepticism, cynicism, bitterness, and a host of other traits that can destroy relationships.

It is doubtful that anyone can find an agony worse than that of emotional pain. Nothing seems more difficult to deal with than the power of rejection, the trauma of shame, the heartache of hopelessness, or the torment created by loss—of a job, a family member, a close friend, or even a pet. And every time we remember it, we feel it all over again.

There are times when we scream, "No, no, no, it didn't happen, it couldn't have happened. If only I had known ahead of time I could have prevented it!" Then the question, "Did I do something wrong to cause this?" And the unending, *why, why, why?* Often a strange and horrible

1. Alan Fogel, "Emotional and Physical Pain Activate Similar Brain Regions," *Psychology Today* blog, April 19, 2012, https://www.psychologytoday.com/blog/body-sense/201204/emotional-and-physical-pain-activate-similar-brain-regions.
2. Maia Szalavitz, "New Test Distinguishes Between Physical From Emotional Pain in Brain for First Time," *Time*, May 6, 2013, http://healthland.time.com/2013/05/06/a-pain-detector-for-the-brain.

sensation flows through the body like an electric current while the whole world seems both surreal and uncaring. People who mean good and want to help come—but do not understand the words to say. The pain only ever seems to intensify, never diminish.

While some people deal with emotional pain and difficult questions better than others, emotional anguish invariably has the power to ostracize us from people around us, usually not because they don't care, but because they don't know how to empathize with people who are enduring mental torture. It also is easy for both sides to assume that the other person's pain does not come close to their own, or that everyone else is free of deep inner pain. Sometimes our own pain shouts so loud we can't hear the pain in others.

One of the reasons we, the authors, speak and write about emotional pain is because of the sheer number of people who suffer from it. It is a real need; for whatever reason, the numbers are staggering. Psychologists, doctors, and religious leaders have addressed it for millennia, yet we believe the issue today warrants another voice (or make that two!). We have chosen to deal with a segment of emotional pain that relates to religion and, especially, to the Christian church.

Most of the pain we have found among Christians has to do with abuse that caused feelings of rejection: shame, neglect, ridicule, disrespect, manipulation, contempt, verbal attacks, and sexual abuse. Some of these actions were deliberate and some unintentional, but the result was the same: believers orphaned from spiritual life and fellowship with God's people. Those affected can suffer from deeply embedded scars (victimizations) without the ability and resources to personally resolve the condemnation and shame that continues to say, "You got yourself into this mess and it's time you do something to get yourself out." Or, even worse, "It was your fault. You've made your bed, now lie in it."

At a domestic violence shelter, a group of adult women who had been severely sexually and physically abused as children discussed church. Considering the levels of trauma experienced, certainly our Savior would find a good market for His ability to bind up wounds and heal the broken-hearted. And indeed, some of the women said church held a little comfort, but only if they didn't share anything about themselves. What a rebuke to the church!

CHRISTIANS AND CONDEMNATION

Christianity is often thought of as something positive, as a *good*, and it should be because it is. It is logical to believe that if it is positive, Christians must also be positive in demeanor and attitude. That may sound good, but the problem is that even though Christianity is *good*, its members still contain far too much of the human disposition toward sin, as we discussed in the previous chapter. We are at the stage of "becoming" not that of "arrival." Life, even for the Christians, is a journey about getting better.

In churches where restoration by grace and the help of the Holy Spirit is not embraced and instead domination (that is, excessive control, authority, and supremacy) is the rule, where both biblical and church-specific standards are the focus of administration and discipline is carried out by demanding leadership, then the Christian, instead of positively journeying in freedom toward excellence in Christ, will usually be sidetracked by feelings of rejection, unworthiness, and negativity.

We know of nothing more detrimental to the human spirit than negativity. When people see God as someone waiting for them to come to a place of perfection before allowing fellowship with Him, it makes God seem impersonal and unfriendly. Somebody to be afraid of. Living in an atmosphere that constantly emphasizes personal righteousness without emphasizing God's help is both frustrating and discouraging. It can ruin a life in the worst possible way—no friends, no fellowship, no hope, no goodness anywhere. Instead, loneliness, constant criticism, hating life, self-justification, and seclusion run rampant.

It doesn't take much research to find that a large number of people wounded in the church were wounded by an overwhelming amount of anxiety concerning their eternal state or by being verbally reprimanded in a way that brought condemnation. In most cases the wounding was the result of loveless attitudes from people who demanded perfection from anyone professing to be a Christian. It's hard to believe that such abuse would come from Christian leadership or a member of a congregation, but it does.

BOBBY'S STORY

At the time, Bobby was ten years old. He didn't respond well to authority figures. He told a local pastor that the reason he attended church was because everybody at home hated him. His perception of any attempts to discipline him for misbehavior was that the discipliner hated him. At church, he constantly acted up and rebelled. His behavior was so bad, it was disrupting the rest of the children and interrupting youth activities. Frustrated and worn out, the consensus of his teachers and the church council was that he be forbidden from coming to church. One council member even suggested that if his misbehavior continued, the entire junior youth program should be suspended.

Upon hearing this report from the council, the pastor asked if any of its members had visited Bobby in his home. None had. "Do any of you know he has no father figure in his life?" None did. "Do any of you know that older siblings and mom are almost never home?" Again, negative. "Do any of you know that the grandmother attempting to raise him is probably in her upper seventies?" They did not. But when the council learned that the pastor had befriended the boy and promised to take him fishing, they accused him of rewarding Bobby for his bad behavior. When an appeal was made to the council to give grace a chance, their response was to point out the necessity of obeying rules. They did eventually grudgingly consent to a two-month trial period to see if it would change the Bobby's behavior.

THE SPIRIT OF JESUS

Bobby's story reflects a systemic problem of the rules and regulations of religion replacing the Spirit of Jesus. A church that is not led by the Holy Spirit has to have a rule for everything. There are countless numbers of Bobby's who should have found healing within the church but did not.

New York Times best-selling author Christine Wicker sounds a much-needed alarm: "A child's open heart is easy tinder for the fiery sermons of evangelical preachers. A thousand righteous conflagrations have burned in mine, leaving behind a residue of guilt, shame, and perfectionism that none of my reclamation efforts has quite cleaned up. I have some of the purging fury that child-converts-turned-apostates use to protect themselves, and I have the despair that goes with it."[3]

Many people have trouble with Christianity because of its absolutes, rules, and requirements. But we have found that their hesitancy about the do's and dont's is usually not the biggest hurdle. Most people know that regulations are necessary for harmony and, for the most part, are willing to accept biblical mandates. No, the biggest hurdle to Christianity is the contest over Jesus and who He is, and the way some Christians try to represent Him, especially with judgmental, critical, and reproachful attitudes. To bluntly sum up such a careless Christian mind-set: "If you are a sinner, you are going to hell."

Let us state something that irritates us perhaps as much as it irritates those who have come to hate religion: far too many Christians do not represent the heart and character of God in word or attitude. Some of us shudder when we see what some people do in the name of Christianity. We would like to police our own ranks but find it hard when free will and free speech allow almost any doctrine and teaching to exist, all in the name of Christ. To our dismay there are those among us who minister with cruel, insensitive, and callous actions.

It isn't Jesus or the gospel that destroys, it is people—people whose temperament are not in line with God's Spirit. From the beginning, the gospel was never preceded by wrecking crew set on dismantling before it began to build.

Harsh preaching, teaching, and discipline appeal to some personalities, but they do not represent God's personality. The strict and even abrasive handling of people suggests to the churchgoer that God is severely upset with mankind—that He wants to be known as One who is set on severe judgment and punishment. It is tough to try to understand why such leaders of abusive churches believe they have the right to unleash critical and condemning attitudes. It seems these leaders are proud and convinced of their position, believing that surely God would never disagree with their views and attitudes. It is even more surprising that some church people

---

3. Christine Wicker, *The Fall of the Evangelical Nation* (New York: HarperCollins Publishers, 2008), x–xi.

continue to listen to cruel and arrogant preaching that does nothing but drive people away from God.

We do realize that not all churches function the same. There are many who are kind and truly interested in ministering to all aspects of a person's life. However, our concern is with exposing those who are causing terrible wounding, who, in what they call "reaching out" to others, are instead selfish, cold, and even cruel in the way they treat people in general. They are the unfortunate reason why it is not unusual to find people inside and outside the church who carry deep emotional scars and open wounds from the church, which the church is making no effort to heal.

Make no mistake, we do understand that the Christian life is not a hearts-and-rainbows story where we all get a go-directly-to-heaven card at the end. God is a God who will judge, and some of that judgment will be severe. But to present Him properly it is important to start with what He says about Himself. He says that He wants reconciliation and restoration far *more* than punishment. That is precisely what the cross is about:

> But God, who is rich in mercy, because of His great love with which He loved us, even when we were dead in trespasses, made us alive together with Christ (by grace you have been saved), and raised us up together, and made us sit together in the heavenly places in Christ Jesus, that in the ages to come He might show the exceeding riches of His grace in His kindness toward us in Christ Jesus. (Ephesians 2:4–7)

It is not a stretch to say that every person God has ever used for His glory came to understand first and foremost the kindness of a loving God. Not one of them labored under a dreadful kind of fear or the heavy weight of condemnation. (See Romans 8:1.)

HARPING ON HELL

By failing to understand the gospel, many trample on God's character and alienate people with hate speech against "unrighteous America." Who is going to come to the God we say is so great and loving if we use such discouraging speech? Not only do judgmental, critical, and reproachful attitudes hurt those inside the church, they also put weapons in the hands of non-Christians who dismiss all of Christianity because of the irrational and erratic people found in its ranks.

One pastor railed about how the church wasn't standing up and re-taking America from the ungodly liberals. He said our founding fathers were born again and meant for this to be a born-again nation, but they—the ungodly liberals—are taking away our Christian rights! Therefore we must arm ourselves, buy guns, and defend our homes from anyone who tries to confiscate our property, because that is what's coming!

This man, like so many others, preaches a message of impending doom. He joins the ranks of religious leaders sounding a panic alarm, not as a constructive warning against the moral and ethical turpitudes sometimes found among believers, but rather as a swooping tirade against culture as a whole. They are marked by almost incessant harping on hell and assertions that they are the only true church. On Monday, they march out into the world having little or no idea what it is that they must do to solve the problems of ungodliness. Instead, they have only alienated and further convinced believers and unbelievers alike to stay far away. Unfortunately, their cultural isolation and self-imposed seclusion are a breeding-ground for abuse. Don't be confused. Hell is certainly something that needs to be addressed as a literal subject. It's the *manner* in which some do it that destroys spiritual lives.

The church is involved in a real battle against evil where casualties are inevitable. And if it's a battlefield, there will be wounded warriors who need compassion and attention. But wherever a hawkish or warlike attitude exists in churches, you will seldom find a battlefield hospital of mercy and healing. Even such a church's sermons, however polished and well-delivered, utterly fail to speak to the hearts of the hurting. They fall on the wounded like cold rain.

If the people of these churches went even a little bit out of their own bubbles, they would find that God has raised up a church far beyond their imaginations; a church that believes in holiness, righteousness, faith, eternity, heaven, and even hell, but a church that also believes that the greatest way to reach people is to tenderly lift them up, heal them, show them mercy—not constantly tear them down with fear.

A CHRISTIAN WORLDVIEW

Unbelievers might look at us and ask, "Well, if the church has all these problems, why are you still in it?" After all, the clash between the Christian worldview and any other worldviews can seem colossally unnecessary, especially when it results in such pain as we've just described! The Christian beliefs of creation, fall from relationship with God, reconciliation and restoration through Jesus, both the Old and New Testaments sanctioned by God, eternal life as well as eternal death, and the current war with Satan and his demons, have caused and continue to cause an appalling amount of nasty debates and separations. It has been the source of dispute for over two thousand years.

Additionally, to the pragmatist, the impoverished condition of the world is ample proof that Jesus and His followers were a hoax. After all, the concept of an all-powerful God and a very bad world are incompatible; unless of course this very powerful God is also a very bad God. And to the secular psychologist, the idea that Christians could provide help to those wounded in the church would be laughable. That would be like asking a lion to stitch up a wounded deer!

We see and recognize the problems of the church and of a dysfunctional world, but at the same time we refuse to accept the non-Christian claim that Christians are irrational and thus can provide no real answers to help hurting people. We recognize that in many cases our revelational knowledge from the Bible and the Spirit of Christ has no value in the arena of current non-biblical "rational" thinking. But here's the reason why a Christian looks to a different knowledge:

> *Even so no one knows the things of God except the Spirit of God. Now we have received, not the spirit of the world, but the Spirit who is from God, that we might know the things that have been freely given to us by God. These things we also speak, not in words which man's wisdom teaches but which the Holy Spirit teaches, comparing spiritual things with spiritual. But the natural man does not receive the things of the Spirit of God, for they are foolishness to him; nor can he know them, because they are spiritually discerned.* (1 Corinthians 2:11–14)

This is why Jesus warned that His disciples would be hated for following Him and His message. It is foolishness to the world, but it's still true, and we continue to bank our lives on it. And He has never disappointed us.

"I WILL BUILD MY CHURCH"

Since the time of Jesus, the church has been made up of sinners and has always had problems. In spite of accusations, we have found nothing to support the idea that the New Testament church was either better or worse than today's church. The church still wrestles with problems. Suppositions, assumptions, and speculations abound, but it is tough to come by hard facts to support the idea that the church is any different from when it first began in terms of its warfare struggles. We say this to challenge the errant perspective that everything in Christianity is getting worse and worse by the millisecond.[4]

Just like the church today, the early church found itself embroiled in dissension, false doctrine, and division on every side. The Scriptures, as well as empirical evidence, support the conviction that God is still wonderfully and powerfully in control of what He started and is still working to make people whole again. Conspiracy theories and a world without hope do not fit into God's kingdom perspective. If, like some believe, the world *is* getting worse, we continue to be convinced that through God's grace the church will remain a healing agent in a broken world.

Much of this book deals with the unethical and immoral control that some people try to leverage over others in the church. Our use of the word control recognizes that it is necessary and even God-given for people to be in control. Paul tells believers in the book of Acts, "*Therefore take heed to yourselves and to all the flock, among which the Holy Spirit has made you overseers, to shepherd the church of God which He purchased with His own blood*" (20:28). It's the *way* control is used when it damages people that concerns us: "*I wrote to the church, but Diotrephes, who loves to have the preeminence among them, does not receive us. Therefore, if I come, I will call to mind his deeds which he does, prating against us with malicious words. And not content*

---

4. This is a most difficult subject because of so many perspectives. When we say the church is still the same, we mean that everything that God established concerning the church is still intact. What has changed is church culture, and there are times when cultural influence starts to change biblical emphasis.

with that, he himself does not receive the brethren, and forbids those who wish to, putting them out of the church" (3 John 9–10).

Although we, the authors, have also experienced our share of pain within churches, this book is built on our firm belief that God has a church, that He loves the people of this world, and that He wants to restore them to His kingdom. It is undeniable that His true church is hard to find and sometimes leaves little evidence of its powerful reality. However, because we have seen the church alive and well, we believe it. Our answer will never be, "just give up on church."

Writer Reggie McNeal makes a similar observation, "The current church culture in North America is on life support. It is living off the work, money, and energy of previous generations from a previous world order.... Please don't hear what I am not saying. The death of the church culture as we know it will not be the death of the church. The church Jesus founded is good; it is right. The church established by Jesus will survive until he returns. The imminent demise under discussion is the collapse of the unique culture in North America that has come to be called 'church.'"[5]

So what does the church need to give up on? What parts of church culture need to "die"? *Where is all this pain coming from?* We'll look at that in the next chapter.

A PROVERB

Good people hate what is false, but the wicked do shameful and disgraceful things.   (Proverbs 13:5 NCV)

PSALMS FOR THE WOUNDED

But the LORD saves his servants' lives; no one who trusts him will be judged guilty.   (Psalm 34:22 NCV)

LORD, you have been watching. Do not keep quiet. LORD, do not leave me alone. Wake up! Come and defend me! My God and LORD, fight

---

5. Reggie McNeal, *The Present Future* (Hoboken, NJ: Jossey-Bass, 2009), 1.

for me! LORD my God, defend me with your justice. Don't let them laugh at me. (Psalm 35:22–24 NCV)

Troubles have surrounded me; there are too many to count. My sins have caught me so that I cannot see a way to escape. I have more sins than hairs on my head, and I have lost my courage. Please, LORD, save me. Hurry, LORD, to help me. (Psalm 40:12–13 NCV)

3

WHERE DOES ALL THIS PAIN COME FROM?

Everyone has a plan 'til they get punched in the mouth.
—*Mike Tyson*

If you were to ask a group of Christians why human beings suffer pain, most would reply, "sin." While yes, that is technically correct, it is akin to saying oranges produce orange juice. It's the obvious answer—but doesn't give the details of *how*, *why*, or *what*, and can even trivialize the pain. Are we talking about your sin, someone else's sin, or just the effect of living in a world where sin, pain, and difficulty exist? There are many areas from which church woundedness originates, and we could in no way make an exhaustive list. However, here are a few key sources:

THINKING THAT NEVER TRIES TO AUTO-CORRECT

There is not a single person on earth who has all the knowledge there is to have of the truth (obviously). All of us are in the process of learning, and each day is an opportunity to grow and mature. Many among us will admit that early in our faith we were zealots for Christ and in the process did some harm. Have we, the authors, ever said something or taught something that needed to be retracted because it didn't present the whole truth? Yes! That is a reality for anyone who wants to stay center-lined with God. There are many things that seem so right in the moment, but in the end prove to be lopsided at best.

However, when we persistently maintain that we should have all the answers to all questions tossed our way *right now*, we put ourselves in a box that prohibits growth because we stick with what seems right and shut our eyes to whether it eventually looks lopsided or not. Bad moral reasoning quickly develops into deception and/or even unethical behavior.

Erroneous thinking can cause huge emotional difficulty. Surprisingly, a great deal of it happens *after* conversion. It usually begins in leaders, no matter their age, who have not developed sufficiently to understand the entire gospel, encompassing God's love, patience, and nature as a Father. Often it's a result of *fear* that forbids them from going beyond their current knowledge and teaching.

In 1958, Lawrence Kohlberg, then a graduate student at the University of Chicago, developed a theory that claimed moral reasoning has six stages of development. It's a widely accepted theory that gives insights into ethical and unethical behavior. Kohlberg based his work on Piaget's Stages of Cognitive Development. Now, we don't mean to give a lecture in psychology, but what we want to point out (which you can study more deeply on your own) is that one stage of development tends to grab people and keep them from moving forward into the next stage, breaking their moral development. And it is an extreme danger for the Christian. The stage is when one learns that "rules are based on principles that if broken have specified consequences. It carries the thought that rules must not and cannot be broken without serious penalties. Rules are the only things that are to regulate our lives."

This stage of understanding is important for the Christian, because there is a law we must understand and follow, but it is not the end of the truth. If anyone gets stuck in this truth, they will become legalistic, will refuse to listen to the opinions and values of other people, will be unwilling to change their thinking, and will not consider other thought patterns that challenge their ideas. They will not be open to expanding any kind of thought processes that don't already fit into their thinking, because that might threaten the rules that they desperately believe they must follow to avoid the serious penalties. As a result they are often negative toward and critical of the people around them. They are generally huddled in a small enclave, shut off from the rest of the world. To venture out and try to understand how other people think is, to them, a compromise of the rules that cannot be broken. They leave no room for the Holy Spirit to help them to be in the world but not of the world. And that's where much of the wounding takes place.

INABILITY TO LISTEN

Yet, whether they are logical and biblical or not, too many people develop a firm basis for beliefs and refuse to have them tampered with. Out of fear of being contaminated by other thinking processes, they prohibit any other moral or ethical views from entering into their belief system. They become stunted in mental, emotional, and spiritual growth. Some can be identified by a narrow-minded, arrogant, and often bitter mind-set. In extreme cases, they refuse to listen to reason, refuse to give mercy, and show no grace.

It is sad to see people who cannot dialogue or hear something contrary to their belief system, especially when others, who by the Holy Spirit and God's Word, sense that something is wrong. That sensitivity from friends or neighbors that something is wrong enables two good things. First, it can cause us to search the Scriptures to find out if we have missed something and if we are wrong. Second, it can affirm our own belief systems and allow us to share warmly the things that someone else may have missed.

INABILITY TO DISAGREE

The daughter of a "pastor's kid" watched her dad go through much pain within his ministry and church. In sympathy for him, she formed unconscious rules that governed the rest of her life, including the rule, "church people must never disagree with the pastor."

When this pastor's kid became a respected adult, she overheard a fellow churchgoer say that a sermon they just heard was painful. Her instant reaction was to punch her friend's shoulder, and then she grew flustered and embarrassed when her friend reacted. She even said she didn't do it, and then said it wasn't that bad. Her rule had taken on a life of its own, and became an embarrassing trap.

Sometimes sensitive children growing up in a rigid and disconnected environment, like this pastor's kid, need to create their own reality to survive. In the process they try to find a safe place where they never hear the words, "What's the matter with you?" Later we see them with severe emotional problems and addictions. Their survival mechanisms, such as "rules" to live by, may be messed up, but the rules make them feel safe. They look for people who won't put them down, contradict them, or make them question themselves or their rules.

ISOLATIONISM

The church attempts to *"give an answer"* for what it believes (see 1 Peter 3:15 KJV), but it has not done well in giving answers for what it does *not* believe. Our biblical illiteracy keeps us from being able to dialogue with issues outside of our own understanding. A poor understanding of apologetics (the theological defenses and proofs of Christianity) and a refusal to look into what others deem truthful has left us with an inability to adequately share the gospel. The result is isolation, intentional isolation. The unconscious rationale seems to be: "Stay as far away from the world's thinking as possible. Get too close and you'll be tainted." This is naïve, irresponsible, and unbiblical.

Thanks to isolationism, we have developed some of the worst problems the world has ever known. Isolationism encourages an "us against them" mentality. It tricks us into thinking that everybody we see at the grocery store is our enemy—or worse, that any Christian who belongs to another church or denomination is out to get us and must be shunned and abhorred. History has shown time and again that in more violent periods of history, churches have even killed others on basis of their beliefs—because the others were in the "them" not "us" category.

Walter Martin once noted that we have become as a society of door-slammers and shade-pullers, afraid to present an argument to the various cults who come to our door. The Scripture challenges us be ready in season and out of season, whether it's convenient or inconvenient, to give an answer for the hope that is in us. But secretly many of us do not want to give an endorsement (that is, support, witness, validation, and approval) either of God or of the local church because we fear rejection. If there is nothing to certify and verify God's power by the indwelling Holy Spirit, and if there is no vibrant hope within us, it is hard to convince ourselves to risk rejection to market something we don't have. These kinds of Christians live a sort of mechanical Christianity that disallows God's power. Some participate in witnessing programs, but the programs rarely bring people to Christ because of their machinelike, non-relational approach.

Those who do respond become notches on the participant's spiritual gun and a number to report to a program director.

As mentioned earlier, we are to be *in* the world but not *of* the world. (See John 17:16.) What does that mean? Precisely that we are to be *insulated* from the world by the Holy Spirit but not *isolated* from unbelievers. How can we be the light of the world if our isolationism and refusal to communicate prevents others from seeing the light? The best way to communicate Christ is to patiently learn the unbelievers' language before we present ours, which involves being, as Jesus was, in contact with the people of the world on their own turf.

It is entirely reasonable that we would have strong opinions and beliefs about certain subjects based upon what we feel is a biblical understanding. However, there is great value in opening our hearts to other people with different persuasions. First of all, it can sharpen our own reasoning for taking such a stance. Second, it allows for the possibility that we might be wrong, or that our argument needs some refining. But probably the greatest value of listening to someone else's opinion is that we honor them and recognize their worth as a human being by giving them a voice. Consider this: one of the first things a dictatorial society does is to take away the voice of the individual—the right to speak one's mind. We seldom question the first amendment of our constitution which we know to be freedom of speech. Yet how many times do we violate this principle within the church by not allowing someone with a differing opinion to share their thoughts?

Isolationism was common and accepted before communication systems brought us massive quantities of information from multicultural sources. Television, the internet, and smartphones now show us a world no one dreamed of even thirty years ago. This cross-culture awareness can actually make one stronger and less likely to be thrown off-balance by differences of race, language, color, and culture. As Mark Twain observed, "Travel is fatal to prejudice, bigotry, and narrow-mindedness, and many of our people need it sorely on these accounts. Broad, wholesome, charitable views of men and things cannot be acquired by vegetating in one little corner of the earth all one's lifetime."[6]

6. Mark Twain, *The Innocents Abroad* (Hartford, CT: American Publishing Company, 1869), 650.

A RELIGIOUS SPIRIT

The religious spirit is an agent of Satan assigned to prevent change and to maintain the status quo by using religious devices, namely, manipulation, domination and control. Without the willingness to listen, Christians embrace this religious spirit, become judgmental, and display an overwhelming lack of compassion. Many of them refuse to dialogue with anyone who doesn't agree with them. In the process, people outside looking in are not only offended, they begin to believe that all Christians are this way. Such was the case with John and his friend:

> John was especially frustrated by Christians who routinely come up with implausible excuses to defend their faith, which they didn't really examine—as if defending the faith with any excuse mattered more than having a genuinely good reason to believe in the first place. John's friend picked up on the subject and went on to say, "Discussing our experiences, we realized we'd both encountered many Christians like this, who color their entire perception of reality with the assumption that they *have* to be right, and therefore the evidence must somehow fit. So they think they can make up anything on the spur of the moment and be 'sure' it's true…. John and I also shared the same experiences in another respect: when their dogmatism meets our empiricism, slander is not far behind. I have increasingly encountered Christians who accuse me to my face of being a liar, of being wicked, but not wanting to talk to God, of willfully ignoring evidence—because that is the only way they can explain my existence. I cannot be an honest, well-informed pursuer of the truth who came to a fair and reasonable decision after a thorough examination of the evidence, because no such person can exist in the Christian worldview, who does not come to Christ. Therefore, I must be a wicked liar, I must be so diluted by sin that I am all but clinically insane, an irrational madman suffering some evil psychosis."[7]

7. http://infidels.org/library/modern/richard carrier/whynotchristian.html (no longer available).

Although we do not agree with the conclusion of John and his friend, that is not our point. Our point is that many people have found an excuse to not pursue Christ because of loveless Christians. It's an age-old problem that we constantly have to deal with, and makes you wonder what gets into some people that makes them think they have the right to slander, insult, and vilify.

SUSPICION

Why are some leaders incapable of listening? Why do some Christians cut you off before you have a chance to share your opinion? Why are some so incapable of hearing any other opinion besides their own? What makes them so hardhearted and why do they make others feel inadequate? In other words, why do they reject the people God wants to save? Why do they reject God's words, "I do not really want the wicked to die" (Ezekiel 18:23 NCV)?

John Bevere suggests, "Not unlike Saul [King Saul], many leaders in our homes, corporations, and churches are more concerned with their goals than with their offspring.... How many leaders have cut off men under them because of suspicion? Why are those leaders suspicious? Because they are not serving God. They are serving a vision. Like Saul, they are insecure in their calling, and that breeds jealousy and pride. They recognize qualities in people that they know are godly, and they are willing to use those people as long as it benefits them. Saul enjoyed the success of David until he saw it as a threat to him. He then demoted David and watched for a reason to destroy him."[8]

FAVORITISM

The church has been warned against putting those who have the greater influence, especially the rich, in places of high esteem, and in the process rejecting the more common people. (See James 2:1–4.) This is not to suggest that the rich are bad people, but they certainly are a group to which many gravitate at the expense of others. No doubt most of us don't realize that we are doing these things, largely because of the pain we fail to see in those whom we are offending. When we allow our culture to dictate what

---

8. John Bevere, *The Bait of Satan* (Lake Mary, FL: Charisma House, 1994), 37.

groups of people we accept or reject, we see "politically correct" thinking at work.

In the world, we make daily decisions to extract ourselves from things we do not like, often in a capricious manner. Unfortunately this pattern follows us into the church, resulting in cliques, divisions, and conflicts. We have followed it so much as a cultural habit that we don't realize when we are shunning fellow believers and causing pain. But we cannot accept favoritism in the ranks of the church. It is not in keeping with the concept of a biblical community.

It's so engrained in the patterns of our lives and hearts that no command will make us suddenly turn and begin caring for the less fortunate. And God doesn't expect that to happen. His plan is much more subtle. If He can draw us into His heart so that we see through His eyes, we are much more prone to care. If you have little concern for the hurting, hang around the Person who does. People who walk with God don't arbitrarily shun other people.

It is difficult to walk with controlling people who try to command your actions and motivations before your heart is involved. When your heart is engaged you have a sense of satisfaction in, as James would say, simply visiting *"orphans and widows in their trouble"* (James 1:27).

OTHER SOURCES OF PAIN

Other sources of pain tied up in the ones in this chapter include:

+ Lack of compassion
+ Insensitivity
+ Dogmatism
+ Inflexibility
+ Accusatory
+ Jealousy
+ Blame

What does pain from these sources look like in the life of the one wounded? Neglect, rejection, abuse, shame, and hopelessness. Everybody has experienced pain, and you could probably add significantly to the list we have made. But the real issue has more to do with how we respond to the pain we are experiencing. As we continue to move through this book it is our expectation that you will see how you can move beyond *your* pain.

A PROVERB

No one else can know your sadness, and strangers cannot share your joy.   (Proverbs 14:10 NCV)

PSALMS FOR THE WOUNDED

LORD, listen to my words. Understand my sadness. Listen to my cry for help, my King and my God, because I pray to you.
                              (Psalm 5:1–2 NCV)

But let everyone who trusts you be happy; let them sing glad songs forever. Protect those who love you and who are happy because of you.
                              (Psalm 5:11 NCV)

4

NOBODY SEES ME

Only when it's dark enough can you see the stars.
—*Ralph Waldo Emerson*

One man joined a local church and was excited to get to work. After a while he somehow got on the wrong side of the pastor and from then on his ministry began to diminish. He was kept out of the information loop that was required to facilitate his work. The neglect was obvious and painful. His excitement for ministry in the church, of course, dwindled significantly.

Neglect from leadership eventually destroys community and leads the church into failure. In this chapter, we will discuss the power of neglect in relation to the health and vibrancy of the church.

THE TERRIBLE POWER OF NEGLECT

We've been conditioned to think in terms of the word "rejection" more than the word "neglect," but in so many ways it is neglect that brings on rejection. This isn't hairsplitting, it's getting to the bottom of why and how certain kinds of pain, in this case the pain of rejection, takes hold.

Neglect can be manifested in a number of ways. People reject people. People reject responsibility. People reject society. People reject God. Somewhere inside of us, in differing degrees, we want to push people away from us while at the same time wanting to be accepted.

Most agree that neglect is dangerous to relationships, but defining or describing it is difficult because it is so subjective. Ask someone why they left a home, a marriage, a school, or a church, and in far too many cases you will find they were neglected, or, at the least, *felt* they were neglected. By the time it's noticed by the offender, it is often too late and the relationship is broken. It's a sobering thought. Neglect is usually never accompanied by hard facts—it's just the way we feel about some relationships and situations. But that doesn't mean it isn't real. It also doesn't mean that people haven't learned to use it as a weapon.

Neglect often comes in very small doses that, if taken individually, would seem to be of little importance. However, over the course of time, the accumulation can be overwhelming. For example, Diane hasn't spoken to Katie for several weeks. Only a ninth grader, Diane has little understanding of what she is doing to Katie. But Katie is waiting every day for a word from Diane, and every day feeling less herself. She has little idea of how to handle something so foreign.

Neglect is one of the easiest forms of censorship, rebuke, and castigation. You don't have to use words. You don't have to write a letter. You don't need to face somebody. All you need to do is ignore them. Neglect is a deadly form of abuse and is highly contrary to godliness. It beats on people with the message that they are irrelevant and insignificant.

In many cases neglect is unintentional. Regardless, it carries the same destructive, abusive power as if it were premeditated. A father neglects his son because he is too busy with work. A mother neglects her family because she is preoccupied with personal interests. A friend neglects those around him or her because relationships are formed only on "my terms." A pastor neglects his congregation because direct and thoughtful interest in people is not as high a priority as writing a good sermon.

Dr. Tania Davidson explains:

Recovering from severe ostracism [a kind of emotional pain that comes from being excluded and unwanted, or a separation that cannot be put back together] can be a challenge, because it affects a person on so many different levels. It impairs four basic human needs: belonging, control, self-esteem, and meaningful existence.

It dramatically raises anxiety levels and causes depression and despondency.... Ostracized people feel isolated and lonely. They often become less active physically and emotionally. Meanwhile, the depth and the gravity of ostracism symptoms are usually not understood. There is a tendency to minimize and invalidate the pain of people experiencing ostracism. Occasionally, some ostracized people will act out in inappropriate ways to try to get those ostracizing them to notice them in any way they can, since even negative attention feels better than no attention. In the most extreme cases ostracism can lead to violence or suicide.[9]

NEGLECT VERSUS ACCEPTANCE

We've visited churches where the message of the gospel was neglected and replaced with, "You've got to do this," or "We've got to do that," as if the entire point of Christianity is a program on how to perform. Directions for living (which are quite necessary) replace an understanding of our deep need for acceptance, both God's acceptance and that which comes out of the fellowship of believers. (See Romans 15:7.) If you have suffered from feelings of neglect by church, whether true or false, you will not get infused into any kind of ministry. You may remain faithful in some ways, but you will pull back from continued involvement because you are not sure of your acceptance, either by God or by the leadership of the church.

At this point, some people make a great mistake by suggesting that human assurance and acceptance is wrong and should never be desired because all we really need is God's approval. After all, what He thinks is all that counts. But what God really thinks is that we need a considerable amount of assurance, acceptance, and comfort from each other: *"Blessed be the God and Father of our Lord Jesus Christ, the Father of mercies and God of all comfort, who comforts us in all our tribulation, that we may be able to comfort those who are in any trouble, with the comfort with which we ourselves are comforted by God"* (2 Corinthians 1:3–4).

Try to get recruits by constantly flagging messages that people will never please God until they get their lives cleaned up, and you won't have

---

9. Tania Davidson, "Recovery from Ostracism," http://ostracism-awareness.com.

enough soldiers to respond to the spiritual war at hand. When a church's goal is modifying behaviors, true discipleship and transformation of the heart are replaced with fleshly perfectionism. Don't miss the point, we would fall miserably short in our commission if we did not want to see lives completely "cleaned up." We certainly do! But we have simply come to realize how demoralizing and discouraging life can be without friendship and fellowship, without someone speaking a word of encouragement into our lives. There is a huge difference between the message that you've got to have a sanitized lifestyle before God will look at you and the message that God is willing to help you get your life cleaned up—that God is a very present help and sees our heart above our failures: *"God is our protection and our strength. He always helps in times of trouble. So we will not be afraid even if the earth shakes, or the mountains fall into the sea, even if the oceans roar and foam, or the mountains shake at the raging sea"* (Psalm 46:1–3 NCV).

This dynamic understanding of God's love and grace does not diminish sin nor take it lightly. It simply adds the dimension of God's care and His desire to help in our inabilities to accomplish any act of righteousness. We need the gospel that tells us that God will never neglect us. King David said of God's character, *"You have also given me the shield of Your salvation; Your right hand has held me up, Your gentleness has made me great"* (Psalm 18:35).

THE RESULTS OF NEGLECT

Neglect anything and it will eventually go away. But where do people go when they are neglected? If they are neglected by other Christians, what will they eventually do with Christianity in general? If they don't find a reason for being, or a vision worth living and dying for through the church, where else will they find anything of value? In the early church, most of the disciples felt they had a message more important than their own lives. And so it has been down through history.

Who knows how many people are looking for meaning and fulfillment and are not finding it? Perhaps millions! This lack of satisfaction and purpose, this disallowing of personal hopes and dreams, causes many to become socially orphaned and disabled. You can find them in minority groups who sooner or later speak in a way in which the world is forced to listen, mostly because of their radical actions. Through them we are com-pelled to face the power of neglect that forced them to react in negative ways. (Of course, not everyone who is neglected, abused, or rejected turns against humanity. And some may do so for a season but, after finding pur-pose, turn out to be builders rather than destroyers.)

When a church recognizes that it's slipping in energy and numbers, it often blames carnal Christians or the last-day events which forecast a falling away. Now, there is nothing wrong with preaching about last-day events, but there is certainly something wrong with blame and scapegoat-ing. Although we don't like to play the blame game, still as Pogo would say, "We have seen the enemy and he is us." Perhaps new people don't stay around because the church is short on vitality and friendship. In towns that have a variety of churches, it is easy to look at them like a car sales lot. Ask someone attending a church how they got there and many will tell you that someone invited them. But perhaps the most common reason why someone moves on, looking for a different church, has to do with a sense that they didn't feel they would fit in. They didn't sense an atmosphere of acceptance. They felt the subtle monster of rejection, but often not from anything specific that they could put a finger on. It was a neglect that was ever-so-faint, but still powerful enough to make them feel unwanted.

We might just say that the church wasn't friendly to visitors and leave it at that. But what happens when a person who knows little about Christianity comes looking for a church? They won't stay unless they be-lieve it is a place of safety and acceptance—and they may not look for an-other one.

The solution is not just about putting in place a new curriculum or enlisting greeters to stand at the door with a big smile. If a church lacks compassion and does not allow and promote caring relationships between people, no curriculum or greeter will overcome that lack. A church exists to accomplish the Redeemer's purpose: caring, happily helping each person succeed, and seeing healing in spirit, soul, and body. If His purpose isn't in the process of being accomplished, it's not our job to support it with atten-dance and finances. If we don't see the obvious fruit of the Spirit when we visit a church, we have to question whether the branch is still connected to the Vine. It's hard to imagine a church that is truly interested in adding to its flock and yet never does.

Please don't think that all of this can be found out in one morning service! First impressions are usually not dependable. Checking out a place for its true spiritual climate will take some time.

HEALING NEGLECT

A friend who is involved in a ministry that deals with emotional difficulties among Christians wrote:

> It's our feeling that the church has abdicated its God-given right, authority and responsibility to minister healing. We have given it over to secular places…. When we come up against something difficult, we are only too happy to refer the problem/people to someone outside of the church.
>
> Much illness, dysfunction, woundedness, etc. is spiritual, so it makes absolutely no sense whatsoever to ask the secular medical community to assume all responsibility for ministering healing.
>
> In this season, God is asking us to recognize what we have given up, to make a shift and to take back what rightfully belongs to the disciples of Jesus Christ—to minister healing in His name, physically, emotionally, mentally and spiritually."

She's right! *"Most assuredly, I say to you, he who believes in Me, the works that I do he will do also; and greater works than these he will do, because I go to My Father"* (John 14:12). Only God knows how a church should start the healing process. We would suggest that a good place would be to take notice of those who have deep hurts or anyone who is hurting—in other words, everyone around you. What's the antonym for neglect? It is "to be noticed, to be accepted." People literally heal when they are made to feel accepted.

Genesis 16 tells the story of Hagar. Sarai gave Hagar, her maid, to her husband Abram to bear him the child she was unable to. The Lord had promised a child to Abram and Sarai, but in Sarai's unbelief she figured a younger woman would have to carry the "child of promise." Despite Abram complying with Sarai's wish, when Hagar became pregnant, Sarai despised her, and eventually cast her and the child away to die. But the Lord saw Hagar. In the midst of her greatest pain and deepest rejection, God saw, and God cared. In fact, in Genesis 16:13, Hagar refers to God as, *"You-Are-the-God-Who-Sees."* What happened for Hagar is available to anyone who has been rejected. There is life and hope and acceptance for you, because there is a God, and He loves you, and He sees you. That goes for anyone and everyone.

Some might say, "I can't make a person feel a specific way. I don't control someone else's emotions. If they want to feel rejected, they will, and it's not my fault." If that were true, why does Scripture direct us to *"be kindly affectionate to one another," "comfort each other and edify one another," "stir up love and good works," "love one another,"* and *"train a child up in the way he should go"*?[10] Words, body language, and sighs matter in communication skills. Even without a common language, or without any language at all, acceptance can be felt.

When a person is noticed and accepted, he or she has a better chance of being healed, and the courage to look up and hold on. There is a Christian leader who has drawn a bit of attention, not that he wanted it or was seeking it but he found it anyway, simply because he calls people on the phone— almost anyone who needs to hear these words: "I was just thinking of you and wondered how you are doing." Some people find it hard to believe that he takes the time to do this. At the same time, he finds it hard to believe that Christians by and large don't tend to do it themselves!

People find healing in just knowing that someone cares. It would be interesting to take a two-question poll of a congregation: "On a scale of 1 to 10, how many people around you genuinely care about what is happening in your life?" And then we could ask the follow-up question: "On a scale of 1 to 10, how much do you care about people around you?" This poll is not to condemn, but to address awareness.

We could only guess at the results of such a poll. But a poll should not be necessary to face up to the truth. Caring is God's nature, and our first calling is to minister His nature to other people. Why so many miss this is

---

10. Romans 12:10; 1 Thessalonians 5:11; Hebrews 10:24; John 13:34; Proverbs 22:6.

perplexing! At the same time, we recognize that we are people in process, and that our propensity toward sin is slowly being overcome by God's love. People will gravitate to people who have a unique quality of life flowing through them, so don't be surprised to find people wanting your time and attention if you have His life to give.

A PROVERB

The wise are patient; they will be honored if they ignore insults.

(Proverbs 19:11 NCV)

PSALMS FOR THE WOUNDED

I love you, LORD. You are my strength. The LORD is my rock, my protection, my Savior. My God is my rock. I can run to him for safety.

(Psalm 18:1–2 NCV)

The ropes of death came around me; the deadly rivers overwhelmed me. The ropes of death wrapped around me. The traps of death were before me. In my trouble I called to the LORD. I cried out to my God for help. From his temple he heard my voice; my call for help reached his ears.

(Psalm 18:4–6 NCV)

People cannot see their own mistakes. Forgive me for my secret sins. Keep me from the sins of pride; don't let them rule me. Then I can be pure and innocent of the greatest of sins. I hope my words and thoughts please you. LORD, you are my Rock, the one who saves me.

(Psalm 19:12–14 NCV)

5

I FEEL BEAT UP IN CHURCH

Have you ever been hurt so bad that your whole body is crying?
Your heart is aching so much, you can't take a breath. You can't
say a word. You can't make a move. Your mind is set on your pain.
You just feel the burning heavy tears streaming down your face.
—*Anonymous*

A shabbily dressed young woman came to church and stayed through all
three morning services and the two evening services. No one inquired
where she was from. Her appearance was unattractive. She looked home-
less with her pack, bandanna, and disheveled clothes. An elegant elderly
lady named Phyllis observed her over a few weeks, and then befriended
her. Phyllis found that the young lady bicycled seventeen miles one way to
get to church, had only a few clothes, no assurance of food, and no family
that would be glad to feed her. She was working and had already put herself
through a college pre-med program, but it hadn't borne fruit. The young
woman slept or studied in a hedgerow behind the church on Sunday afternoons. After the evening service, she rode her bike seventeen miles home
in the dark. She knew she wasn't dressed right, but there wasn't any way to
get to church if she dressed right. She had been told her bike-riding wasn't
ladylike, that riding on the highways was "asking for it," and that if she was
really serving God she would not be in this position.

Phyllis, with her husband Tom, "adopted" the young woman. Phyllis
and Tom understood poverty and abandonment, and they made sure this
wasn't an adoption in word only. They took her into their home for a year,

fed her, and let her use their vehicle to go to work. They talked with her, encouraged her, showed her life skills, and gave her emotional balance. Phyllis may have dressed like an elegant lady, and she was, but she was also a tough warrior who identified the broken and refused to ignore them.

REJECTION THAT DESTROYS

There are basically two kinds of rejection. The first deals with likes and dislikes, opinions and preferences. A person may like bananas but reject asparagus. Someone else may prefer one political candidate and reject another. These are the normal aspects of decisions everyone makes daily.

The second kind of rejection is dangerous and devastating. By definition, this kind of rejection is "the refusal to accept" or better yet, "the absence of caring." It's the rejection that shuns other people. It has its own peculiar language: "Dropped like a hot potato." "Keep your distance." "He got a 'Dear John letter.'" "He just threw her aside like a ragdoll." "She was blackballed." "He's on the blacklist." "I was given the cold shoulder." "He acted like I wasn't there." "They threw him under the bus." "Shake him off, get rid of the guy." It has the ability to destroy both mental and emotional health. It is so strong that it alters social life, rational thinking, and sound decision-making.

Rejection implies that some people are just unacceptable. Many of us know how it feels when rejection brings on apprehension and self-doubt, and then confusion and fear. When we witness a rejection, it causes us to question both the one who rejected and the one who was rejected.

THE TORMENT OF REJECTION

The real torment of rejection is its ping-pong nature. The rejected turn around and reject others. Those who are personally well-acquainted with denunciation are often the ones who begin their own lifestyles of the same. Many become fierce in their dislike for those who have rejected them, which opens the door to unforgiveness and vengeance. Rejection is the ball that always gets returned.

Rejection forces questions like, "Why don't people like me?" "Why don't they want to be around me?" And then the big one, "Why am I so different?" And this is where the pain goes deep: "What's wrong with *me?*" "Why am I so repulsive?" "Was I born this way or did I do something to cause this?" "How did I get to be this way?" "If I tell you who I am on the inside and you reject me...then what? That is all I have; all I am." Exasperation and often hatred quickly follow; both self-hatred and hatred of those who have rejected.

Listen to this story:

> My mother used to introduce me as "Betty, my mistake." I cannot tell you how it affected me. I thought somehow I wasn't really supposed to be here on earth. It was only when I turned my heart to Jesus and accepted the fact that He died for me that I started to be set free. I was released from the terrible path of rejection and low self-esteem that had begun as a child and resulted in an abusive marriage as an adult. Even as I received the truth, it took me several years to actually accept that God really loved me.[11]

What causes rejection and what causes the soul of the rejected to wither? Why does it affect people, families, whole societies with intolerable behavior, including violence, rape, and murder, and whole nations with war?

On what seemed to be a normal day in Isla Vista, California, Elliot Rodgers took the lives of six people and injured thirteen others before committing suicide. In a video recording he made before the murders, he explained his feelings of rejection. He felt shunned, ignored, and disregarded. He was an object that no one wanted. While it is difficult to understand the process of Rodger's thinking, his actions cannot be, and must not be, condoned or justified. Today's news includes so many stories of school shootings, theater killings, and gang violence; and when the life of the offender is traced back, we often find a person who has been relentlessly rejected. In the ever-increasing impersonal nature of our culture, and the crumbling of the family unit, we certainly have conditions in which to look for blame.

People who fall through the cracks become targets of the enemy. Those who are increasingly being attracted to radical organizations, anarchists, the drug culture, gangs, the cults and the occult have often suffered from

---

11. J. Betty Carr, *You're Loved No Matter What* (San Diego, CA: Black Forest Press, 2000), 4.

heavy amounts of rejection. A lot of them have some kind of church background. And for numbers of them, the rejection started in a church.

Certainly, all responsibility for vehement rejection cannot be put on churches. In many of the kinds of difficulties above, it was the church who rushed in to give love and support to those who had been hurt and abused. But if we could take a group of new Christians, before they had ever attended a church, and guide them through a few basics of the New Testament before telling them to find a church, what would be their expectations? Having no previous biases, would it cross their minds that one or more of them could be excluded from fellowship because something seriously wrong in their past was uncovered? What would they think if they found arrogant attitudes and caustic remarks that facilitated anger, not peace? What if they were looking for: *"You shall love your neighbor as yourself"*; *"But love your enemies, do good, and lend"*; *"By this all will know that you are My disciples, if you have love for one another"* and didn't find it?[12] What if they found just the opposite—rejection and arrogance?

Again, it is true that some churches can't meet the needs of some people, but that doesn't mean a loving church can't help in some way. When a church purports to offer the full gospel, we want to believe they will do so. If a problem becomes overwhelming, we hope the church would at least help the hurting to carefully find others who can assist them. A church that will network with other churches promotes utilization of people with different giftings or special abilities in order to bring wholeness and healing. A healthy church does not fear losing members and their money. They are primarily interested in their members maturing and reaching out to others.

There is nothing that gets to the bottom of deep issues as quickly as patience and care. These two characteristics can prevent a tremendous amount of pain. They give a point of trust within a maelstrom of fear and punishment. They become a beacon of hope for those who need acceptance and kindness. All it takes to do this is one to two people who think acutely and have an understanding of His character.

John is another person who fell victim to loveless religion. When he was in his early teens he used to hunt birds on his grandfather's farm on

---

12. Mark 12:31; Luke 6:35; John 13:35.

Sunday afternoons after church. When a man in his church discovered this, he reprimanded John by telling him that if he continued to do so, he would die and go to hell for violating the Sabbath. This along with a number of other condemning statements eventually led John to leave the church. He was subsequently branded rebellious. In the years that followed, John found it impossible to believe that God loved him. He struggled for more than fifty years to understand how a loving God continually appeared angry with him. In his heart, far beyond the pain, there was something that always seemed to say that God loved him, but he couldn't grasp onto it. John's rejection by people in the church led him to believe his cup was always empty. He saw the worst in almost everything, including himself.

To understand the message of this book, withhold evaluation either of John or the man in his church just yet. Instead, simply take this to heart: John suffered needlessly for over fifty years.

THE PECKING ORDER

A friend wrote to us:

Let me tell you the grisly source of the term "pecking order." We raised "free-range" chickens for eggs, with about four hundred to one thousand hens in each room of our three-room chicken house. In a flock of chickens, pecking is a way of both establishing dominance and of finding the weak one. Chickens vary in their ability to fend off those who are aggressive. Some are queen-of-the-mountain, others less so. The "less so" then look for someone else to pick on, someone less than themselves. And so a "pecking order" is established. The weakest or most frightened one is doomed. Chickens will actually chase the weak ones over obstacles and through a crowd to land more pecks. And what they like best is meat and blood. The antagonist chicken will aim her pecks at the weak one's soft spot, eventually ripping it open. Once the blood starts, multiple chickens "flock" to the feast, overwhelming the weak one's attempts to defend themselves. They don't stop pecking until all the blood is gone and rigor mortis sets in. Then the flock leaves the corpse alone.

Some weak chickens just learn ways to stay out of the way. They get scrawny because they can't have free access to food, but they sneak some of it while the others aren't looking. They don't lay eggs. They get sick easily. They always have skin showing because the pecking breaks off and pulls off their feathers. But they are alive. They just have to avoid the other chickens. It works for weak people in church too.

Why do chickens act so ugly? Why do we? Why is mankind creative and beautiful one moment, and destructive and ugly the next? Science has come a long way in appreciating the uniqueness of the human body as well as the human mind. But for all the time spent on study and examination, human complexities still baffle us, especially in efforts to unravel the mysteries of human awareness. The intricacies of a single human mind will no doubt continue to perplex both scientific, philosophical, and even religious investigation for a long time to come. So take seven billion of these minds and put them together on a rather small planet where they will continually associate with each other. Then, divide them into different-sized groups and place some of them together in a building in which they intend to minister and worship God. When you get that many people in that small of an area you're bound to have differences and disagreements. And often those dissimilarities become breeding grounds for severe hurts and pains.

But why? "Why can't we all just get along?"[13]

From a biblical point of view, the gospel is both for those who have been rejected and for those who do the rejecting. For comfort we add that no one knows better the terrible power of rejection than God Himself: *"Then those of you who escape will remember Me among the nations where they are carried captive, because **I was crushed** by their adulterous heart which has departed from [rejected] Me"* (Ezekiel 6:9). *"They turned against God so often in the desert and grieved him there. Again and again they tested God and brought pain to the Holy One of Israel"* (Psalm 78:40–41 NCV). *"So Jesus also suffered outside the city to make his people holy with his own blood. So let us go to Jesus outside the camp, holding on as he did when we are abused"* (Hebrews 13:12–13 NCV).

---

13. As Rodney King said after the fallout from his arrest on March 3, 1991.

If we ponder the sufferings of Christ, there is no room to accuse God of not knowing our pain, and that makes it believable that He, as a good God and good Father, wants to eliminate our own personal pain and rejection. It's not just that He's been through it, but also that He doesn't want those He values and loves to *stay in it.*

THE SIGNS OF SPIRITUAL ABUSE

It would be accurate to call Jesus the great socializer, especially if one realizes that caring to meet with and talk to people is really ministering. Socializing is really a time to speak into someone else's life, or to let another person speak into your life. Think of the many churches where it is hard to get people to leave after a service is over. They love socializing!

It's nice to know that when a pastor reaches out to his people with a lunch, a dinner, or a few minutes on the phone, that *all* are included—both rich and poor, old and young, educated and uneducated. In one case a young man was led to believe that the pastor was interested in helping him personally. However, he could never get him on the phone to make an appointment. Pastors who don't return phone calls cause rejection. Can you imagine Jesus saying to one of his disciples, "Sorry, Peter, I just don't have time for you."

Now, it would be unfair to suggest that a pastor can get to know everyone in his congregation personally. Many churches run well over two hundred people, some even into the thousands and tens of thousands. But it is not unreasonable to rely on assistants, associate pastors, and members of the congregation to make up the slack. People are very discerning when it comes to the authenticity of another person's character. If a pastor has deep genuine love for his/her congregation, the people will feel loved, despite not always having personal time with the pastor.

For example, one pastor had several families begin attending his church after they came out of a very controlling and abusive church. One new congregant told the other, "I don't know our new pastor very well, but what I do know is that he loves me."

We have watched ministers put a great deal of time and effort into their sermons and administrative responsibilities, but put very little time into people, including their own families. Some churches (by no means a majority or even close to it) don't seem to find interest in anything more than that a sermon was preached and an offering was taken, and then with a sigh, "That's out of the way for another week."

Some churches are like farm auction houses. They look the sheep over carefully before they bid on them. One pastor commented that he would like to take about sixty people out of his congregation of about three hundred and just pastor the small group. If you've ever walked in his shoes you might want to say, "Amen." But although the other 240 may be difficult to get along with, they are still people who need to get a better handle on life and especially on Jesus. They are flesh and blood just like you and me, with a will, mind, and emotions. They are real, although for one reason or another, they are quite often treated as nonentities. Touch one of them, regardless of color, economic soundness, or social acceptability and you will find that their skin is warm just like yours and mine. And perhaps even more important, look at them and realize that they were created in the same image and likeness as you and me.

When Pastor Smith came to a new town, he had a certain flair that suggested he was energetic enough to get this tired church up and running again. But right from the start, it became obvious to some that his agenda was more about himself than about the gospel and the congregation.

It is frustrating to find men like this, leaders who have little or no time for others, unless a person can benefit them. Their traits are easy to see for what they are when all lumped together. However, one small disturbing mannerism here and there is often left to the casual acknowledgment that, "He's only human like the rest of us." And we agree—to a point. It's far too easy to become picky and start a process that ruins ministry. On the other hand there are warning signs that need to be addressed concerning leaders.

Here is a shortlist of some of the telltale signs that, if not corrected, can lead to spiritual abuse. We don't want this list to be used to beat up on any leader who is trying to do his best but has some bad habits. This must not be taken to be a witch hunt to ferret out negligent leadership. It is, instead, a list of warning signs:

+ A casual attitude toward people in general.

- Domination over almost all conversations.
- Failure to return phone calls without an explanation why.
- Carrying out discipline from the pulpit.
- Railing on people in private.
- Railing on the church for failure to promote the church.
- Railing on the church for lack of involvement.
- Railing on the church for financial reasons.
- Eliminating people from the church who exhibit exemplary leadership.
- Developing an inner circle that is impossible to penetrate.
- Dining only with those of influence.
- Threatening people with spiritual ruin if they leave the church.
- Saying they will get back to you but never do.

When you look at this list, a number of damaging traits are easily seen—primarily neglecting people because of an inordinate self-identification, fear of losing control, and insecurity born out of previous rejections. If some or all of these attitudes prevail in your church, it certainly is a call to intercede on behalf of those in authority. If these attitudes persist over time, one should certainly be open to the Holy Spirit leading one into a safe and healthy church.

WHAT TO EXPECT WHEN YOU LEAVE

You will almost always feel better when you're out of a strained relationship. But the *process* of leaving a relationship might not make you feel better for a number of reasons. And a relationship with a church is no different—and perhaps even worse. Leaving a church can seem like leaving God. In abusive situations, some have been led to believe that it is really love that allows a preacher or teacher to pound hard on sin even if it pounds hard on the person. They are convinced that it's God's love that strikes blows into hearts and minds, and will continue to do so until every aspect of sin has been removed.

There is a strong custom that claims you cannot leave a church unless you leave on good terms with the pastor and the church. However, abusive churches will not allow the parting to be on good terms. Arbitrarily telling someone that they need to go back to a previous situation and "make things right" can make things worse on both sides. Each situation of spiritual abuse demands its own survey—no situation is the same. Sometimes, you have to leave and not look back.

Abused people feel that church and God are basically the same thing. But, having the desire to continue to respect and worship God, they also know they cannot stay in a church that destroys. If you're in that situation, where can you go? Chapter 15 explores in a little more detail what biblical leadership looks like and what a healthy church looks like.

A PROVERB

Don't ever forget kindness and truth. Wear them like a necklace. Write them on your heart as if on a tablet. Then you will be respected and will please both God and people. (Proverbs 3:3–4 NCV)

PSALMS FOR THE WOUNDED

LORD, tell me your ways. Show me how to live. Guide me in your truth, and teach me, my God, my Savior. I trust you all day long. LORD, remember your mercy and love that you have shown since long ago. Do not remember the sins and wrong things I did when I was young. But remember to love me always because you are good, LORD.
(Psalm 25:4–7 NCV)

The LORD tells his secrets to those who respect him; he tells them about his agreement. (Psalm 25:14 NCV)

His anger lasts only a moment, but his kindness lasts for a lifetime. Crying may last for a night, but joy comes in the morning.
(Psalm 30:5 NCV)

I LIVE IN SHAME ALL THE TIME

Analytical psychology...can lay bare where the roots of man's estrangement lies; but it cannot offer forgiveness.... Psychiatrists have realized that there are no techniques whereby they can dissipate real guilt feelings and their associated shame.[14]
—*John McKenzie*

Debra had been a strong Christian for more than forty years. She raised a Christian daughter as a single mom. One day while walking through a friend's home she noticed a book on shame and asked what it was about. Her friend briefly shared the content: that Jesus bore her shame on the cross and that she no longer had to bear it herself. Debra burst into tears. Debra confessed that she had been carrying the shame of an abortion for years. She received the truth, prayed with her friend, and Debra was delivered from her shame that very day.[15]

It is difficult to understand why a person in a church had to undergo shame for all those years when Jesus had already set her free. Debra's friend explained, "I can tell you why: every year on one specific Sunday, her pastor preached on the evils of abortion, attacking mothers for murdering babies for their own convenience and bemoaning all those precious lives lost. The pastor even said in the sermon, 'Some of you who have had abortions before you became Christians have come to me and asked me to stop

14. John G. McKenzie, *Guilt: Its Meaning and Significance* (Nashville, TN: Abingdon Press, 1962), 126 and 179.
15. We highly recommend *Shattering the Shackles of Shame* by Pat Hulsey for anyone dealing with guilt and shame.

preaching like this because it hurts you. I can't help it if you get hurt. I have to preach the truth. That is more important.'"

What the pastor said had a grain of truth, which makes it all the more devilish. Yes, it is true that when the Holy Spirit exposes our sin and errors, it *hurts*. But that is not the same thing as pouring salt on the wound of a tender soul suffering from guilt. There is never justification for intentionally wounding others with harshness, judgmentalism, and guilt-tripping.

The pastor's message did nothing to help this woman whom Jesus wants so very much to forgive. This pastor didn't care about the heartaches and hurts in the lives of others. His rigidity was pharisaical and counters everything about the gospel for which Jesus paid an unbelievable price. This heartless pastor had an incredible opportunity to witness and encourage the love of God working in women's lives. But he missed it, and instead heaped more shame and sorrow on already deeply hurting women.

SHAME AND GUILT

Nobody does surgery on a foot because of a throbbing tooth. The pain of a toothache has a known location because of our bodies' amazing neurological system that pinpoints the source with amazing accuracy. We know to visit a dentist instead of a podiatrist. But when emotional pain is found in the soul it is far more difficult to determine its source. Even the best of analytical minds fail to understand the deep recesses of the soul. The pain is there, but understanding is not. We feel it but can't deal with it.

So it is with guilt, and especially shame. The longer it's there, the wider it spreads until one small spring has drenched acres of the past. "The trail of guilt becomes more difficult to track when our footsteps are blurred by the winds and wash of time. Eventually guilt is not directed toward a specific deed at all, but only generally toward the 'past.'"[16] When one small sight, smell, or other stimulus comes at us, the past rushes forward like a flood. For the most part, guilt is the emotion associated with some wrong done in the past, but shame not only contains the guilt from the past, but goes further to suggest a guilt-based identity. Guilt says, "I did something bad." Shame says, "I did something bad, and now I'm a bad person."

16. Thomas Oden, *Guilt Free* (Nashville: Abingdon Press, 1980), 169.

Guilt does not reflect directly on one's identity nor diminish one's sense of personal worth. It emanates from an integrated conscience and set of rules. It is the reflection of a developing self. A person with guilt might say, "I feel awful seeing that I did something which violated my values." Or, the guilty party might say, "I feel sorry about the consequences of my behavior." In doing so the person's values are reaffirmed. The possibility of repair exists and learning and growth are promoted. While guilt is a painful feeling of regret and responsibility for one's actions, shame is a painful feeling about oneself as a person. The possibility for repair seems foreclosed to the shameful person because shame is a matter of identity, not a behavioral infraction. There is nothing to be learned from it and no growth is opened by the experience because it only confirms one's negative feelings about oneself.[17]

Shame is a state of mind developed through events from the past, especially owing to both personal mistakes and the mistakes others have assigned to you. Shame might seem a small thing were it were not for the multitudes who are shackled to the past by feelings of condemnation. One woman's story provides a painful example:

> The programming by the church I once attended told me that I was a sinner saved by grace. Evil at the core, but saved. I wondered how that worked! How can evil get into heaven? And why would I look forward to spending eternity with these people? When I asked questions, they got mad. I thought that's what students were supposed to do…ask questions of their mentors!

> I was shamed for saying Mom and Dad were abusive. The church said that is dishonoring to my parents, and I'm cursed for saying it. But to say they weren't abusive was a lie. It was a catch-22: I had to lie and say they were good parents, or I had to tell the truth and be considered rebellious.

> They told me my pain was "because I hadn't dealt with 'it,'" whatever "it" was. Sometimes it seemed like "it" was the person

17. Merle A. Fossum and Marilyn J. Mason, *Facing Shame: Families in Recovery* (New York and London: W.W. Norton & Company, 1986), 7–8.

talking to me, pressing the trigger on the pain reflex. Or, "it" must be unforgiveness, and that I'm rebellious and not willing to admit it.

John Bradshaw describes shame as "a state of being, a core identity. Shame gives you a sense of failing and falling short as a human being. Shame is a rupture of the self with the self. It is like internal bleeding.... An inner torment, a sickness of the soul. A shame-based person is haunted by a sense of absence and emptiness."[18] Lewis Smedes, Professor at Fuller Theological Seminary, says shame is a "vague, undefined heaviness that presses on our spirit, dampens our gratitude for the goodness of life, and slackens the free flow of joy. Shame...seeps into and colors all our other feelings, primarily about ourselves, but about almost everyone and everything else in our life as well."[19]

The apostle Paul also wrestled greatly with guilt and shame. He acknowledges his guilt with these words: *"For the good that I will to do, I do not do; but the evil I will not to do, that I practice"* (Romans 7:19). Don't forget, this is one of the mighty men of God—used by God to convey the gospel message perhaps more than any other person! But listen to Paul again, this time in the midst of his shame: *"O wretched man that I am! Who will deliver me from this body of death?"* (Romans 7:24). Paul was so devastated by the pain caused by his guilt and shame that he referred to himself as having a *"body of death."* He was miserable and dejected, a state of mind we would never have expected in a man God used so mightily.

But that is the case with all human beings. Either we strut with arrogance and pride, at least for a while, or we are depressed with deep feelings of inadequacy. And these deficient feelings almost always lead to isolation, which we defend by convincing ourselves that at least it's better than the stress of fronting a face in public.

Most of us have seen people who are obviously uncomfortable in a crowd. Their speech, demeanor, and behavior betray their uncertainty; their obvious self-consciousness makes it apparent that they are uncomfortable.

18. John Bradshaw, *Healing the Shame That Binds You* (Deerfield Beach, FL: Health Communications Inc., 1988), 10.
19. Lewis B. Smedes, *Healing the Shame We Don't Deserve* (San Francisco: Harper Collins, 1993), preface.

They look nervous while talking with others. Many of those people are struggling with shame.

Shame most often affects those who are perfectionists, especially those who are afraid of God's displeasure. It probes like the opposition's political campaign manager, scrutinizing every detail of a person's past in order to disqualify him from an electoral position. The devil constantly scrutinizes our past in order to take away our God-given rights and subsequent peace of mind. Shame is not casual fire from the devil. It is not a blip on our radar. Shame is warfare at its most vicious state. It is Stage 4 cancer in the soul. It is a full-fledged, incessant, raging, deadly assault on our most vulnerable weaknesses.

THE LYING VOICE OF SHAME

Kevin, a young pastor, was hired by a struggling church as their children's ministry director. The church had been declining in finances and attendance for over a decade, but a few staff transitions promised a fresh start. However, eighteen months after Kevin was hired, he was brought into the pastor's office and let go. In subsequent meetings Kevin was berated and told that he was the reason the church numbers were still in decline, and that out of protection for the entire church and finances, he had to go. Character assassination quickly followed. The pastor told Kevin that not only was he the sole cause for their current church struggles, he would never succeed in any ministry ever, and would likely find himself working at a coffee shop or a lawn service in the future.

These words hit Kevin hard. Kevin had felt the call to ministry as a young boy, and subsequently attended Bible college and seminary. He just wanted to serve the Lord and His church. But were these words true? Would Kevin truly be the source of pain and failure for the rest of his life? A season of pain ensued as these words festered in Kevin's heart and mind. He felt a tremendous burden and shame that he was the source for the church's decline and struggle. One day, he was recounting the pain of these words to a mentor and fellow pastor. "Kevin," the man replied, "the only reason those words hurt and still hurt is because you believed them." A lightbulb went on for Kevin and a season of healing began. He embraced what was true. He believed that God had called and anointed him, and he rejected the words of his former pastor. Kevin had lived in shame, believing that he was every bit the failure and cause of pain he had been told he was. Kevin hadn't done everything perfectly, but the Lord began to move him beyond the insecurity and embarrassment of the situation and into the confidence and boldness of his calling once again.

Ephesians 1 says huge things about our identities and who we are: we were chosen "*before the foundation of the world,*" to be "*sons by Jesus Christ to Himself,*" "*blessed…with every spiritual blessing*" and "*accepted in the Beloved*" (verses 3–6). Our identity is found in our adoption by God through the work of Christ. But shame changes our identities. It's like trying to get the smell of fire out of clothing. The shame-filled person can't shake this sense that they are worthless, that they deserve little. It lingers and is absorbed into every fiber of their being.

Shame prepares the soil for other enemy seeds. To see yourself as a bad person because of someone else's arbitrary conclusion about you is yielding yourself to a lie. And to unreasonably believe there is something inherently wrong with you destroys a potentially rich life. You can hear the self-criticism in the voice of the one who says, "I hate myself." Or the person who says, "I just want to die." It is true that circumstances bring people to the point of shame and hopelessness. But when a person understands why they are suffering such debilitating pain, it is far easier to take steps to remove it. Make no mistake, the pain and its roots of guilt and shame can be removed.

(Please note that we do not intend for this book to be in any way a replacement for counseling or other professional help as it's needed. Instead, our goal is to provide snapshots of what emotional pain looks like and guidance toward where that pain might be coming from. If something resonates with your own experience or your observation of a friend or relative's experience, please do not hesitate seek professional help.)

SEEING SHAME'S SOURCE

HEREDITARY SHAME

Man's original transgression produced in him and in all succeeding generations a nature bent on immorality, generating the reality that "*all have sinned and fall short of the glory of God*" (Romans 3:23).

In the biblical account of the beginning of the world, God creates two people, Adam and Eve, and places them in a beautiful garden. *"And they were both naked, the man and his wife, and were not ashamed"* (Genesis 2:25). They had unlimited resources and could eat from all of the trees of the garden except one, the tree of knowledge of good and evil. Satan, in the form of a serpent, went to Eve and challenged God's word:

> *"Has God indeed said, 'You shall not eat of every tree of the garden'?" And the woman said to the serpent, "We may eat the fruit of the trees of the garden; but of the fruit of the tree which is in the midst of the garden, God has said, 'You shall not eat it, nor shall you touch it, lest you die.'"*   (Genesis 3:1–3)

In the following dialogue, Satan convinces Eve that the forbidden tree would really bring her closer to God, that by eating she would be *"like God"* (verse 4), that things she didn't know about her realm would now be hers to appreciate and enjoy. Once Eve succumbed, she convinced her husband to eat with her. And as Adam did, both of their eyes were opened to things they had never seen before, and they knew that they were naked and tried to hide. They were ashamed.

Soon shame led to fear and fear to blame: *"Then the man said, 'The woman whom You gave to be with me, she gave me of the tree, and I ate.'… The woman said, 'The serpent deceived me, and I ate'"* (verses 12–13). Adam may not have said it then, but he was certainly implying, *"God, if You really think about it, it was really Your fault for giving me this woman in the first place. I wouldn't be in this mess if it wasn't for her."* It was the first blame game in human history.

It is at this point that the power of darkness began to cover the earth, and Adam and Eve were cast out of the garden, covered in shame. This is just a brief summation of the creation and fall, but there are two things to glean: First, this story is not a fable, it's a reality. It begins the process of answering the question of why the world is as bad as it is and explores how many of the issues and shame we currently face are ultimately inherited from the original fall of man. And second, the story leads us to an understanding of God's desire for restoration and reconciliation—or in other words, His desire to remove our shame from us that we might fellowship with Him and walk with Him once again.

PERSONAL SHAME

Although our shame-based nature came to us from Adam, shame doesn't become a horrible thing until it is activated by sin. It was not until we made a decision against a recognized standard that disgrace and dishonor shadowed us, or someone else's wrong decision placed blame upon us.

One prisoner describing her personal shame said, "I could hide my sins from everyone but myself. No physical torments can match the torments of an accusing conscience. An accusing conscience means hell on earth. No earthly wealth, human love, music, fun, or intoxication can dispel or comfort the agony of its gnawing teeth. My sins were finding me out. I was suffering for every sin I had ever committed. Sin was breeding a moral ulcer. A diseased character is worse than a diseased body. My character was suffering. I could not escape my sin."[20] Miraculously, she was set free and became a strong leader in a prison church.

GENERATIONAL SHAME

A parent acting out of his or her shame says things and does things that give rise to shame in future generations. "When children have shame-based parents, they identify with them. This is the first step in the child's internalizing shame."[21]

Generational shame can be recognized when a person from a shame-based family says, "I will never treat my children the way my parents treated me," but then goes on to do exactly the same things his parents did to him. "If you do not deal with your shame, you pass it on to your children and they pass it to their children. Shame then becomes multigenerational, meaning it is firmly entrenched within the family and passed from one generation to the next."[22]

---

20. Patricia Hulsey, *Shattering the Shackles of Shame* (Colorado Springs: Harvestime International Network, 2003), 50.
21. Smedes, *Healing the Shame That We Don't Deserve*, 41.
22. Hulsey, *Shattering the Shackles*, 60.

The power of generational influence, although it doesn't release its victims from accountability, is a stronghold that through the power of the Holy Spirit can be broken. Proverbs 26:2 says, *"The curse causeless shall not come"* (KJV). In other words, the curse of shame, along with all other destructive emotions, has a cause that needs removal. It begins by recognizing that everything harmful was planted in us by rebellion at the beginning of creation. That rebellion carried in it Adam's shame. So how do we deal with both shame and rebellion?

The most common way is to try to deal with it ourselves by resolving to do better. Our sincerity is certainly there, but we will usually end up disappointed like the New-Year's dieter who ends the year several pounds heavier, not lighter. There are certain habits and behaviors so embedded in our personality that all the self-help in the world won't fix. Your whole family may be controlling and manipulative. Your parents grew up this way. Their parents grew up this way. Now you have fallen into the same pattern. No matter how hard you try to change, you keep falling back into the same behavior. It has become multi-generational and can only be broken by the power of God's intervention.

Start by becoming involved with God. Persistently move into anything that gives you a better understanding of who He is and how He deals with our lives. In other words, run after Him. Everybody that has ever done so has found He wasn't far away at all.

INFLICTED SHAME

A shamed person usually doesn't really realize how the shame got there. Listen to the person who says in their misery, "I'm just a bad person." Then ask why they believe this and you will probably get the answer, "I just am."

Shame is inflicted by people who arbitrarily typecast another's identity. The bully makes note of a small boy and imposes the name "weakling." The father who thinks his son is lazy says to him, "You will never amount to anything," and the son believes it. The college group sees a freshman caught up in a bundle of mistakes and calls her a "loser." A mother with a painful past tells her daughter, "You were the product of rape, so you were an accident. God didn't plan for you to exist." Patricia Hulsey explains: "Shame is not something I learned about through research. I didn't read a book or go to a seminar on the subject. I agonized with its intensity when as a child I was told I was no good, stupid, and would never amount to anything."[23]

We would like to believe that most people who have been branded with false identities would recognize and reject them. But everywhere we turn we find of people who believe their mistaken identity. That's why many will say, "I don't know who I am," "I feel like I'm just going through the motions." Shame is the product of how we feel about ourselves. Feeling that we are bad, no good, and worthless sets the stage for a shame-based life.

INDUCED SHAME

One of the most potent and negative forms of induced shame comes through child sexual abuse and incest. The sexual predator grooms the victim (male or female) to believe that the abuse is their fault—that they caused it, they started it, they made the abuser do it, or they asked for it. And that means their identity is bad. This manipulation rips away their original identity and gives them a shame-based identity that causes them to withdraw from both God and others. They are often threatened into not telling others what is going on. So there is no voice to contradict what the abuser is telling them. They are alone, isolated by what they are told about who they are. Depending on the victim's persona, the identity is changed one way or another—but it is changed. There is no going back. But there is going forward. Even atrocities like these are not outside of Jesus' capacity to heal, restore, and release from the pain of the memories.

These people feel like damaged goods, like they have no worth or value left. There is great grief and shame. Somewhere along the line they wonder why God didn't stop it if He really loved them. This kind of abuse doesn't go away by reading a book, or attending a church, or being a part of a Bible study. It requires the intervention of God's love and kindness, and that comes through people who express His Father-heart. They must first hear the words from their heavenly Father saying, "It was not your fault, there's nothing you did to deserve what happened to you." They do not need to

---

23. Hulsey, *Shattering the Shackles*, 1.

hear the shaming words, "Well, what did you do to make it stop?" "You must have wanted it." "Why didn't you tell someone?"

Those men or women who are seduced or sexually attacked in their adult years do not need to hear this either. What is washed away by Christ's blood must stay gone. The abused person's shame-based and grief-based identity will not change without someone to speak into their new identity, giving the ex-victim the vision and courage to become a new person. That is who and what Jesus is about. Those who don't know God's heart, will always see this person as an ex-victim. Keeping a victim a victim, because they *were* a victim, is an attitude that God hates. There is a new identity and purpose in Him for all who believe in Him.

DISCRIMINATORY SHAME

Discriminatory shame is observed in types or classes of people who are inclined toward certain kinds of cultural prejudice, partiality, and outright bias. When one person shames your identity, it's bad enough, but when a whole group does, it's devastating. Children seem to have a natural talent for this. "Nobody likes Susie because she's so fat." "We've always called Johnny 'Dumbo' because of his big ears." "The kids that come from Southside just don't fit in with the kids that come from the north end."

All it takes are a few words from someone who has no conscience and someone gets hurt—often terribly hurt. Bullying by peers can end in suicide or murder. And yet, recognizing and maintaining personal values is hard when the crowd is going the other way, and risking rejection by peers has never been easy. Ask any middle-schooler. "A person gives up responsibility for some of his or her actions by identification with a socially approved norm of behavior. When this happens, the individual....feels little guilt when orders are executed from that collective will which, in fact, may go against his or her own personal norm of conduct."[24] This happened in Germany (and many other nations) during World War II. Countless numbers of soldiers tortured and murdered people because their superiors told them to do so. Their minds told them that their first duty was to obey what they were told even though their consciences opposed their actions. Many

---

24. Bradshaw, *Healing the Shame That Binds You*, 25.

of those soldiers died the inner death of shame even though they went on to live long lives after the war was over.

Other kinds of discriminatory shame can be attributed to groups or individuals with wealth and/or education. James said not to discriminate between the rich and the poor. (See James 2:3–4.) Paul told the rich to not be proud and contemptuous of others. (See 1 Timothy 6:17–18.) They wouldn't have mentioned it unless they had found it to be a common problem in the early church.

Suppose someone comes into a church while engaging in an inappropriate sexual lifestyle. The words they hear in that church can either shame them out of the church forever, or offer the love of Jesus and, in the process, bring them to repentance and wholeness.

UNWARRANTED OR FALSE SHAME

Sometimes unhealthy leaders use shame for the purpose of manipulation. People will do almost anything to avoid feelings of shame. If a person can make you feel ashamed by pointing out that you failed to heed church standards, they are one step further on the road to controlling you. If you admire and want to please a church leader and he points out how you have disappointed him and you feel ashamed, he has power over you. Some of us never grow from this childlike position of powerlessness.

False shame enters our identity when we are convinced that we have done wrong, when in fact there is no valid ethical or moral violation revealed by either God's Word or His character. Rather, it was an action or inaction that went against an organizational expectation, such as failing to send in your tithe on the first of the month, failing to give enough in offerings, or failing to regularly witness to unbelievers.

We certainly believe in tithing, offerings, and witnessing. We believe in them very much, but when a pastor says at offering time, "Everyone who is tithing, stand up," we guess it's to get non-tithers to tithe so they will be able to stand up too. It's shaming them into giving. It makes those in the congregation feel that acceptability depends on giving, and giving enough. It suggests rejection if we fail to comply. Such leadership forces nonbiblical rules on the congregation, and it prevents many from learning the joy of both tithing and giving. Keep in mind, *forcing* is the issue. We have a responsibility to show people the Scriptures, but not the commission to forcefully compel them to respond. It's the Holy Spirit's job to work in people after they have learned the truth of Scriptures.

There are also telltale attitudes from leadership that, if you are sensitive, you see readily. One is a somber attitude meant to portray a sense of spirituality. It seems to say that we must eradicate joy because we are not supposed to enjoy this life. This controlling attitude is ridiculous, because if the universe is an extension of God's energy and love, and it is, then we were made to be full of energy and love.

All of us are aware of various church organizations that hold certain standards of behavior. This is right to do. But some of their behaviors are not validated in the Scriptures. They have been established to protect the beliefs of the organization, but they are not backed up by the Bible. They are the social norms that a particular church or denomination finds acceptable. They involve cultural acceptance, not acceptance by God into His kingdom. Such practices may include commands for dress, dancing, women's makeup, church attendance, witnessing, movies, hair length, clothing, entertainment, coffee, drinking Coke, and a host of other things. They may be well-intentioned for the most part, but if one feels bad for violating any unbiblical restrictions, it is usually a signal that that one is experiencing unwarranted shame.

SECRET SHAME

Everyone has done something in their life for which they are not proud. It may have been something that they've taken to the Lord, confessed, and received forgiveness for, but it is still something they don't feel free to discuss with other people. It could've been a divorce, a bankruptcy, or a moral failure. Everything forgiven does not need to be communicated, especially if it unnecessarily opens old wounds.

It's not necessarily a problem to have a secret in your life. Many of us have had failures that we don't want to talk about. If the failure was a violation of God's Word and we've confessed and received forgiveness, there is now no shame, simply because He took all of our sin and shame on the cross. The right to keep things to yourself is important. Some people want to know too much about you. You do not have to "tell-all" to be a Christian.

However, given that the right to privacy is legitimate, as confessed failures are "cleansed by the blood," it is still quite possible that the Lord would give the freedom to share these failures as a part of our testimony of God's love and forgiveness. But the key realization is that you don't *have* to.

SHAME FROM DEFORMITIES

What is it like to be deformed, physically or mentally? Isolation, rejection, loneliness, and exclusion are just a few of the things that place deformity between those who have it and those who do not.

Some of us can't perform as well as others. There is great shame in being told we cost other people something because we exist. There is great shame in knowing that people don't want to look at your deformity, mental or physical. Or that they are inconvenienced or irritated by your presence. We seem unable to embrace the idea that the handicapped may very well be around us so that the works of God might be revealed in them. (See John 9:3.) Maybe they are there to help us learn to love as He loved!

One person wrote to us:

I have PTSD [Post Traumatic Stress Disorder], but I don't dare share that at church. It makes people not want to be friends with me. Maybe they think I will explode or something. I don't know. But I do know that the shame of it makes it so I can't find help, except from the medical or psych types that would like to prescribe drugs. I don't want drugs. I want friends. Friends would help me heal a lot faster.

SHAME LEADING TO HOPELESSNESS

The devil finds great joy in bringing the ugly elements of the past to memory: the thoughts of an abortion, a failed marriage, the damage done through drugs and alcohol, the shame of being sexually abused, and whatever other event for which we now feel saddened. The fallout is hopelessness, career inhibition, fear of responsibility, the lack of intimacy, and failure to thrive. In some cases it even results in lost marriage, lost friends, lost kids, lost peace, and lost place.

For those who feel deep remorse for the past, but do not see the differ-ence between godly sorrow for sin that looks to the cross, and remorse that cannot move beyond condemnation, Satan's demons try to make us believe that remorse is sent from God to show His deep displeasure. This is the counterfeit lie that leads to hopelessness. If, indeed, we mistakenly believe that the shame comes from God and we can't get rid of it and its haunting memories, we then think it must be "just due" for our sins. Consequently, we lose heart and enter despair.

Notice how shame leads to despair and despair leads to hopelessness. It's a cycle that repeats itself over and over again until a person is complete-ly worn out. Hopelessness is an ungodly belief, a delusion, and the lie of the enemy. It says, "You and you alone have this kind of situation and you are to blame." Then a mixture of thoughts begin. "I failed so often it's no use to try." "If the end is as bad as this, I don't want to continue the journey."

There is nothing, other than the gospel, that can deal with guilt, hope-lessness, and shame effectively and permanently. But it's not a matter of simply saying a few words and watching it fly away. The reason God doesn't arbitrarily take guilt and shame out of our lives by a single prayer is because its roots must also be eliminated. Over time and with revelation, God will make it clear why we have been overloaded with bondage, and show us both how and why we got into the situation in the first place. That's how He quietly and privately mentors us why to avoid it in the future. *"For godly sorrow produces repentance leading to salvation, not to be regretted; but the sorrow of the world produces death"* (2 Corinthians 7:10).

> It is abundantly clear that no man lives free of guilt [and shame]. Guilt [and shame] is universal. But according as it is repressed *or* recognized, so it sets in motion one of two contradictory process-es; repressed, it leads to anger, rebellion, fear, and anxiety, a dead-ening of the conscience, an increasing inability to recognize one's faults, and a growing dominance of aggressive tendencies. But con-sciously recognized, it leads to repentance, to peace and security of divine pardon."[25]

---

25. Paul Tournier, *Guilt and Grace* (New York: Harper and Row, 1962), 152.

comes from God. Absorb that, and you can see that ⌐ondemnation are part of the spiritual warfare used against us. ⌐ not know or to forget that the enemy of our soul is an accuser of God's people can be deadly. It's a fast and sure way to fall into condemnation, and into false shame and false guilt. So, then, do we have the right to demand of ourselves (in spite of outside and inside voices) that we believe that we are accepted by God? Absolutely! If we come, His promise is acceptance. To believe anything less is to put Him in a box. He is the one who works in us to bring needed change so that we might become more like Him—holy.

PROTECTING OUR IDENTITY IN CHRIST

One of Satan's chief goals is to classify people into identities that don't belong to them. Is it any wonder why some people act out and appear to not be themselves? If they can't see or believe in their real identity and are told that they have a different identity, they tend to act contrary to who they really are.

> Shame is associated with the loss of respect by others and the eradication of self-respect. It prohibits intimacy with God because we feel unworthy. Unlike guilt, which is resolved by confession and repentance, shame becomes an identity.... Shame torments you internally through your conscience and externally through condemnation by others. Shame moves into your life and establishes a base of operations resulting in what some psychologists call 'a shame-based' personality, meaning that every facet of your person is affected by shame's deadly poison.[26]

It takes time to be assured that God is not behind false guilt and shame. This becomes quite clear by learning the distinctive voice of the Holy Spirit. We know of nothing better than God's Word, prayer, and the fellowship of caring believers to bring an understanding of the Father-heart of God. King David learned to recognize God's voice by its characteristics and qualities—including the characteristic of gentleness: *"You have also given me the shield of Your salvation; Your right hand has held me up, Your gentleness has made me great"* (Psalm 18:35).

---

26. Hulsey, *Shattering the Shackles of Shame,* 11–12.

Note how the Holy Spirit works within the human spirit:

"When the Holy Spirit discloses the matters pertaining to God He does so not to our mind nor to any other organ but to our spirit. God knows this is the sole place in man which can apprehend man's things as well as His things. The mind is not the place for knowing these things. While it is true that the mind can think and conceive many matters, it nonetheless cannot know them…. From this we can appreciate how highly God esteems the regenerated spirit of man."[27]

Alastair Roy, director of Cleansing Stream in Ireland, tells how false guilt was ruining his life. Listen to his incredible story:

One of those areas where God healed me in recent years was in the area of "false guilt." Now the Holy Spirit will bring us to repentance through guilty feelings. But false guilt is not from God. False guilt is from the accuser. But it is very subtle and can deceive us into thinking it's our guilt. And Satan can take circumstances that occur in your life and exploit them to his purposes. Satan took circumstances that occurred in my life and somehow made me feel responsible, until God intervened.

When I was twenty months old I was seriously scalded in an accident in my home. I pulled a kettle of boiling water over myself, almost died, was four months in the hospital, and still bear the scars fifty-five years later! My father blamed my mother for leaving me exposed to that danger and in all my life I never knew him to love her, to care for her, to sleep with her, or to respect her. When I was eighteen years old (1967) I left home to join the police force (Royal Ulster Constabulary). My mum and dad parted and eventually divorced.

A few years ago Pauline and I were at a ministry training conference in England and got to talking to a person taking the course. I related what I've just told you and the Lord seemed to show me

27. Watchman Nee, *The Spiritual Man, vol. 2* (New York: Christian Fellowship Publishers, Inc., 1968), 88.

through him that I had taken onboard responsibility for the break-up of my parent's marriage. Now, rationally, I knew it wasn't my fault. But somehow in my soul I had taken on a perception in my life that it was. What had really happened was that Mum had left the fire guard off and nipped out to get coal for two minutes. I had pulled the kettle over myself and dad blamed her! It wasn't her fault! It wasn't his fault! And it wasn't my fault. I was less than two years old, for goodness sake! But over the years I had embraced false guilt.

And you know Satan's clever, he knows about deception and bondage. Over the years he reinforced my false guilt. In 1971 I was a young twenty-two-year-old police sergeant on the border with the Irish Republic. It was in the early years of that thirty-years' terrorist campaign in Northern Ireland (The Troubles). One morning I detailed a young constable, Davey, under my command for duty at a security checkpoint in the town of Newry. I told him to wear his bulletproof jacket. He didn't want to—they were cumbersome things in those days—and it wasn't compulsory so I didn't insist. A couple of hours later Davey was shot in the back trying to prevent a terrorist bomb attack. He died in my arms! He was nineteen years old and his wife had their first child a week later. If he'd been wearing his flak jacket, he may have lived (we'll never know). It wasn't my fault, but I felt responsible. False guilt was reinforced!

A couple of years later Pauline and I were going to a dance in a town nearby and I asked my friend Sgt. Jimmy Hunter to swap duties with me, so I'd be free to go. I.R.A. terrorist gunmen ambushed Jimmy's patrol car and Jimmy was shot dead in the front passenger seat of the vehicle where I should have been sitting. I didn't know until the next day and refused to believe it. I drove to the hospital where they had taken him, pulled out the freezer tray in the morgue, and Jimmy, my friend and colleague, was lying there in full uniform, very dead! It wasn't my fault, but false guilt was reinforced yet again.

We all have different stories but the enemy has one strategy: False guilt!

As you can tell by Alastair's stories he was in deep emotional pain over very real tragedy and false guilt. Yet today he is free from shame and now can go through life full of joy.

AN UNFORGETTABLE STORY OF GRACE

In the Old Testament while Israel was planning on moving into the land that God had promised to them, the inhabitants of Jericho stood in their way. Joshua had assumed Moses's leadership and set about spying out the land for an invasion. Two spies were sent to Jericho and soon found secret refuge in the house of a family where Rahab, one of the women in the house, was a prostitute. Rahab, along with the rest of the city, knew of the coming invasion, and she was frightened. When it was discovered that the spies were staying with Rahab's family, the king of Jericho immediately sent word to Rahab to *"bring out the men"* (Joshua 2:3). Rahab told the messengers that the men from Israel had been there but that they had fled. All the while the two were hiding in the house. When it was safe, Rahab said to the spies:

> *I know that the LORD has given you the land, that the terror of you has fallen on us, and that all the inhabitants of the land are fainthearted because of you. For we have heard how the LORD dried up the water of the Red Sea for you when you came out of Egypt, and what you did to the two kings of the Amorites who were on the other side of the Jordan, Sihon and Og, whom you utterly destroyed. And as soon as we heard these things, our hearts melted; neither did there remain any more courage in anyone because of you, for the LORD your God, He is God in heaven above and on earth beneath. Now therefore, I beg you, swear to me by the LORD, since I have shown you kindness, that you also will show kindness to my father's house, and give me a true token, and spare my father, my mother, my brothers, my sisters, and all that they have, and deliver our lives from death.* (Joshua 2:9–13)

Because her house was built into the city wall, Rahab helped the men escape to the outside through a window. They agreed that before the assault began, she would hang a scarlet cloth in her window. Consequently, she and her family were saved.

The most beautiful part of this story is that Rahab was visited by God's grace. When her heart turned towards God, she was saved. She went down in history as one of God's great people of faith, right next to the great patriarchs—Abraham, Isaac, Jacob, Joseph, Moses, David, and many more. Read it for yourself in Hebrews 11. She's included with the great men and women of God: "*By faith the harlot Rahab did not perish with those who did not believe, when she had received the spies with peace*" (Hebrews 11:31).

We wish we didn't have to say that some people, some Christians, do not believe that God's grace can be extended to a prostitute like Rahab. But it is true. It's also true that many in the church want to classify sin in varying degrees, making one better or worse than another, and ultimately believing that perhaps an eternal hierarchy is being set up based on "good living" while here on earth. But the Bible is clear: man looks on the outside, but God looks on the heart. Rahab and Sarah stand side-by-side in God's book of honor. One lived an admirable life while the other, not so much. There is even more to Rahab's credibility because of her response to grace. Rahab was also one of Christ's ancestors. (See Matthew 1:5.)

When it's put in perspective, not one of God's great men and women in the Bible can claim any more grace than anyone else. The grace that was extended to Abraham, Isaac, Jacob, Daniel, King David and all the rest of the patriarchs was no different than the grace extended to Rahab. The scarlet cloth that saved her life can now be seen as the crimson blood that saved her soul.

It all begins with walking with God. "*Enoch walked with God three hundred years, and had sons and daughters*" (Genesis 5:22). In the process he got to know God personally. It is from this close walk that Enoch's righteousness began. We also can walk with God. We don't have to clean up our act before He will walk with us. We begin this walk with all of our weaknesses and failures, all of our bad habits, and everything both good and bad. We begin with Him loving us just as we are. And in that, He leads us in His kindness, love, and acceptance of others.

Just as I am, without one plea,
But that Thy blood was shed for me.[28]

---

28. Charlotte Elliott, "Just As I Am," 1834.

All God wants is a willingness to become His friend. If you lay before Him every good thing you have ever done, it's not good enough. God's most profound word to humanity is, "Since the standard for your reconciliation and restoration is so far beyond your ability, by simply recognizing your condition and receiving my love in Jesus, *that* will begin our relationship." One of the first things people say after coming to God through Jesus is, "I've never felt so free."

To be free...

+ Let God love you into an increasing personal relationship with Him.

+ Let Him prove His love to you in His ways, not yours.

+ Go to Him when nothing makes sense and you think He might have walked out of your life.

+ Go to Him when your strength is failing and your righteousness is collapsing.

+ Cry out to Him when you are desperate.

+ Quit trying to impress Him.

+ Cry out to Him when you realize there's nothing you can do to change yourself.

Beware of these tactics that come from the enemy to try to destroy your identity:

+ You are not strong enough; you will eventually go back to your old ways.

+ All of this is a sham. Wait and see, God won't help you to become a new person. That's your responsibility.

+ There is no such thing as a new identity; you are what you are.

+ If you've got a new identity, why do you act in old ways?

+ You can't possibly make it to the end with God.

+ There is too much sin in your past to ever change.

+ Christianity wasn't made for you. You are not good enough.

- God saves certain people because they are chosen, others such as you He wants nothing to do with.

God's promises to you:

- Greater is He who is in you than He who is in the world. (See 1 John 4:4.)

- I will never leave you or forsake you. (See Deuteronomy 31:6.)

- I've prepared a home for you in heaven. (See John 14:3.)

- I sent the Holy Spirit to help you and not to condemn you. (See John 14:16.)

- I would that none be lost, and since you agreed with me for salvation you are forever saved. (See 2 Peter 3:9.)

- My plans for you are for good and not for evil. (See Jeremiah 29:11–13.)

- Remember that the enemy goes about like a roaring lion seeking whom he may devour. You are not going to be devoured. (See 1 Peter 5:8; 1 Corinthians 1:8.)

- You are so close to me that I have called you by name. (See Isaiah 43:1.)

- My love will always remain in you. (See John 15:10.)

You have nothing to fear, because fear, anxiety, depression and discouragement never come from God. There are other kinds of shame not on our list. Since this is not a technical treatise on the subject, we hope the elements we did discuss will help in understanding a very real affliction of Christians and non-Christians alike.

A PROVERB

The LORD's blessing brings wealth, and no sorrow comes with it.

(Proverbs 10:22 NCV)

PSALMS FOR THE WOUNDED

I will praise the LORD at all times; his praise is always on my lips. My whole being praises the LORD. The poor will hear and be glad. Glorify the LORD with me, and let us praise his name together. I asked the LORD for help, and he answered me. He saved me from all that I feared. (Psalm 34:1–4 NCV)

The LORD is close to the brokenhearted, and he saves those whose spirits have been crushed. People who do what is right may have many problems, but the LORD will solve them all. (Psalm 34:18–19 NCV)

7

I FEEL USED

Everyone knows what it feels like to be criticized and rejected, often by the very people in our lives we desperately want to please. We were born and raised in a worldly environment which chooses favorites and rejects seconds. And since nobody can be the best at everything, we all were ignored, overlooked, or rejected at times by parents, teachers and friends.[29]
—*Neil Anderson*

I thought it was true that no human should lord it over me, but they beat me down so much! They were bigger than me. My brains, salvation, and worthiness were questioned if I suggested such a rebellious thought as that I was being put down. I was reminded that rebellion is as the sin of witchcraft, suggesting I'm dangerously close to losing my relationship with God if I even say I feel "lorded over."
—*Jean DeHaven*

The very essence of a "group" requires leadership. God has always used men and women to lead His people. However, His leaders were to be people willing to develop a relationship with Him so that through His imparted wisdom and understanding everyone would remain safe from abuse. The Bible does not allow any human being to "lord" it over another. Nor does it condone leaders who instill fear of man into their followers.

---

29. Neil Anderson, *Today's Devotional from Freedom in Christ Ministries*, December 3, 2014.

It is all right to fear fire when it is out of control. It is valuable to fear water if you don't know how to swim. But it is needless to fear something or someone that under normal conditions can't hurt us. However, when rational thought dissipates, fear can quickly trick us into false belief. For example, in Waco, Texas, in the early 1990's David Koresh was the leader of a sect called the Branch Davidians. He claimed to be the Messiah and taught his followers to fear both government and churches, alleging that these two entities would destroy them if they did not follow Koresh himself. Once the fear established itself, he continued its use for purposes of control. His messages emphasized the need to stay together with him for protection against an evil world. It worked, but with shocking consequences. After a 51-day standoff with the federal government for a number of offenses including weapons charges, David Koresh (Vernon Howell) and seventy-three of his followers died. Only nine others survived. One of the survivors, after twenty years, still believes that Koresh was a manifestation of God in the flesh. Even men and women with apparently good hearts can fall prey to unfounded fear.

Deception lurks in the shadows of fear and no one should think they are exempt. Too many leaders today treat their followers like cattle to be wrestled to the ground and branded with the letters of the leader, instead of being the shepherd who never leaves the sheep alone or unattended. Manipulative leadership is perhaps one of the greatest weapons of wounding that Satan uses against those in the church. It's a weighty topic, but our hope is to find freedom on the other side.

A TWISTED USE OF FEAR AND REJECTION

Some church leaders make it plain that if you were to leave their church, you would be outside of God's will and suffer His wrath. And, if you don't fall in line with their teaching, you could be excommunicated from their church—the "only" church that can save you. Such leaders are playing on one of mankind's greatest fears: being denied salvation. That one fear has the ability to manipulate, not only the gullible, but the intelligent as well. But motivation by fear always ends in disaster.

A woman was told that if she left her church she would die and go to hell. She felt empty, wanting something she knew she didn't have, and so she eventually walked into a different church in search of the truth. After the pastor of that different church spoke with her, he wondered at how much fear she must have felt when she walked through the door this new church. He thought, "Here's a woman who was willing to go to hell to find the truth." That was one courageous woman!

Any time a leader can convince followers that only a select few have access to divine knowledge from God and that the leaders are the special ones who can represent others before God, then the allegiance of the followers will shift from God to the leader. A love of God born of experiencing His personal love cannot and will not exist in such a situation. Instead, the joyless, mechanical environment will develop a sense of paranoia and obligation. Men and women will not think for themselves under the weight of such deception and manipulation. Instead, they will fear the leader and they will fear rejection. Rejection and fear almost always operate side-by-side. When ostracized by a particular church, even if not excommunicated, there is the fear of losing what you thought was your family.

Many pastors control by communicating there is no possibility of a personal and intimate relationship with God without a specific leader, a mediator. Mankind's fall from Eden and consequential inherited sense of alienation from God allows someone to come along and say, "I will represent you myself." People who are experiencing a spiritual void will respond quickly to a self-proclaimed authority who seems highly spiritual. They will believe lies like, "If you were listening to the Lord as I do, you would agree with me. Since I have been appointed as God's leader, I interpret any opposition to me to be opposition to God. You must be walking in the flesh and must repent. I sincerely advise you to submit to my authority."

The implication of such lies is that submission to the speaker's authority is the only way to grow spiritually, or even just to continue in community and fellowship. Leaders who use lies like that will also lie that they are being misunderstood when accused of being controlling. They might dig the hole even deeper by saying things like, "Any negative feelings you have about my leadership or my words are from the enemy. You're letting him lead you around and guide your thinking. I am only here to help you. My words are from God. The reason you don't like them is because you are rebellious and cooperating with the enemy."

How can a person feel anything but alone and worthless when only a select few have a voice, or the ability to express themselves? The Bible makes clear that the veil was torn in the Holy of Holies the day Jesus was crucified so that all could have unrestricted access to life, love, and intimacy in a relationship with God. In this context, believers are to be a powerful force, each as a different part of a body, working together for the good of the whole. A good pastor and shepherd will equip and encourage his or her congregation to hear the voice of God for themselves and be obedient to it.

BEATEN INTO SUBMISSION

From the beginning of time, power over people has been a highly prized goal. Alexander the Great, Hitler, Mussolini, Saddam Hussein—they all wanted power over people. The same power struggle evinces itself in churches, especially among leaders. Many leaders feel they have a God-given right to direct the church, and see themselves as called to do whatever it takes to bring it into submission.

Take the leader who, when challenged over almost anything, will react strongly and harshly. They know that by using fear, anger, shame, and humiliation they can arbitrarily shut down virtually any challenge. Or take the leader who rebuts critique by saying, "I'm God's spokesperson!" as if to say, "Your words don't count no matter what you say." When you hear something like that, then you have a right to raise more than just an eyebrow. Or take the leader who does not have a close relationship with God, but does have a charisma that draws people in. No matter their charm, such a leader will always be seeking power, not God's glory.

The very nature of leadership (that is, God-ordained leadership) may seem less than gentle even when it is done correctly. Leadership is one of the most difficult responsibilities in life because our fleshly nature doesn't always respond properly. Far too often we find pastors who are accused of abusive control when in fact they are operating within biblical guidelines. They are trying to do their best to give God-inspired direction. They are simply exercising assertiveness and decisiveness. (For more insight on what a godly leader looks like, see chapter 14.) Those with a demanding personality and a power-grabbing agenda will attempt to whip people into shape. How far this is from Jesus' admonishment that those who are greatest among us shall be the servants of all, and His words "*feed my sheep.*" "*Be sure you know how your sheep are doing, and pay attention to the condition of your cattle*" (Proverbs 27:23 NCV).

CONTROLLING OR CONTROLLED?

Once a pastor is wounded by a congregation, he or she often determines never to let it happen again by developing a dictatorial leadership style. Their realized or unrealized thought is, *I will never again subject myself to this kind of control.* And in the process they sometimes become what they despise—controlling and manipulative.

Now, there is certainly a sense that you must become controlling in order to keep from being controlled. However, to some leaders, any disagreement is perceived as a personal challenge to diminish and devalue the leader's character. And congregations lose confidence in leaders who feel threatened by disagreement or leaders who won't allow anyone else to lead alongside them for fear of being usurped. These are the leaders who feel humiliated if they are not constantly honored and instantly obeyed without question. Do you know who else had this leadership style? King Saul.

> So David went out wherever Saul sent him, and behaved wisely. And Saul set him over the men of war, and he was accepted in the sight of all the people and also in the sight of Saul's servants. Now it had happened as they were coming home, when David was returning from the slaughter of the Philistine, that the women had come out of all the cities of Israel, singing and dancing, to meet King Saul, with tambourines, with joy, and with musical instruments. So the women sang as they danced, and said: "Saul has slain his thousands, and David his ten thousands." Then Saul was very angry, and the saying displeased him; and he said, "They have ascribed to David ten thousands, and to me they have ascribed only thousands. Now what more can he have but the kingdom?" So Saul eyed David from that day forward.
>
> (1 Samuel 18:5–9)

Saul's jealousy of David eventually accelerated to the point that he hunted him down in order to kill him. His bitterness knew no bounds, and it was the result of turning his heart from God, seeking his own power, and becoming paranoid about the position of his throne.

RESPONDING TO FAULTY LEADERSHIP

There was a man who was profoundly discouraged about a number of things happening in his church, things he felt definitely needed improvement. Every time he attended church he was distracted by these things and found it almost impossible to worship. He became angrier as the months passed, especially because he saw no progress in correcting what he thought was wrong. At the same time the Holy Spirit would not allow him to say anything. He had walked with God long enough to know God's voice and to know that he had to obey. This man wrestled for a long time with feelings concerning his pastor's lack of response to what he felt were glaring problems.

It was one of the most difficult things he had ever done, to simply sit there, bothered by the situation and feeling there was no way to respond. He even looked around and wondered why everyone else seemed oblivious to the things he saw. He wanted to talk to people but knew the potential for bringing doubt and concerns into the lives of others who might be destroyed by the knowledge. He even wanted to talk to the pastor but felt cautioned against doing so. Month after month he wrestled, but slowly he began to see changes in the things he was concerned about. He was delighted. He realized that if he had addressed those situations prematurely, before he allowed God to deal with them, he may have hurt, wounded, and discouraged others. He's a man who knows Proverbs 6:19 quite well; that among the things the Lord hates is the person *"who sows discord among brethren."*

It's always good to wait a while so that we can raise our sights a little higher. It prevents us from shooting ourselves in the foot. There are certainly times God allows inconsistencies in the church because He is calling you to be an intercessor for that situation. It often takes time and opportunity to discover the true heart of a leader. Perhaps the best way to approach this problem is to throw out assumption and accusation aside along with anger, rage, and feelings of injustice, and wait to see what God does in revealing the truth.

THE PERFECT STORM

So far we have addressed this issue from the perspective of the church-goers, but for the rest of the chapter let's consider what can go wrong in a church from the perspective of the pastor. Our friend Mark, a pastor, wrote to us about an extremely agonizing situation he experienced in his church. His story gives clarity about the difficulties leaders must sometimes face. They, too, often feel alone.

> It was the most painful chapter in my life.... To see God's church almost consume itself in animosity. There are no winners in this battle and hell gets the spoils. In my thirty-three years as a minister I had never been through a church split. People come and go, and sometimes they go disgruntled for various reasons important to them. At the heart of many hostile departures is often offense, selfishness, and revenge. Other times, folks who left just need a fresh start for personal reasons.
>
> The storm I was about to experience could be called "a perfect storm." It started to brew in both the men's ministry and in the young adult ministry. The issues were over the ability of some leaders to transfer their allegiances to new associate pastors, and also over some voluntary leaders who desired to become paid staff at a time when it was not the church board's monetary priority. Soon after, four associate pastors left the church for other ministries. Subsequently four areas of the church were affected; the women's ministry, music ministry, and the two ministries that were already having difficulties, the young adult ministry and the youth ministry. To further complicate matters there were also parking problems, staff problems, and some heavy financial troubles as well. I did and continued to do everything I knew to solve the problems. Soon struggles grew in every ministry of the church.
>
> Behind the dissension were two people. One was a woman with a full-time position in the church. The other was a man who was a volunteer leader in the church. These two people, not related, were once admired, trusted, and faithful people in the work of the ministry. Then something very difficult to explain happened. They

suddenly became ruthless enemies of my wife and me. They started making false statements, innuendos, and railing accusations against senior leadership. The church board and I worked to find a solution to the situation but to no avail. Soon a good segment of the congregation began to listen to the dissidents and echo the similar sentiments. These two, John and Betty, were intent on dividing the church and encouraged people to leave, and many of them did. Both of them became involved in poisonous conversations toward pastors and staff. No one seemed to know quite why John and Betty's attitude strangely became hostile and intensified in the months to come. Many felt that John and Betty wanted to tear the church apart.

John personally stepped up his hostility and viciousness aiming it at my wife while deepening his negativism and bitterness. Betty eventually resigned but in her resignation letter continued to lash out at my wife and me. Then later Betty accused me of firing her. John was finally fired for "actions harmful to a Christian organization." After this, John and Betty organized and engineered a full onslaught of revenge to oust us from the church by taking their fight to the church body. Betty worked by sending email barrages to attendees and going to denominational officials. John worked the church by sowing seeds of slanderous statements. They used innuendo and deliberate misrepresentations for several months. Their animosity pervasively trafficked itself throughout the church. They were influencers, sounded believable, and appealed to the idea of suspecting pastors of wrongdoing.

Now a group, they sought every possible way to force us to leave: letters, threats, many emails, withholding tithes, home meetings, four or five off-site organizational meetings, demeaning name-calling, conducting lobby wars and "prayer meetings," sending church people to me to demand I leave, threatened petitions, and church-wide phone campaigns.

They freely advertised in and outside the church how bad for the church we were, and that, due to the attendance and financial downturns, we needed to leave. It was very sad because a large number of people we loved—who received from our ministry and who at one time loved us—believed what was perpetuated by these two and their growing number of supporters. The full intensity of these attacks went on for four to five months. Painfully two former associate pastors were recruited and joined their voices in the anger against us. They were people I had chosen, given places of ministry, defended, esteemed, and loved. John went to prominent locations in the church during and around services times to tell his stories to anyone who would listen. There wasn't a move I made or a word I said that wasn't criticized in those awful months by someone in the divisive group. Everything about me personally and professionally was slammed by negativity.

It was heart-wrenching for the congregation. Folks took sides—which we never wanted, but which seemed to be the forced result of a splitting congregation. Some agonized because they did not know what to believe, especially when I did little publicly to defend myself in comparison to the very public campaign directed against me. Many who were undecided were contacted so many times that they were eventually won over. Scores of people who once loved and appreciated us were targeted until they also joined the ranks of the rebellion. The church's reputation in the community was damaged. The fellowship fabric was shattered, and people scattered to any number of other churches. Folks left the church angered at me, and other families felt they could no longer stay because of the ungodly negativity taking place. Some have not returned to any church at all.

You might imagine what we went through emotionally, spiritually, and physically during these painful months. I questioned whether God wanted me to stay, but He did. I felt every assurance from the Lord to remain in my position, even when my mind and body wanted to leave. I questioned my call, but God reassured me. We both were greatly hurt, but we resolved to walk in integrity and not respond to the carnality shown by many of the antagonists. The collateral damage was tremendous. Many, many innocent people were dismayed by it all; teenagers and children, young

Christians and more, did not survive those terrible months. The church was torn apart. Church relationships that had existed for years were shattered. Families were divided as some stayed and others left. A few months after he left the church, John called one of our secretaries and bragged that in the church he now attends there are more than fifty former attendees he led away. He seemed *proud of what he did.*

LOOKING BACK

Looking back, what could I have done differently? Where was I at fault? 1) I failed to pick up on John's behavioral changes. He seemed to turn on a dime against us. I falsely assumed that with encouragement he would be the same helpful John he had been. I was wrong. 2) I failed to understand how deceptively and energetically Betty would act in her revenge. For example, I was ready to keep her when she, in essence, fired herself.

Eventually God begin to speak to me and to the congregation, "Be fused with My Spirit...not confused with the words of man, and you will wear the garland of triumph. Do not allow the hindrances the Evil One has sown to confuse you. If you will be diligent, you will be blest. You will overcome. You will have an increase of love, of purpose, an increase of peace. My joy in you will be your everyday strength."

Then encouraging, inspired words from many others raised our faith for God to strongly move in the congregation, and He did not disappoint. The church sought God and He came with power, love, and hope. In the ensuing thirty months and more, scores of people were miraculously healed. The district who had received evil reports about me now gave me opportunity to share about the outpouring at our district ministries summit.

I am so glad I was not led by God to take the fight to the pulpit, although I must confess I wanted to many times. The church still hasn't recovered fully in attendance and finances from the split. It's hard for people to recover. It's hard for pastors and their families to recover. It is as if there's a collective traumatic battlefield effect, but God is restoring the church. Each Sunday, new faces and a new energy is bringing in His *"new thing"!* (Isaiah 43:18–19).

I'm still healing. It was the most painful chapter in my life. Even writing this opens those wounds a bit, but if it will help others to survive such difficult times, it is worth it. My wife and I started from day one to forgive these people, no matter what, but many we cannot trust again.[30]

I love the Lord with all my heart. It's a profound privilege and joy to serve the Lord and to pastor His church. There's nothing I enjoy more than being in His presence. If I have nothing better to do with my life but to love, serve, and enjoy Him, I will be very happy. I hunger for more of God with a hunger that will never be satisfied till I arrive at His throne. Unfortunately, church life is littered with pastors who were abused by their congregations, and congregations who were abused by their pastors. Sometimes it's difficult to determine which one is the abuser because things become so complicated, distorted, and carnal. But God knows. In that we take confidence.

The following is from a person who had first-hand access to Mark and his church:

I watched firsthand what happened to Mark and his wife as a result of outright lying and falsehood against them. It cut them to the quick! Their heart broke in two and the tears were endless. The questions a pastor asks of himself or herself are relentless: "What did I do to deserve this? How could someone I loved and cared for so much, someone I prayed for, supported and helped during times of crisis, seek to take my life?"

The Scripture that states, *"Strike the Shepherd, and the sheep will be scattered"*[31] is so very true! The fields are littered with the ema-

---

30. There is a powerful false conception about forgiveness that insists "trust without conditions or boundaries." However, to work through the forgiveness issue is one thing, to trust someone again is quite another. More on forgiveness in chapter 9.
31. Zechariah 13:7.

ciated bodies of good men and women, shepherds, who sought to serve the Lord but have been cruelly struck down! Sometimes they survive the attack and go forward to shepherd God's sheep. But many, perhaps most, never make it. You never hear of them again. The despair and heartache become too much. No one truly understands the depth of agony men and women go through as they pastor God's flock. It can be brutal.

Later Mark wrote to us again, concluding: "The thing I'd say about the subject now is that there are many, many pastors who have gone through horrendous situations like we did—and many worse than ours—at the hands of their boards and congregations. In no way do I minimize the abuse at times pastors give to people, but there are many times when it's the other way around. The trail is littered with many disillusioned but called persons who have been very ill-treated."

THE ALIENATING POWER OF PRIDE

It is frustrating when a person who has been faithful in serving the Lord, has been supportive of his pastor for years, and has ministered in the church all this time, suddenly changes. After something happens that causes negative attitudes or some event takes place in which a root of bitterness takes hold, they become a sower of discord and a hateful opponent of leadership. They establish friendships among people who will agree with their point of view and do everything in their power to uproot and get rid of the current leadership. What's the cause? Often, pride is.

> Satan's desire is to work in the local church, to hinder its ministry; and to do this, he must work in and through Christians or professed Christians who are a part of that fellowship. Pride is one of his chief weapons. If he can get a pastor proud of his preaching, a Sunday school teacher proud of his class's growth, or a church officer proud of his experience and leadership, then Satan has a foothold from which to launch his attack.[32]

---

32. Warren W. Wiersbe, *The Strategy of Satan* (Wheaton, IL: Tyndale House, 1979), 67.

The kind of pride and arrogance that tries to destroy God's work can be seen in the new pastor who comes to town saying, "We've decided to come to this place and plant a new church because no one is preaching the gospel here." It can be seen in the pastor who related that his church would never be a mega-church because his own church preached the gospel—implying that larger churches simply "tickle people's ears" and never preach "real righteousness." It can be seen in the pastor who concluded that most churches were not preaching the *true* gospel. (When asked for an example, he could only come up with one—and it was in his own town.) It is seen in the pastors who believe that the bigger the church, the less it is concerned with preaching the Bible.

(In one case, a church with a constituency of several hundred was down the road from a church of ten thousand. In a staff meeting, the executive pastor suggested the team come up with a strategy on "how to combat" the mega-church down the road.) And perhaps worst, it is seen in the vague accusation that many, if not most, churches are "feel-good" churches that preach "fluff," in that they don't address God's wrath and the subjects of hell and punishment.

The authors of this book have traveled extensively for years and have found few of the above broad-brushed statements to be true. In fact, we are pleased to report that God is doing great things today and many people are responding no matter what the size of the church. It would be foolish to assume that backslidden churches do not exist, but that's not the point. The point is that to take what one assumes to be true about some churches and people, and generalize that to claim that most churches have corrupted the gospel, is falsehood. And every word of criticism will have to be accounted for. Wise men and women seek to know the truth by personal examination, which is difficult and requires listening to both sides in nothing less than humility and gentleness. This is what is required of leaders.

Some leaders truly feel they are doing God's work, carrying the banner of Christ and upholding the integrity of the church, while all the time they are being used by the enemy to tear down the foundations of the local church. In a time of cultural crisis, their righteous indignation carries them too far and their self-justification keeps them from coming back. It's a hotbed for unbiblical extremism. Usually oblivious to how manipulative and controlling they have become, such leaders are, in a way, spiritual demagogues.

Demagoguery is when a person or group of people work within the framework of a state, a country, a church, or any kind of organization to raise up a group from within in order to eventually conquer the existing group. These leaders, really false leaders, use prejudices, false promises, false claims, and inaccurate statements to champion their cause. They are often masters at using emotions to control their audience. Adolf Hitler promised to change the drastic conditions that Germany fell into after WWI. Large numbers of people were out of work, others faced poverty, and a general unrest prevailed. People listened to him. In Italy, Benito Mussolini promised the same. Mussolini appealed to the masses with the promise that he could fix everything that was wrong with the country. These men were demagogues (people who are intent on overthrowing another group of people in unscrupulous ways). They rise up at convenient times when there is unrest, confusion, fear, and instability.

So it often is in the church. Someone gathers people around them who are disgruntled and want to see change, but does so through slander, false statements, fabricated lies, and deceptive statements. When they are able to form a large enough and strong enough faction, they either leave the church with a significant following, or overtake the church itself. They will actually sacrifice the entire body to get what they want. They don't care who gets hurt or even destroyed.

THE GREATEST KING ALSO FELT ALONE

King David speaks of a man who was his close friend and advisor, who dined with him, yet turned against him:

> All who hate me whisper together against me; against me they devise my hurt. "An evil disease," they say, "clings to him. And now that he lies down, he will rise up no more." Even my own familiar friend in whom I trusted, who ate my bread, has lifted up his heel against me.
>
> (Psalm 41:7–9)

Sometimes it is hard to know the root of the problems that tear people apart. Quite often, however, anger, bitterness, and unforgiveness lie at the source. Common phrases from such spiritual demagogues are:

...you hurt somebody who was close to me

...you didn't take my advice

...you opposed me publicly

...you dealt unfairly with me

...you ignored me

...you judged me wrongly

...you think you are powerful enough to play with my emotions

...you didn't give me the position I wanted or deserved

...you neglected me, and as a result I'll find a way to get back at you.

There is a generation that is pure in its own eyes, yet is not washed from its filthiness. There is a generation—oh, how lofty are their eyes! And their eyelids are lifted up. There is a generation whose teeth are like swords, and whose fangs are like knives, to devour the poor from off the earth, and the needy from among men.   (Proverbs 30:12–14)

Out of the mouth of babes and nursing infants you have ordained strength, because of Your enemies, that You may silence the enemy and the avenger.   (Psalm 8:2)

Arise, O Lord, do not let man prevail; let the nations be judged in Your sight.   (Psalm 9:19)

No matter where we turn in life or in the Bible, we find people torn apart by someone's selfish and even evil intentions. Again, we look at King David who banished his son Absalom had killed the man who raped his sister and then fled from his father. By the time Absalom was allowed to come back, the hook had been set. Bitterness had taken root. He saw his father as a weak leader who needed to be dethroned. At this point Absalom went to work persuading the people that David was a bad king. He literally stole the hearts of the people. Absalom was good at working on the young men of the city, and soon was able to lead a revolt against David. It was a futile mistake and Absalom lost his life. God hadn't left David. (See 2 Samuel 14–19.)

If you intend to serve God you may well face the pain of isolation. It would appear that the universal characteristic of healthy leader is having, at some point, walked through the fiery trial of loneliness and rejection and come out the other end still determined to serve God and love people.

A PROVERB

Every day is hard for those who suffer, but a happy heart is like a continual feast. (Proverbs 15:15 NCV)

PSALMS FOR THE WOUNDED

I am tired of crying to you. Every night my bed is wet with tears; my bed is soaked from my crying. My eyes are weak from so much crying; they are weak from crying about my enemies. Get away from me, all you who do evil, because the LORD has heard my crying. The LORD has heard my cry for help; the LORD will answer my prayer. (Psalm 6:6–9 NCV)

The LORD defends those who suffer; he defends them in times of trouble. (Psalm 9:9 NCV)

I praise the LORD because he advises me. Even at night, I feel his leading. I keep the LORD before me always. Because he is close by my side, I will not be hurt. (Psalm 16:7–8 NCV)

8

I CAN'T FORGIVE

Use me, God. Show me how to take who I am, who I want to be,
and what I can do, and use it for a purpose greater than myself.
—*Dr. Martin Luther King Jr.*

The following story is from a man who has spent years trying to forgive:

My grandfather was of strong personality, so much so that it
was probably more of a detriment to him than a blessing. It certainly had a lasting impact on his children and grandchildren who
grew up in his shadow.

He had many fine qualities, but many shortcomings as well. He
was born in 1896, was of German descent, and knew the lessons of
life that come from hard work. He married and raised a family of
two boys and one girl, who became my mother.

My grandfather was "instrumental" in my religious upbringing,
taking his grandchildren to church every Sunday without fail. He
was a man not only of strict religious conviction but the type who
believed that a man's handshake in commitment was as strong and
binding as any written contract. He tried to instill this in his progeny and showed, without reservation, his disappointment if one of
them fell short of his expectations.

He also did not have much faith in politicians (a rather insight-
ful and proven position that holds with me today). He believed
that instruction from the world was of little value. It was only what

Christ, the Apostles, the biblical patriarchs, and what he himself had to say that was of much "meat." He was not easy to love but he did have a tremendous impact on my spiritual life. His influence is still with me.

My grandfather saw only in black and white. He didn't suffer physically from colorblindness but sometimes did see poorly in spiritual matters, which affected his compassion for people who didn't agree with him. Such it was with most of his beliefs. He seemed to always have biblical support against which no sound defense could be proffered. God's word was black or white, a man was hot or cold, and there was no in between.

I felt his prejudice of judgment, and was hurt deeply by his rejection. Through his lens on life, I felt I was unacceptable and destined to hell.

I don't hate him but neither do I forgive him as completely as I seem to be able to do with many people in life who have wronged me. I don't believe anyone's wrongs should be explained away by the era or mind-set in which they were raised. Were that to be a deciding factor in forgiveness, no one would ever be held responsible for their actions. Forgiveness is something only God can truly give. Man may (and should) try to mimic God in such treatment of others, but in reality, few ever forgive without some sort of caveat, some prejudice in so doing. Forgiveness is almost always conditional. My grandfather cannot be exonerated. Maybe that is the better word to use in regards to my feelings about him. I forgive him as best I can but he, like everyone, must give account for his actions, and it is only God—not me, nor any man or woman—who ever absolves another.

NO EASY FIXES

We believe forgiveness is the only way forward. But we know it's no easy fix.

A woman had been repeatedly raped by her uncle from the age of seven to seventeen. He threatened to harm both her sister and her mother if she said anything. The very mention of his name would cause her to vomit. If some well-meaning Christian had come along and said to her, "You just need to forgive him for what he did," when he was totally unrepentant, it would have been unfair, unrealistic, and unbiblical. Legally, from a biblical standpoint, she can turn the debt he owes her over to God to begin to release herself from the pain of what was stolen from her. But imagine what pain we would cause her if we said something trite like, "You've got to forgive or God won't forgive you." We may mean well but we are only causing more pain.

Forgiveness has as much to do with the health of the forgiver as it does with the one who is forgiven. Forgiveness is about walking away from the hurt without ever needing to look back. Forgiveness was never meant to exonerate the one who created the wound. Nor does it mean a person must now return to an unjust situation or deny that that situation was unjust. Forgiveness is not saying it didn't happen. That would be a relinquishment of our rights. It would also be a lie, for the offense did happen. In releasing someone, we are not releasing them from all justice. But we *are* releasing them to God's justice, not ours.

Legally, the offender owes a debt to the offended. But we can turn the debt of our offender, who has never repaid their debt, who is not around, and who has never shown repentance, over to Jesus. The debt still exists, but the ownership of the debt and the associated pain are transferred to Jesus. Transferring the debt disconnects us from the debtor. They no longer have control over us because the tie is broken. It is much cheaper to release a debt to God than to be continually angry.

We know the principle of repentance requires forgiveness. But keep in mind that repentance, or any other issue that needs to be dealt with in our lives, has more to do with sending up a flare to God, asking for help: "God, I'm in trouble, I need your help. I don't want to walk this way." Neither repentance nor forgiveness are magic buttons that we can push or magic words that we can say and suddenly see results. If we want to see ourselves truly set free, we cannot short-circuit or misunderstand His often slow way of doing things to bring peace and freedom.

There are literally thousands of people everywhere who have experienced the kind of pain we're talking about—perhaps including you. You may have been in the congregation, or you may have been in leadership where terrible wounding took place. Because of this, the thought of ever stepping foot inside a church again is almost inconceivable. Church only reminds you of your pain.

Others have decided to stay in the church, but their souls feel dead. They now have difficulty relating to other people because the pain of a former experience has never been healed. (Pain not dealt with properly will never go away.) They believe that if they ever shared their pain with somebody else, they would hear the same unfortunate words, "Well, you just have to forgive. If you can't forgive, you won't be forgiven."

Something about that statement feels so wrong. It seems so unfair and unjust. And it is. Because hidden within we know that there is no forgiveness without repentance. Repentance and forgiveness are inextricably related in the Bible. You do not find one without the other. Unless the offender repents to the offended there is no release of the debt.

You can't truly forgive someone unless they have repented.

THE HAZARDS OF IDENTIFICATIONAL REPENTANCE

There's a very popular way of helping people to forgive called "Identificational Repentance." The ministry we are associated with, Cleansing Stream, once practiced it without question. In effect, it's where the person ministering says to the person who has been abused, "I am going to stand in the place of the one who has hurt you. I'm so sorry for what I did to you. I hurt you. I wounded you, and I stole your innocence. Would you please forgive me for what I did?" The normal response from those ministered to is tears and release. The only problem is that there has been *no real repentance* from the actual abuser. It is simply a device to release the pain of the one abused.

There was a girl, not associated with our ministry, who was carrying a great deal of pain. She had been repeatedly raped by her father while growing up. Now a teenager, she had been told that she simply needed to forgive her father in order to go on with life. In obedience, she went through the process of saying that she forgave him through an Identificational Repentance session. The girl, believing that everything was right with her father, went home to visit, and told him that she forgave him, whereupon he raped her again.

Chris Hayward, director of Cleansing Stream Ministries and co-author of this book, later noted,

> When I heard about this, I grieved terribly, thinking, *What have we done? What are we doing that is creating such a wrong impression in the eyes of the one we pray for?* From that point on I decided we were not going to do Identificational Repentance as it is traditionally done. Instead, we would address the abused stating, "I wish your abuser could stand in front of you the way I am now doing and tell you the words I am going to say—'I'm so sorry for what I did to you, it was so wrong. It was unjust and you didn't deserve it. There's nothing you did that made me do what I did. It was not your fault.'" At that point we would speak the words of repentance stating how sorry we were for what they had endured. Of course we were not the abuser, nor had the abuser spoken those words. In the ministry session, it did serve to help recall the memories of the event, but it did nothing to deal with the pain of unforgiveness. To accomplish that, we now introduce them to the High Court of Heaven saying, "Every one of you would love to hear your abuser saying these words to you. You would love to see them apologize, repent before you sincerely, and ask you for forgiveness. But the truth is most of you will never hear those words in this lifetime. Most of you will never have your abuser stand before you and truly repent before you and God. If they did, you and I both know you would be obligated to forgive them. If someone steals your coat, you can get another one and it would seem a small thing to forgive that person even if you never saw them again. But if someone takes a part of your life away and steals your innocence, how can you ever get that back? And if that person who did that never repents before you, how can you possibly forgive them?"

In many Christian circles wounded people hear, "Just forgive!" And although something deep inside them may say, *this is so unfair, this is not right, this is unjust,* in order to accommodate the people praying and supporting, they mouth the words of forgiveness. Afterward, inside, the pain never really goes away because something unjust has just taken place, another denial of justice. We must come to realize there is an inextricable link between repentance by the one who offended and forgiveness from the one offended. And if someone does not repent, then how can we forgive?

So what are we saying? Are we saying that you don't have to forgive—that you can just forget about it? No. In order to be released from the great pain of abuse, one must forgive vertically—not horizontally. The horizontal may never happen. In other words the person who abused you will most likely never ask for forgiveness—but we do have a way for freedom to take place, and that way starts first with God and the jurisprudence practiced in the High Court of Heaven. We know that God is good, loving, faithful, and just. Because of this we know that we can approach Him because of our relationship with Him through Jesus Christ. It is on this vertical level that we can release our pain and receive our healing.

THE HIGH COURT OF HEAVEN

When you received Jesus Christ as Lord and Savior, you have entered into the High Court of Heaven. Accompanying you on one side was the devil, your Accuser. (See Revelation 12:10.) On the other side is your Advocate, Jesus. Entering the court, the Judge of the universe, Father God, asks for the charges. The first one to speak is the devil who begins to recite all of your sins before God, starting with how unworthy you are, and accusing you in every possible way. The Judge then asks how you plead. Before you can say anything, Jesus steps between you and the Father and says, "He is guilty of all charges." Before you can respond, the Judge states that the penalty is death. Inside, you *know* that the judgment is fair in front of such a holy God. But at that point Jesus approaches the Father and says, "Father, you know that he has believed in Me, he has entrusted his life to Me, he knows that without Me there is no hope. He has trusted in the fact that I went to the cross and paid for all of his sin. He has received that truth." At that point the Father says, "I realize this. I grant a pardon."

Did this really happen? Yes, in truth it did. We have an Advocate before the Father, Jesus Christ Himself, who has legally paid the debt. (See 1 John 2:1.) We have believed in Him and have received reconciliation and freedom with God. That High Court still exists for our benefit. We may enter at any time we wish. We are not playing word games. The Scripture says that we have access into the Holy of Holies through the blood of Jesus Christ. (See Hebrews 10:19.) There is a court in heaven where justice and love rule. We can come to that court any time and present our case.

As you walk into that court today, you can say to the Judge who is your loving heavenly Father, "Father, I'm in pain. The weight of the abuse I have received is crushing me. It is tearing me apart. I know I can't be the judge and jury. So I'm asking you, can I bring all of this pain, all of this judgment, all of the bitterness, and all of the anger I feel to you? Can I turn my case over to you?" At this point, your heavenly Father will say, without hesitation, "Yes, I will take all of your hurt, all of your pain, all of your judgments. I will take your case. I will do everything in my power to bring your abuser to a place of repentance. But if they do not repent, justice will be served."

Then you can respond in a declaration: "By turning this case, this debt, over to God, I realize that I'm releasing all of my judgments, all my pain, and every sense of injustice that has happened to me that is associated with this debt. And I've turned it over to the One who can release me from my pain and bring justice."

There are four particular Scriptures people use in stating, "You must forgive": Matthew 6, Matthew 18, Ephesians 4:32, and Colossians 3:3. One says that we must forgive even as we have been forgiven. But what was the basis for our forgiveness: didn't we have to repent before God? Jesus died on the cross for all of us, but for us to receive salvation we had to repent. In another Scripture, Jesus said from the cross: *"Father, forgive them, for they do not know what they do"* (Luke 23:34). Who is He speaking to? It wasn't to those who were abusing Him. They were still abusing Him and were unrepentant. Jesus was speaking to His Father. It was a vertical relationship, not a horizontal one. Certainly, He was referring to His abusers, but His words were to the Father and not to those who were harming Him.

Stephen asked God to not hold a charge against those who were stoning him—he said nothing about personally forgiving them. Because Stephen was the one offended, he had a right to do with the debt what he wished.

He could outright let it go, or he could turn it over to God. A company that holds the mortgage on your house has a right to sell that mortgage to anyone they choose. In the same way, we have the right to convey the debt owed to us by the abuser to God, who then holds that mortgage or debt.

When we release a debt to God, we are not eliminating the obligation these people have to God for committing the sin, we are simply releasing them from any judgment that we would hold against them. In other words, we are not holding them accountable any longer, we are simply turning them over to God, who will hold them accountable.

Let us illustrate: suppose a man murders your closest friend. That person caused great offense. You can release that offense to God because the pain is too much to bear. When you do that you are releasing your right to judge any longer. However, the murderer still has offended God and until he repents he continues to be guilty of murder. In effect we have released all the pain and judgments to God, but the murderer must still give an account.

Forgiveness is a legal transaction based on repentance. But what about the Scripture that says, "If you forgive the sins of any, they are forgiven them" (John 20:23). This can be best understood by a paraphrase of Jesus' prayer on the cross: "Father, I'm releasing, remitting (sending away) my legal right for justice to you." When we remit (forgive) sin we do not remit to the person and say it never happened, for that would be a lie. We are remitting it to God because He is the One who will eventually judge. For another example, Nehemiah confessed the sins of his former generation, but he didn't repent. God was simply asking that generational sin be acknowledged. Nehemiah did, however, repent (turned away from) for his own sins.

Do not think we do not need to forgive. We are saying it's the way people require you to do forgive that is not right. To restate, an unrepentant person cannot be legally forgiven on a horizontal level. But they can be forgiven on a vertical level we have with our Father and righteous Judge. It is our Father's pleasure to release us from the pain associated with the case (He takes it upon Himself) and blesses us with life.

In the case of the girl who was again raped by her father after telling him that she forgave him for what he had previously done to her, she mistakenly believed that reconciliation was now possible because she had chosen to forgive. What she failed to recognize was that her father was completely unrepentant. No matter how much she wanted to, she did not have the legal right to forgive him without his repentance. As we began the section saying, forgiveness without repentance is not possible. The two are plainly linked together, you don't find one without the other. And it is unwise to assume because one has given the case to God (forgiven vertically), that the forgiven one is now trustworthy, especially if there has been no repentance. If an offender really wants to have forgiveness there has to be repentance.

Tragically, the possibility that the person who offended you would come to you in deep repentance (meaning he or she has turned away from their abuse) is highly unlikely. (See Matthew 18:35.) But you can find release from your pain even though the offending party is totally unrepentant. Our love for God and our trust in His justice enables us to turn our case over to Him, knowing that He will do with it what is necessary, and at the same time relieve us of our pain (see 1 Peter 5:7), and that He will do everything in His power to bring the offender to the place of repentance. But even God cannot force someone to repent. If they refuse to do so, some day justice will come.

LET US RESTATE

So that we do not create misinformation or appear to minimize forgiveness, please keep the following in mind. Although the abused often suffers greatly from the abuser, there is still the need for both to come to terms with the offense. We would hold that the abuser should repent and ask for forgiveness, although far too often that doesn't happen. The pain suffered by the abused is often compounded by those who misunderstand forgiveness. But the abused still has a responsibility to handle life's circumstances correctly.

And if the abuser does legitimately ask for forgiveness, with God's help, the abused can stand willing to allow the abuser to repent before them and to offer forgiveness. Yet, and this is important, that repentance does not demand reconciliation and fellowship. There still may be good cause for distance and protection from further abuse. Also keep in mind that by saying "sorry" the abuser still isn't off the hook. *Sorry* is not repentance. It may start the process, but it is not repentance.

Pastor Jack Hayford teaches, "A *just* God never *just* forgives." The forgiveness offered through the atoning work of the cross is for those who come in repentance. If it were not so, there would be no need for evangelism. God's heart is to forgive everyone, and His provision stands ready. In addition, His mercy is infinitely grander than your sin.

When you can stand in the presence of the Lord and nothing comes to mind but worshiping Him, you have found freedom. When heartaches, bitterness, and jealousies are kept from raising their ugly heads, you are free, at least for the moment. When these amazing moments calm our soul and become larger and longer over time, freedom is no longer an aspiration but a reality in the making. Stop! This sounds like heaven. And to a great degree it is. However, those who are increasingly becoming free find that freedom is a direction and not a state of mind. Because of the constant battle with the flesh and the devil, it's hard to nail freedom down and make it stay in place. The closer we stick to God, the easier it is to experience freedom. But it is hard to stay close to God. Anybody who says it isn't has already gone to heaven. It's important to put forth effort but perhaps the most important thing is to stay open to Him. This is essential for those who feel they must always be doing something *for* God. Great freedom comes with the knowledge that God wants to do something for us first, just because He wants to.

QUESTIONS FOR THE WOUNDED AND THE WOUNDER

Here are some helpful questions to ask ourselves when we know that we want to seek forgiveness, but can't quite figure out how.

Questions to ask when we have been hurt and are willing to have the hurt removed:

1.   Is my offense based on direct involvement, or am I picking up the offense from someone else?

2.   Am I absolutely certain of the facts? Or is my information taken out of context and/or pre-judged motives?

3. Have I spoken directly with the offender to hear his or her heart?

4. Am I willing to release all judgments and pain to God?

5. Have I given time for the Holy Spirit to first bring conviction to the other person?

6. Have I asked the Lord to reveal any hidden motives on my part?

7. Have I repented of any personal wrongdoing?

8. Before confronting, have I asked the Lord for His timing and His manner; have I asked Him for what, when, where, and how?

9. Have I shared my offense with anyone else, causing further division?

10. Will my actions be a demonstration of love?

Questions to ask when we have been the offender and are willing to admit it:

1. Have I prayed and asked the Holy Spirit to reveal my true offense?

2. Have I asked the Lord to reveal the manner by which I am to ask forgiveness?

3. Am I willing to allow the offended party to share the full extent of the pain I caused?

4. Am I willing to ask for their forgiveness rather than just telling them "I'm sorry"?

5. Am I willing to ask for their forgiveness without telling them how they have also offended me?

6. Am I willing to agree and empathize with their pain?

7. Am I willing to ask the Lord to help change my character (heart) as a result?

Because you picked up this book, it is quite likely that you were once wounded in a church. We certainly want to help you to understand how and why these things happened, but we would be doing you a disservice if we did not offer you a way to deal with your previous hurts and pains.

Because of this, we want to provide you with a prayer in which you can use your own words to take the hurt and pain to the Lord, to convey that hurt and pain to Him, and to be released of any bitterness, unforgiveness, and judgments that resulted from it. The act of this prayer will not release the people who offended you from accountability. Only God can do that. It is meant to acknowledge and then release you of your own personal pain.

A Prayer of Release:

Heavenly Father, it is my choice to be a forgiving person. I know my case is just, but I can no longer carry the weight of judgments. The pain is just too great. Therefore, I release into Your hands all of my hurt, bitterness, anger, and pain. I further release into Your hands all my judgments and all those who have abused me in any way. I leave them all with You, for You are trustworthy and good and You will take care of any abuse against me or Your people. I thank You that You will do everything in Your power to bring these people to a place of repentance. I also realize that if they do not repent, justice will come by Your hand and not mine. In the name of Jesus, amen.

A PROVERB

The plans that good people make are fair, but the advice of the wicked will trick you. (Proverbs 12:5 NCV)

PSALMS FOR THE WOUNDED

I was in trouble, so I called to the LORD. The LORD answered me and set me free. (Psalm 118:5 NCV)

I am sad and tired. Make me strong again as you have promised. Don't let me be dishonest; have mercy on me by helping me obey your teachings. (Psalm 119:28–29 NCV)

It was good for me to suffer so I would learn your demands. (Psalm 119:71 NCV)

PART II: THE HOPE

9

WILL I EVER GET PAST THE PAIN?

Don't stop feeling just because you were hurt. Don't stop dream-
ing just because you had a nightmare!
—*Anonymous*

Seldom do we come across someone who writes, not just informative-
ly, but inspirationally and insightfully as well. It's even harder to find
someone who can articulate efficiently and effectively after going through a
lifetime of extreme difficulties. Jean DeHaven is one of those unique people.

Jean stuck it out with Jesus where many would have run. With faith
nearly gone and hope a fleeting concept, she didn't give up. Today she understands abuse from the world and sadly from the church as well. What
makes her material both so interesting and provocative at the same time
is her genuine love for the church. She has no desire to castigate it or rail
against its leaders, but she is quite willing to speak to its abuses when
needed in order to strengthen it. Jean is open to addressing difficult issues,
while at the same time careful not to grieve the Holy Spirit. She is almost
overly concerned that what she says brings life and not death.

After attending a Cleansing Stream Retreat, she began the emails that
have become so helpful in writing this book. Her insights, though written
through painful memory, have been both delightful and heartbreaking.
She has the ability to relate deeply to so many of us who have suffered at
the hands of poor and deceptive teaching as well as the sometimes careless
and wanton attitudes of by religious leaders. We are thankful that she has

not given up on Jesus because of abuses in the church. We're also so thankful for her insights throughout this book and her willingness to share them with us. We wanted to begin Part II: The Hope with Jean's thoughts on how she was able to get past the pain.

A TESTIMONY OF GETTING PAST THE PAIN

Some days are so taxing. Some days it is just hard to get started. The spiritual obstructions manifest themselves in an increased physical difficulty of getting around. I wake up and question how much longer I can do this. Yes, God has always been there. Yes, wonderful progress has been made. But I have been so leaky, giving out, that I repeatedly come close to giving up. However, Psalm 37:7 says, *"Rest in the LORD, and wait patiently for Him."* Jeremiah 31:5 speaks of hearing a voice of trembling and panic, of terror, and not of peace. But God tells Jeremiah to refrain from weeping, *"for your work shall be rewarded"* and his children shall return from the enemy's land (31:16). He assures Jeremiah that He will create a nation from the blind and lame. (See 31:8.)

Feel like you qualify? Then it's exactly as it should be.

It feels unfair that life should be so hard for me and not for others, but I don't know if I see into other's lives accurately enough to know if that's true. I have to be careful how I measure my fruit. I sometimes get so tired of only seeing buds, a flower here and there, and then interminably green apples. But I must remember that it wouldn't be there at all if I hadn't, in spite of the agony, taken Him up on His offer to be with me, and put my back into it.

It's hard to trust in a good future when one dreads the nights, but it has to be done. We may look at the mountain ahead and tremble. But when He asks us to climb a mountain, it's to increase our intimacy and dependence on Him. As I reflect on the seasons of deep pain and trauma in my own life, I can clearly see several themes that are helpful in overcoming and moving into the fullness of the future God has for me.

IDENTITY

First, understanding your identity in Christ is crucial. It does matter what kind of father we had in life, but God, the incorruptible Father, supersedes that experience and will do so for eternity. Our sonhood and daughterhood is the position we work from. He has called us friends, not slaves. (See John 15:15.) He asked that we be filled with His joy. (See John 17:13.) What a high-octane tankful to run on!

Defining identity through the eyes of others is a setup for constant pain. Identity comes from a legal right to be a distinct person. Revelation 12:10 refers to Satan as the *"accuser of our brethren."* We have to believe God recognizes our identity, even when self-doubt or external accusation knock on the door for attention. When your identity feels challenged, and thoughts and feelings of worthlessness and hopeless come, know that these are not of God. Confidently choose to let God define you through His eyes as He reveals what your identity is. Psalm 15:2 commends speaking truth in our hearts. When we rebel against the devil's lies, a holy rebellion takes place. When we embrace our God-given identity and shut out the voice of the enemy, it's like seed falling on good soil. Be careful what judgments about yourself that you hear, from any source, and do not rehearse them to yourself, even if it makes you feel better. Self-pity is a toxic spiritual waste. It is bondage.

Despite what others say about me, I am humbled at how passionate God is about me. I don't know why disabilities occur. But I am amazed at God's description of Himself, that He is *"jealous"* for me. (See Exodus 34:14.) That means I am His, warts and all, disabilities or not, and He wants me. He wants my attention and welcomes it. I not only have *permission* to live with Him, but He *wants* me to live with Him. I am His child, chosen, set apart, royalty, the apple of His eye. As I keep truth before me and place more weight on His words than on man's words, health and wholeness come to my soul, and they will come to yours, too.

EVERY THOUGHT CAPTIVE

Second, we must bring every thought captive to the obedience of Christ. (See 2 Corinthians 10:5.) Sometimes we have to raise our swords and swing hard to assault thoughts, leading them captive instead of letting them take us captive. It *is* possible, because the Word says it is, and it must be done. Just because a thought comes and our flesh leans into its pressure, doesn't make it true. However, sometimes it does make us want to hide, make us fear we have fallen short, and make us grieve unnecessarily.

I have come to see that if we analyze life too much, we squeeze the good things out of it. Some thought processes are non-productive at best. Some downright destroy joy and peace. When we don't understand, when we fail or are humiliated, the self-questioning begins. It's amazing how little it takes to start a flood of obsessive thoughts. And when negative memories are recalled, they can potentially destroy the vision God has given us. Second-guessing past actions, like always staring into the rear-view mirror, distracts us from oncoming hazards and opportunities. Each negative thought has a message of destruction, and the constant rehearsal of the message hammers against the soul.

Now, it is true that intense betrayals and injuries have shaken me to the core, and self-protection does seem to be the natural response, but often it is demon-assisted. God's love has a different message about my painful memories, a message that can only be seen through the cross, a message that is freeing, pure, practical, and truthful, a message that builds up, protects, and banishes our vulnerability to its conclusion. The purity and wholesomeness of His love is a mighty shield for war and life. Internal false witnesses can be as loud and unrelenting as tinnitus, but they must be taken captive and brought into obedience to Jesus.

Often we experience pain from hearing negative words from others because somewhere inside us, we believe what the person said was true. Ignoring these thoughts and giving them to Jesus takes away their control. It's amazing how intense distractions can be! Fight them with a counter-distraction, by sitting back, counting, and savoring the foundational people in your life. Those resilient, independent coworkers, those struck with wisdom who have been willing to share with you. If you take the time to bring them to mind, you might find they were salted into your life over the years right when you most needed them. Health comes as we focus on how we have been blessed and take the other thoughts captive.

So remember who Jesus made you to be and speak out loud to yourself the truth of your identity. Thankfully, my mind has a limited number of things it can think about at once, and that helps.

FULL OF COURAGE

The third theme I have found in moving past pain is learning to deal with discouragement. Discouragement points to reasons to give up and tries to tell me it's "common sense" to not try any more. But if we stop, we miss the dawn. There is a joy in successful endurance. We cannot listen to the judgments of ourselves by ourselves or others (see Psalm 26:4–5) because they are false witnesses (see Psalm 27:12) that destroy the vision or heart-call God has given us. Proverbs 13:12 says, "*Hope deferred makes the heart sick, but when the desire comes, it is a tree of life.*" When we walk through seasons of pain, hope often feels deferred. Our hearts feel sick because a situation seems inescapable, and the weight seems too much to bear. Yet God calls us to be strong and courageous, to be filled with desire, and He will produce life in the midst of what seems like a wilderness.

The disappointment of expecting love where we have a right to expect it but not getting it, is excruciatingly hard to bear. Our Father says He is love, and He is not dangerous. If we repeatedly encounter things that don't feel like love from people we thought would "be true," it's an opportunity for growth or decay. Remember that the devil departed from Jesus "*until an opportune time*" (Luke 4:13). It helps to bury my head in Jesus' lap, so I can't feel, hear, or see anything else. Depending on Him to take care of the conflict is also placing oneself in a position of trust. The woman with the issue of blood and the whore, both of whom sought Jesus, got what they wanted, and never had to address those who rejected them again.

HAVING BOUNDARIES

Fourth, I have learned to separate what's my job and what's His job. Some things are outside your boundaries and are not your responsibility to judge or fix. He reminds us that we are not just ancillary fluff. Every living being needs a point of peace and rest. You and I qualify. Most of us need reassurance, a sense of protection, a quietness that says He can handle anything that comes our way. We can find ourselves in situations where wrong is being done, and we want to "fix it." But sometimes we cause ourselves unnecessary weariness when we try to handle something that was never ours to deal with. Matthew 11:30 says, *"My yoke is easy and My burden is light."* If we are carrying something that is hard and heavy, perhaps it was not something we we were supposed to be carrying at all. That is not to say that hard and painful things don't come our way, because they do, but sometimes we insert ourselves into problems and issues that were His to carry all along and not ours. Rightfully assessing what is my part in a situation, and what is His, is life-giving.

One lie I too easily believe is that I have to be hyper-prepared for crisis all the time. It is true that stressors are unavoidable. But my habit has been to apply more force, demand more of myself. While "setting one's face" for a particular situation is appropriate, as Jesus did on the way to Jerusalem, maintaining hyper-preparation as a lifestyle is destructive. We were made for Eden, not hell. I am accountable to the Holy Spirit for my reactions. Because of the way God set up biblical boundaries, I am not to control others. I can influence, but not control. Those biblical boundaries do leave me with the responsibility to control *me*, by not letting my mind dwell on destructive things (e.g. nightmares, bad thoughts, revenge, etc.), and focusing on what builds me up the most and the fastest.

The self-reliant belief that I have to protect and guide myself actually works against the trust and life in Jesus. Spiritual vertigo is worse than physical vertigo. Some of the most damaging distractions are those with the biggest emotional punch. Who better than ourselves to get an emotionally intense thought string going, questioning our cooperation with God, our spiritual growth, our usefulness…the list goes on and on, mushrooming with the enemy's additional accusations. But if the Holy Spirit is to bring freedom to our dulled thinking, then emotions that destroy must be dealt with also. What matters is what the Holy Spirit does in restoring our will, mind, and emotions. Do these aspects of our being welcome Him? After all, He is not a predator. If He's knocking at the door, there is a reason for Him knocking at a boundary line. It's up to us to calm ourselves and open the door. The cacophony of the soul can be quieted by intentionally resting in His peace.

LEARNING TO FORGIVE

And finally, forgiveness and God's love is an important key to moving past pain. Forgiveness doesn't negate the wrong someone has done to you, but it takes the hook out of your own soul that ties you to that pain. Psalm 26:2–4 says it's more than letting go of an offense or a fear of future experiences. It's demanding of myself that I look at His loving-kindness instead.

We are told to put down the weights that keep us back: "*Therefore, we also, since we are surrounded by so great a cloud of witnesses, let us also lay aside every weight, and sin which so easily ensnares us, and let us run with endurance the race that is set before us, looking unto Jesus, the author and finisher of our faith*" (Hebrews 12:1–2). Unforgiveness is one of those "*weights.*" It keeps us from moving forward quickly, if at all. But when we lay down our offense, and keep our eyes fixed on Jesus, He meets us with all the grace and love that we could have ever hoped for.

There's times when all we want is to be quieted in our soul by another's words, looks, or touch. We aren't asking for the world to stop clamoring. We're just asking for that reassurance, like that which comes from a child crawling up on daddy's lap. As an adult, that often looks like credibility and gracious speech from a compatriot. (See Ephesians 4:29.) Both are gifts from Him to relieve the sandpaper feeling in our hearts. However, even when we are forsaken by friends, God holds us close with His love. It is very difficult, even unspeakably agonizing, to be rejected no matter what one does to try to restore a relationship. It is critical to grab hard onto Jesus and our memories of the times He has intensely interacted with us in the past. The freshness of the relationship and the quality of His maintenance is like going to a safe place and finding someone willing to wipe the blood off our faces and bind up our wounds after a fight.

God's love is inflexible, harder than diamond, and of much greater value. Tougher than any pain we have or will encounter. When the Rock, Jesus, falls on those pains, their power shatters. He is good. No assault can change that. And we are given the opportunity to draw nearer to this good and constant Creator. The invitation I dared not hope for is here.[33]

THE CHURCH NEEDS YOU

As Jean described, sometimes we get so tired. Things just haven't gone right. If God doesn't come through, we know all is lost. We may question ourselves as to why we are in this situation, but He knows our heart, and He says, "Enough. Peace!" At the worst times, we have to face the fact that He has not pulled our life support plug even when we so much wanted Him to pull it. Our physical heart refuses to stop beating, the lungs won't stop working. Because the situation is so intense, we do have to withdraw to regain our equilibrium, but if that is what it takes, we have to do it. People don't understand the evisceration of having walls and dreams torn down. He does. He understands why the pain makes us gasp. Of all people, He understands. And He doesn't condemn us for it. Unlike our experiences with some people, He says "Enough. Peace!"

---

33. From Jean DeHaven, without whose story and insight this book would not have been written.

Sometimes the fact of the new creation needs to be enforced, and it isn't comfortable. Looking at the mountain that needs to be climbed can be daunting, but looking at only the next few steps keeps one upright. Yes, by taking sightings and adjusting course periodically we stay on track. Even pausing for a breather helps—but we cannot go back. Why does He think challenges are good for us? Perhaps because we are His progeny, His new creation. The business is owned by "Father and Sons." The business needs active participation by all business partners to succeed. We are His new creation and we have the right to participate.

You are needed in His church. It is a grave mistake to believe that some people are too broken to be of any value to the church. If that were true, nobody could serve in the local congregation. God does not qualify us before He uses us. He uses us and, in the process, we get qualified. As the adage goes, He does not call the equipped; He equips the called.

Whatever has paralyzed your life, your past does not have to define your future. In the midst of pain, it's hard to believe there is hope. But in His grace, God sends people to help. *"Blessed be the God and Father of our Lord Jesus Christ, the Father of mercies and God of all comfort, who comforts us in all our tribulation, that we may be able to comfort those who are in any trouble, with the comfort with which we ourselves are comforted by God"* (2 Corinthians 1:3–4). Most of us who are in the midst of pain and suffering need help. One of the reasons God formed the church was to help those who are in trouble. But if the enemy can get a person to believe that they don't need church, he can prevent the opportunity for God to use people in a personal way to provide the help those people need.

The early disciples were shocked that God would use them. And knowing their backgrounds, we would agree. We recognize that there are qualifications for working in the church as found in the New Testament. But personal brokenness does not negate a person from personal service. In fact, depending on the type of service, it can be extremely helpful to others and healing to themselves. For instance, a person who has been broken through the loss of a spouse might be the perfect person to help those who are grieving in a similar manner. Is this not the beauty of redemption? That it's the exact place where we were broken that God makes most lovely through the profound sympathy we now have for others? He knows where we are, what we've been through, and how best we can be put to use in His kingdom. No matter how broken we are, He won't let us go without giving us a calling.

And this pursuit by God? There is no word for it. The ferocity of His commitment, the personal extension through Jesus expressed toward all people—He is intent on not letting His dream die. He just won't give it a rest! He circles around us, waiting for the right moment to show us something, to create a new understanding in us. None of us knows how big the outworking of His work in and through us will be. Dream! Your dreams could come true.

> In an effort to account for the illness, we can ask endless questions: Did I miss God's will at some crucial point? Is it my lack of faith? Am I harboring sin? How long will this last? What should I be doing that I'm not now doing? Self-examination easily deteriorates into self-accusation.
>
> Even when we experience grace to rest and wait for God to make His will clear, well-meaning family and friends may not. They encircle us with cure-alls, advice, interrogation, and reproof until the free air of the Spirit is stifled. We may come to feel increasing guilt and responsibility for our sickness in such an atmosphere. Fuller Seminary President David Allen Hubbard warns such unwelcome sickroom visitors that "blame bordering on rejection is no comfort to those whose sense of worth is already worn paper thin by the chafing cords of pain and inadequacy."
>
> Whether the attacks come from outside or inside ourselves, the Lord of Life would have us resist them. Even when he needs to use his rod of correction on us, he will never do it without simultaneously rescuing us with his staff. His Spirit is rightly called the Comforter.[34]

---

34. Ray Beeson and Ranelda Mack Hunsicker, *The Hidden Price of Greatness* (Wheaton, IL: Tyndale, 1991), 102–103.

A PROVERB

The LORD hates the sacrifice that the wicked offer, but he likes the prayers of honest people. (Proverbs 15:8 NCV)

PSALMS FOR THE WOUNDED

When I am afraid, I will trust you. I praise God for his word. I trust God, so I am not afraid. What can human beings do to me?
(Psalm 56:3–4 NCV)

People, trust God all the time. Tell him all your problems, because God is our protection. (Psalm 62:8 NCV)

God is in his holy Temple. He is a father to orphans, and he defends the widows. God gives the lonely a home. He leads prisoners out with joy. (Psalm 68:5–6 NCV)

10

WHY DO I FEEL SO UNSAFE IN CHURCH?

The two most important days in your life are the day you were
born and the day you find out why.
—*Mark Twain*

An audience at a retreat in Pittsburgh was invited by the speaker to ask God what their true identity was. At the end of the retreat, the speaker asked if anyone was willing to come forward and share what God said. A young woman stepped up. She said, "My previous identity was that of a whore. My mother was a whore. I was a whore. But, when I asked the Lord who I am and what is my true identity, He said 'You are a teacher.' I'm going to get my teacher's certificate and I'm going to teach. I am no longer a whore."

All of her life she had seen herself a certain way. It was introduced to her by her mother, then it was confirmed by all of those around her. She began to practice what she thought was her identity. God had something else in mind. He had never created her to be what she thought was. Once she sought for her true identity, He gave it to her and she would never be the same.

The deep reason why true Christ-seekers feel unsafe in church is not because their identity is rejected by God. He promised that *"If we confess our sins, He is faithful and just to forgive us our sins and to cleanse us from all unrighteousness"* (1 John 1:9). No, they feel unsafe because the *church* rejects their identity. As Jean described in the previous chapter, a loss of identity is devastating. This chapter contains important firewalls to protect your identity from anybody who would tear it down.

IDENTITY AND PROTECTING OUR DREAMS

When our identities are painted over by others, we look in the mirror and see ourselves as they paint us. They may have been merciless in their branding: ugly, treacherous, liar, causer of evil, betrayer...the list goes on. The people who did the painting did not supply the paint. There is an enemy with a massive paint factory whose name is the Accuser and who often uses Christians to do his dirty work. But Jesus has a way of removing paint like a leaf-blower removes leaves, or a blow-drier removes water. He doesn't hurt us.

Firewall: Safeguard your own God-given identity. Declare to the enemy of your soul that you refuse to allow yourself to be branded in any negative way. The gospel gives you the right to declare these false identities liars because of your identity in Christ. When the accusations come, ask yourself, *Would Jesus allow and accept those same words if they were thrown at Him?*

Sometimes it seems like everyone's got a plan for our lives. They "advise" without understanding what is really happening deep inside of us. They believe that if you do something outside of your comfort zone, it must not be God's will. Sometimes the dream that is conceived in us by God can be drained of enthusiasm just before it is time for it to be born. People don't realize their words can short-circuit what God is doing through our dreams. The dream has to take on a life of its own, demand the right to be born, to breathe, to exist. If we allow people to tear apart our hopes and dreams before they ever get to know us, dreams might never be born. It is hard to leave behind the people who short-circuit our dreams because they are often the ones we are closest to. But if the dream is to live, we have to.

All dreams require an incubation time, time to be thought through and developed before they're shared. If you share them prematurely, people will ask you questions that you cannot answer and the dream will be aborted.

The life of Nehemiah, cupbearer to the king, is a classic example of this. When Nehemiah first heard that Jerusalem's gates had been burned, he wept. His heart was broken. He then began to seek the Lord and dream about what was possible and what needed to be done. When Nehemiah came before the king, his countenance was so sad, the king questioned him. Nehemiah explained his distress. The king then asked him, "What do you want?" Nehemiah was able to give a detailed list of what would be required to go back to Jerusalem and rebuild its walls. (See Nehemiah 1–2.) If he had tried to answer the king without having time to think through the process he would've had little to say and perhaps would have lost the king's help. Instead, the dream was given time to incubate and the king gave him permission to proceed.

Sometimes we give away our dreams prematurely, having not thought through the process. If we share these dreams with unsafe people they can tear them apart and discourage us from ever beginning the process. After Nehemiah began to build the walls there were people who stood in strong opposition. However, Nehemiah's vision was strong and had God's blessing. No amount of attempted discouragement would dismay him. The walls were built.

Firewall: Allow your dreams to begin to mature before you share them with others, otherwise you may be branded as a dreamer and not a person of action.

If we allow others to determine our identity, then we will never reach our destiny. If we lose our destiny, we have lost our value and we rob ourselves and the body of Christ. The key, of course, is discovering what our true identity is before God. Jesus asked the disciples, "*Who do men say that I am?*" (Mark 8:27). They all got it wrong except Peter who replied, "*You are the Christ*" (verse 29). Peter's words will be remembered forever because he got it right. Identity is important to God.

Firewall: When we discover our true identity, we will fulfill our destiny. Only God knows our identity, and only He can give it to us when we ask.

THE BEGINNING OF A NEW IDENTITY

There is a very real and powerful war going on concerning the souls of men and women. In Romans 7, the apostle Paul shows what we are up against. Most of us know the pain of trying to fix ourselves. Paul described it as wanting to do good but never really overcoming the problem, and wanting not to do bad but always doing it anyway. (See Romans 7:19.) This results in guilt, condemnation, and just plain frustration. Who knows how many have quit serving God because they could never accomplish what they felt was expected of them. How sad that these people never really saw their new identity before turning back!

Again and again Paul mentions in his epistles the concepts of being "in Christ" and of having "Christ in us." It is the "in Christ" message that gives "new life" and new identity. New life does not mean fixing up the old life. New life in Christ is not a spiritual workout regimen to take the old life and work really hard to make it better. Being "born-again" is really just that. We are born into a new identity which is in Jesus. It's almost similar to being born on a new planet where the memory of our old ways are never able to touch us again. The grace of God makes this canceling of the past a reality when identifying with Christ. But if we fail to recognize this "new" life, we easily slip into a mode of working hard to try to please God, and find ourselves back in a former worthless identity. As much as it may be well-intentioned, Paul taught that it simply doesn't work. We can never rise to a personal righteousness that pleases God.

So then, how do we attain the righteousness that is necessary for a relationship with Him?

Once it is understood that we are in Christ, and that Jesus sent the Holy Spirit to fulfill the promise and the dynamics of Christ in us (see Colossians 1:27), God is no longer just a heavenly Being at an incalculable distance. His presence fills our entire being. And, as we have mentioned many times, this is where the power of God is available to do what we can't do on our own. It is also the place where we lose old identities—*loser, failure, no good, disappointment, black sheep*—and gain new ones—*loved of the Father, a child of God, redeemed, a friend of God, kings and priests unto God.* (For more details on your new identity, see Galatians 1.)

GUARDING YOUR IDENTITY

The first generation disciples knew who they were "in Christ." They were, in every way, identified with Jesus. Later generations, however, began to identify with Paul, Apollos, and Peter instead. Their identity began to lose the impact of the risen Christ. We have the same problems today when our chief identity is with a particular church, Presbyterian, Baptist, Nazarene, etc., or with a movement such as evangelical, charismatic, Pentecostal, or emergent. Paul confronted those whose identity was with dietary laws, wealth, or nationality—today, the equivalents seem to be the faith movement, the prosperity gospel, positive confession, etc.

If you sense this tendency, please read Paul's inspired words carefully:

So now, those who are in Christ Jesus are not judged guilty. Through Christ Jesus the law of the Spirit that brings life made you free from the law that brings sin and death. The law was without power, because the law was made weak by our sinful selves. But God did what the law could not do. He sent his own Son to earth with the same human life that others use for sin. By sending his Son to be an offering for sin, God used a human life to destroy sin. He did this so that we could be the kind of people the law correctly wants us to be. Now we do not live following our sinful selves, but we live following the Spirit.

(Romans 8:1–4 ncv)

God is saying through Paul that right living is necessary in order to get to know Him. But the law is without power to save us. If we put our trust in the law and our fulfilment of it, we will inevitably fail. We must put our trust where the real power is: God. He did what the law could not do. If we want to live right, we must go to Christ and trust His power in us.

This is so important, let us say it again. When we receive God's gift of righteousness offered through His Son Jesus, the Bible says we become a new creation. Becoming a new creation is not a process by which God makes improvements on who we were before we met Him. We are not better people *because* of Christ, we are new people in Christ: "Therefore, *if anyone is in Christ, he is a new creation; old things have passed away; behold, all things have become new*" (2 Corinthians 5:17). Being a new creation in Christ means being a new person, with a new heart and new desires. God doesn't just improve our hearts, He puts a new heart in us. The biblical word for "new creation" is *regeneration*, which is a Greek translation of *palingenesia*, from *palin* (again) and *genesis* (birth). *Regeneration* simply means "new birth." We are regenerated, born again, the moment we put our faith in Jesus Christ. This new birth is not an improvement on who we used to be; it is a supernatural experience in which we become a completely different person because we have a completely new heart. We protect our identity when we realize that our new heart is not something we planted ourselves and must constantly monitor with our own know-how. No! Our identity is founded in a new heart, a new birth, given by One whom we can't see, but who is renewing our spirit day by day.

> So we do not give up. Our physical body is becoming older and weaker, but our spirit inside us is made new every day. We have small troubles for a while now, but they are helping us gain an eternal glory that is much greater than the troubles. We set our eyes not on what we see but on what we cannot see. What we see will last only a short time, but what we cannot see will last forever.   (2 Corinthians 4:16–18 NCV)

Our question to you is, what is your true identity? Who do you think you are? Where did you get your present identity? Did it come from your parents? Did it come from your friends? Did you receive it because you made a mistake in life and from that point on it became your label? Or have you received your identity from God? He is the only one you were created for and only He knows what your destiny needs to be. If you have never asked Him, we would suggest that you pray the prayer at the end of this chapter. He is a loving Father, and as one of His children it would be His delight to share with you how to head in the direction to best fulfill your life.

MAKING OTHERS FEEL SAFE IN CHURCH

Even in compassionate, loving churches, there are some people we can't help, at least at the moment. They come only for pity and a handout or, more often, to deliver an agenda. They don't want to be a part of society, let alone a part of the church. They are masters at what they do to get a few dollars here and a handout there. Regardless, our job is not to castigate but to determine godly principles for dealing with such situations. There should never be a negative attitude toward them, but rather a recognition that these people, too, are suffering from the effects of a broken world.

Some people may look strange, but have no agenda that would disrupt the church and just want to participate and be loved. Take the case of the "Glitter Lady." At least that's what the church women called her after she left her first church service. She had come, probably for a handout, with glitter all over her face and in her hair. They kindly asked why she was covered in glitter, and she responded that Jesus had given her such a beautiful morning, she just had to celebrate! It quickly became apparent that she functioned at about a ten-year-old level. Her glitter was the expression of a child's joy. When the church did some investigating, they found she lived in a house with holes in the exterior walls, roof, and floor, with her handicapped son. There is much more to the story, but the short version is that the Glitter Lady fought hard for years to keep herself and two sons together and off welfare. She had very serious heart disease, with asthma and diabetes. She passed away since then at the age of forty-three. The Glitter Lady. Now, the church could not magically fix her situation, but notice that there was no reason why she couldn't be loved and love in return. And so that's what they did.

Charles and Leah had the unfortunate experience of having a traumatized delivery when their son was born. Lack of oxygen produced limited cognitive ability. Their son would never enjoy a normal life. His mental and intellectual skills were damaged. And he was an easy target for humiliation. To see the world make fun of a person or disregard him or her as having little value is one thing, but for a church to reject Jimmy and his family is shocking. And yet that is what happened. How is it that God's love, grace, and mercy doesn't make it into some churches?

Today, Jimmy is a part of a vibrant and patient church. Even though his social skills are lacking he's a great guy. Obnoxious? Yes. Sometimes overbearing? Yes. Otherwise, just a person who wants to be loved and accepted, which he gets at his new church. It's difficult to understand how and why some within the church can miss not only the responsibility, but the incredible blessing of having Jimmy among them.

There will be all kinds of people that walk through your church door. Most will be in pain of some kind. Far too often people stay chained to their feelings and emotions simply because they are not aware that there is hope and freedom for another kind of life. Others suffer mental and emotional pain that some people and some churches are either unwilling to or incapable of dealing with. And unfortunately the church often stigmatizes these difficulties more quickly and more harshly than secular circles, who are often eager to offer help to anyone with such needs. Some Christian circles don't look favorably on individuals seeking counseling and medicine for mental health. This needs to change. It takes work to create a safe place for people like the Glitter Lady or like Jimmy and his family, but it always comes with blessings, too.

A PRAYER FOR IDENTITY

Heavenly Father, I may have the wrong label on me. I may not have my identity correct. I know You love me and You care about my future, so please share with me who You see me to be, who I am to You. Help me to see for what purpose You created me.

Take time to listen to the Lord in order to allow Him to share His thoughts with you. It may come through prayer or by reading His Word. Very few of us ever hear an audible voice, but it is quite likely that you will be impressed or inclined to move in a specific direction which will continue to define your identity. Give God time for this to take place.

A PROVERB

My child, listen to what I say and remember what I command you. Listen carefully to wisdom; set your mind on understanding. Cry out for wisdom, and beg for understanding. Search for it like silver, and hunt for it like hidden treasure. (Proverbvs 2:1–4 NCV)

PSALMS FOR THE WOUNDED

The LORD is pleased with those who respect him, with those who trust his love. (Psalm 147:11 NCV)

Let those who worship him rejoice in his glory. Let them sing for joy even in bed! (Psalm 149:5 NCV)

Praise the Lord*! Praise God in his Temple; praise him in his mighty heaven. Praise him for his strength; praise him for his greatness. Praise him with trumpet blasts; praise him with harps and lyres. Praise him with tambourines and dancing; praise him with stringed instruments and flutes. Praise him with loud cymbals; praise him with crashing cymbals. Let everything that breathes praise the* Lord*. Praise the* Lord*!* (Psalm 150:1–6 ncv)

11

I CAN'T KEEP UP WITH ALL THE RULES

Fairy tales are more than true: not because they tell us that dragons exist, but because they tell us that dragons can be beaten.
—*Neil Gaiman, paraphrasing G. K. Chesterton*

From one of Chris's experiences:

Debra and John were attending a church down the street. It
seemed to be a very vibrant place but took God's Word out of context to such an extent there was little room for joy and peace. If you
had any personal challenges, they were pretty much brushed aside
with the comment, "Just obey the Word and get on with it." In
fact, they borrowed their slogan from Nike: "just do it." Members
lived under a high level of expectation to perform.

When Debra left that church to attend ours, she was distraught,
depressed, and feeling rejected. She came from a very rough child-
hood and background. The previous church really didn't want her
anymore because she was such a high-maintenance person. When
she began to attend our church, my wife and I were certain that
she would be calling me every day for prayer and advice for at least
a year. We weren't wrong. Debra's personality was overbearing,
loud, boisterous, pushy, and obnoxious. She was barely tolerable.
But I was convinced that if she was placed in the garden of God's
grace she would flourish and grow. Fortunately, we had a very understanding and gracious group of believers in our church. When

Debra asked me if she could attend the Cleansing Stream seminar and retreat I was only too glad to say yes.

John, her husband, wanted nothing to do with it; he was a man you could call Mr. Milquetoast. He faded into the background on spiritual matters and let Debra take the lead role in just about everything. But two days after the retreat, John came bursting into my office and demanded, "What did you do to Debra?" I asked him what he was talking about. He explained that Debra had come home the Saturday evening after the retreat and told John to sit down. He obediently pulled up a chair. Then Debra grabbed a pail, filled it with water, and came over to John. Taking his shoes and socks off, she began washing his feet. With tears in her eyes she apologized to him for being such an obnoxious wife and for being so pushy and controlling. John told me that day in the office that whatever she got, he wanted some of it too.

Debra was changed because of God's love and grace. Within a couple of years Debra became my lead intercessor and used her vibrant personality to intercede for those in need. She was still assertive, but reflected God's love in all that she did. She had flourished in the garden of God's grace.

THE FAITHFUL GOSPEL

Debra had finally absorbed the faithful gospel. What do we mean by that? Well, much of the abuse coming through Christian leadership is the result, in part, of a poor understanding of the gospel. It comes from leaders who do not properly understand the relationship between the Old and New Testaments. Certainly, most know that the gospel is good news. However, it is not unusual to find a Christian who can't explain it further. To say that the gospel represents salvation through Jesus, although correct, is not the gospel. To say that the gospel means that we have hope, although correct again, is not the gospel. What, then, is the gospel? The following explanation of the true gospel, though somewhat theological, will help us to understand why so many people are unable to keep up with rules.

First Corinthians 15:1–4 gives a very specific definition of the true gospel:

> *Moreover, brethren, I declare to you the gospel which I preached to you, which also you received and in which you stand, by which also you are saved, if you hold fast that word which I preached to you—unless you believed in vain. For I delivered to you first of all that which I also received: that Christ died for our sins according to the Scriptures, and that He was buried, and that He rose again the third day according to the Scriptures.*

This could be summarized by saying that the gospel is the work God did for us in the death, burial, and resurrection of Jesus Christ. Romans 1:3 states that the gospel is *"concerning His Son."* In other words, the gospel, the good news, is what God did for us in the person and work of Christ.

In a direct sense, the gospel is a Person. The gospel is not information, an idea, a law, or a moral code. Although these things are important, it is God in the flesh who became a Payment for sin, an Advocate to the Father, a Protector from the enemy, and the only Way to please God. This means we are not to try to take on a "good" life without the life of *Christ in us*, the life we obtained the moment we said "thumbs up" to Jesus.

It is a regrettable commentary on the biblical illiteracy of modern-day Christianity that so many see Jesus as an extension of the law. Only those who do not understand the proper relationship of the Old and New Testaments would teach that. To see Jesus as the One who came to reemphasize righteousness through the law and make sure everyone knows that disobedience to the commandments results in hell is a very mistaken view! If that were Christ's intent, He would be nothing more than a messenger of the law, harping on what people must do and how they should live in order to obtain salvation.

But instead, Christ came to reveal the righteousness available to those who want a righteousness beyond themselves and their good works. It's a personal relationship, not a fee-for-service process. *"For what the law could not do in that it was weak through the flesh, God did by sending His own Son in the likeness of sinful flesh, on account of sin: He condemned sin in the flesh, that the righteous requirement of the law might be fulfilled in us who do not walk according to the flesh but according to the Spirit"* (Romans 8:3–4). The point here is not that the law ceases to exist, but that the fulfillment of the law comes by the indwelling Spirit through what Christ did on the cross. If we were free from the righteousness of the law, we would still be enslaved to our sin. Real freedom comes from Jesus who fulfilled the law in our place and is capable of keeping us free of sin and its terrible consequences.

Again, this is so important to understand if we are to avoid being put into a straitjacket of rules and regulations. Just doing the mechanics of obedient living in order to obtain salvation is not getting saved. It's a living death.

If Christ had failed, we would continue to be dead in sin, separated from a life God intended for us from the beginning but which we lost through Adam. There would be no hope of reconciliation with God because we can never achieve a level of goodness that deserves God's life in us. Although the Bible teaches about good and evil, it never advocates a personal attempt at being good outside of God's help through the Holy Spirit because that would be impossible. As hard as we may try, it is impossible to keep the law. Our efforts fall far short of God's requirements, and like the apostle Paul groaned, "The harder I try to do good (and good is good), the worse I get (and bad is bad)." (See Romans 7.) And then, his painful cry, *"O wretched man that I am! Who will deliver me from this body of death?"* (Romans 7:24). The true gospel is that Christ, the Person, will deliver those who cry out to Him.

"BUT I'M A GOOD PERSON!"

Most Christians agree that God's laws are important. However, the requirement of the Old Testament law was not just "try to keep the law since it's important," or "do your best til you need some rest." No, the requirement was *absolute* righteousness. Galatians 3:10 states, *"for as many as are of the works of the law are under a curse, for it is written 'Cursed is everyone who does not continue in all things written in the book of the law, to do them.'"* Note the words *"everyone"*, *"continue"*, *"all"*, and *"perform"*—the only way for anyone to escape the curse of the law was to continually perform, for a lifetime, every single thing which the law required.

Many people say they keep the Ten Commandments, or at least that they have come close, or that they are pretty good people. People who say such things are misled into thinking that their effort, which produces less than absolute righteousness, will somehow satisfy God. It is an old problem. The rich young ruler had it:

> *Now a certain ruler asked Him, saying, "Good Teacher, what shall I do to inherit eternal life?" So Jesus said to him, "Why do you call Me good? No one is good but One, that is, God. You know the commandments: 'Do not commit adultery,' 'Do not murder,' 'Do not steal,' 'Do not bear false witness,' 'Honor your father and your mother.'" And he said, "All these things I have kept from my youth." So when Jesus heard these things, He said to him, "You still lack one thing. Sell all that you have and distribute to the poor, and you will have treasure in heaven; and come, follow Me." But when he heard this, he became very sorrowful, for he was very rich.* (Luke 18:18–23)

This man figured he was doing pretty well. But Jesus, with a word of knowledge, exposed his heart issue that kept him from eternal life: a love of this money that made him rich. However good his actions, this ruler was still motivated by an idol, his money. (See also Romans 5:12–21.)

The religious Jews of Jesus' day also deluded themselves into thinking they were righteous. Jesus addressed them in His famous Sermon on the Mount. He showed them that the requirement was far above what they supposed it to be. He pointed out that the intention of the heart was equal to the action in respect to sins such as murder, adultery, and dishonesty. The motive was as important as the act itself. In other words, He raised the bar for righteousness far higher than people had come to believe it was, so high it became utterly unattainable. He showed that the righteousness of the law required absolute purity, absolute honesty, absolute justice, absolute mercy, and absolute love for God, none of which are attainable by sinful men.

As Galatians 3:10 says, as many as are under the works of the law are under a curse. But note what comes next in the Galatians passage: *"Christ has redeemed us from the curse of the law, having become a curse for us (for it is written, 'Cursed is everyone who hangs on a tree')"* (Galatians 3:13). Christ became a curse for us. How? By becoming a curse when He was hung on a tree. In other words, the fulfilment of the law was accomplished by the death of Christ, because only His death could satisfy the requirement for total, utter, complete obedience. When He fulfilled the law, He welcomed into His presence all those who couldn't but wanted to be righteous.

> Jesus came to break the power of religion—to set us free from the law. The basis of most religion is thinking that following a set of correct beliefs and rules is pleasing to God, a way of earning His favor. Jesus taught us a better way. He taught us that it is God's love, not His rules, which bring us into a right relationship with Him. His favor comes through grace, not through religious works and rituals. God wants relationship, not slavery. I personally believe that God is bigger than our belief systems or any denomination.[35]

He fulfilled the law for us and then sent the Holy Spirit to help us live a proper lifestyle.

FIRST CHRIST, THEN THE SPIRIT

Those of us who are not in constant denial eventually recognize that our attitudes and actions are much out of control. Our conscience is always notifying us of the moral and ethical codes we break, at least until the point where we have shut our conscience down so many times it doesn't work any longer. (See 1 Timothy 4:1–3.) Rules show us right from wrong, but the rule itself could not make us good. That's why something had to come along to solve the problem of mankind's inability to live up to a standard. That something was Someone who could generate control in our inner spirit by linking His Spirit to us: *"He did this by ending the system of law with its commandments and regulations"* (Ephesians 2:15 NLT); *"And this is the secret: **Christ lives in you.** This gives you assurance of sharing his glory"* (Colossians 1:27 NLT).

The law had no other reason for existing than to lead us to the "indwelling Christ," who now imputes His righteousness to His people. *"Therefore the law was our tutor to bring us to Christ, that we might be justified*

35. Michael Dye, *The Church: Helping or Hurting?* (Auburn, CA: Genesis Publishing, 2015), 289.

by faith. But after faith has come, we are no longer under a tutor" (Galatians 3:24–25). The law was good in showing right from wrong, but it failed to impart to us Christ's life. Human nature wants to believe we have power over sin, but eventually we find that we have no strength against it. Consider the drug addict, the gambler, or any other person with a habit they can't get rid of. Christ's first advent was to conquer sin on the cross. He then offered the strength to overcome through His indwelling Spirit in the believer.

Now, we must be careful because, as vital as the work of the Holy Spirit is in helping us walk in righteousness, it is in no way the fulfillment of the law. In spite of the presence and the influence of the Spirit in our lives, we continue to sin and fall short of the absolute requirement of the law. *Only Christ's work* fulfilled the law, and it is critically important people do not confuse that fact with the work of the Spirit in their own lives. If they do, they will find themselves striving to do and to be what is impossible to do and be.

> Christians can and ought to enjoy complete deliverance from the power of Satan and demons as a result of Christ's perfect work of redemption. But what believers can and ought to enjoy and what they actually do enjoy are two different things. When Christians fail to recognize what they have in Christ and refuse to appropriate the resulting privileges, they invite defeat and can be held captive by demonic forces to a pitiable degree.[36]

God is the heart-changer who changes us on the inside and makes the Holy Spirit available to us so that we have special control in order to deal with the outside. It is Christ's righteousness that gives the ability to live correctly. You can't have the Spirit without truly acknowledging Christ's life and death.

If this seems a little confusing, don't worry: it is a mystery that every believer wrestles with! How can Christ live inside of us? These are spiritual things that we come to understand by developing spiritual life in Christ.

---

36. Merrill F. Unger, *Demons in the World Today* (Carol Stream, IL: Tyndale House, 1972), 183.

RULES DON'T LOVE US LIKE CHRIST DOES

To recap, fulfilling the law is no longer the prerequisite for righteousness. Christ would take its place and through His death (see Romans 8:3–4) and life (see Romans 5:10), its demands would be fulfilled. But the tragedy is that the law can be, and often is, used by unscrupulous and pharisaical leaders to gather people under their leadership.

We do understand that there are people who are sincerely attempting to do good by feverishly following the law. But as sincere as they are, wherever law is emphasized over grace, there is a failure to understand the power of Christ's indwelling life. Knowledge of the Old Testament Scriptures, a little charisma, and a dash of boldness in a leader have deceived many into believing that they can be saved by the works of the law. But by bringing people under guilt by misuse of the Scriptures, while at the same time appearing to want to help them, some leaders twist the Scriptures into impossible lifestyles. Their followers become fearful to the point of not going anywhere or doing anything that is not a part of a spiritual exercise for fear of transgressing the law.

Rules don't love us like Christ does. This is huge! There is no life in a rule. Life is in the Rule-Giver. Even though the laws of God are good and necessary, we don't sense love from someone who only tells us the things we must do in order to be accepted. We don't sense Him when we are only introduced to rules and regulations. Christ's personal concern makes life come "alive," which is then followed by our desire to follow Him into His righteousness.

You can't tell a person that Jesus loves him if that person does not see God's love standing before him. Contentious and combative people cannot represent Jesus. Most often they scare others far away from Him. What makes someone think they can attack anyone, let alone God's people, and assume no one is watching?

The Pharisees of old as well as those of today use traditions as law to either control people or to justify behaviors that would profit themselves or make themselves look good. Some of these "you-must-not" laws were even used as charges against Jesus: not healing on the Sabbath (see Matthew 12:9–14); not helping parents because the means had already been dedicated as a gift to God (see Mark 7:11–13); not gathering grain on the Sabbath (see Matthew 12:1–2); and not eating with sinners (see Mark 9:11–13). Nothing has changed through the years. We still have religious leaders who claim Christianity, but we see little, if anything, in their teaching and behavior pertaining to the Holy Spirit and His desired work to provide help and comfort for every human being who wants it.

The gospel was meant for people to feel *good*, even excited and constantly joyful. It really is good news! It was meant to declare that we serve a good God, a great God, a kind God, a patient God, a loving God, and a God who helps us in our weaknesses. It was also meant to declare that the Holy Spirit will mess with our lives if we fail to yield to His warnings, and that that is a part of God's loving protection and not just an angry response to sin. The gospel was not meant to cause people to be joyless, deflated, depressed, mechanical, overwhelmed, fearful, discouraged, oppressed, worried, anxious, and all kinds of other disorders that we have seen in abundance in far too many uncaring churches.

DECEPTIONS ALONG THE WAY

There are some very good men and women among us who are prone to make mistakes in teaching and preaching because of a strong desire to see others live holy lives—which is good. We cringe when we see people living in sin. Many of us would like to grab them by the collar and shake them until they realized what they are doing. But nobody can force holiness on another person. We must each become aware of the phrases that might reinforce a reliance on self and our own good works, and not on God. They are easy to use and easy to believe! Here are a few such phrases:

"We believe that Jesus is our example for living in truth." This statement, although it seems true, is actually misleading. It goes back to the law by using the word "example," meaning that we are now to follow Jesus by simply trying to do the things that He did. By "living in truth," do we mean "truth" as a statement of facts or as a Person? Are we subjecting Christ's powerful—but brief—time here on earth to a list of do's and dont's that condemn or save us? Christ flipped the world upside down because He is God. He calls us to follow Him, but He does not call us to be God. We cannot be left alone to clean up our act before God will let us in the house

and sit us down to dinner. Is Jesus our example? Of course He is! But it's our relationship with Him as a Person, not a list of rules, and the work of the Spirit that allow us to see our sin in the first place. To follow Jesus successfully can only be done through the aiding and powering of the Holy Spirit. It can never be accomplished by scrubbing ourselves down first.

"A true believer will consistently seek the light and avoid sin." As good as this sounds, it still echoes the law because it fails to recognize the inner power of the Holy Spirit. It denies how He, with our cooperation, helps us to both seek God and come to a place of obedience. Nobody obeys God without His help.

"Our obedience to His law is rewarded by blessing. Our crowns and rewards at the judgment seat will directly relate to our practice and obedience to His Word." Does this mean that if we want a blessing, we must accomplish something? Does this mean "No performance, no blessing?" Not at all! Certainly we have a responsibility to maintain a righteous lifestyle, but only with God's help. Far too many people feel they cannot approach the Father and ask for a blessing because they are not sure of their obedience level. If you live with a perfectionist mind-set, you will be miserable, always guessing where you stand in God's eyes—unless, of course, you adopt the unbiblical idea that by hard work you can enter a state of sinless perfection. Any perfection we ever achieve only comes through the perfection Jesus achieved on the cross, and is lived out by recognizing both 1) Christ gives the gift of salvation necessary for eternal life, and 2) He delights in our asking for His help in living fittingly in this life. Our motivation for living faithfully should always be gratitude for the lifesaver that was thrown to us, not a petty calculation whether our lifesaver is cleaner or a better color than someone else's.

"We are to love God with all of our heart, soul, mind, and strength and we do this by seeking and keeping His commandments." These statements really do not reflect the Scriptures. Loving God comes from being thankful and appreciative of His love. *"We love Him because He first loved us"* (1 John 4:19). He chose us, He delivered us, He set us free from the power of sin, and He has given us precious promises and the further promise of eternal life. Who wouldn't dance and sing His praises for having received such grace? We didn't start this journey with God by performing a "to do" list.

We simply received His love and His Holy Spirit who now indwells us. If we didn't come into this walk by our performance, how can we possibly maintain it by our performance? It's like being told that God has changed His mind, and is now saying to us, "You got here by grace, but now you must stay here by the law."

If we accept the truth that by grace we receive salvation, why do we let ourselves be persuaded that we have to work hard to maintain it? "Perform" means that we have a "to do" list that we must accomplish. It doesn't matter whether or not that "to do" list is following a set of rules as outlined in the Old Testament, or set of regulations that some Christian leader is telling us to do.

One of the wonderful purposes of the Holy Spirit in us is fitting us into the image of Jesus, changing and developing our character to reflect His love. The whole message of the Scriptures is that redemption, reconciliation, and restoration are for the very purpose of once again receiving God's character. And the only way to receive His character is to receive Jesus.

Living out the Christian life is not fulfilled by obeying His commandments. Living it out is receiving His life through the Holy Spirit, who enables us to reflect His strength, love, and character. His law is now inscribed upon our hearts, and His law is not a burden (see 1 John 5:3), just as His yoke is not a burden. One thousand times over, please understand, we are by no means insinuating that anything the Bible calls sin can now be undertaken because of grace. Instead, our point is threefold. First, we cannot add rules and regulations that do not come directly from the Scriptures. Second, we cannot make the Scriptures say things that they don't say. And third, we cannot force the tenets of the Bible on anyone.

UNREASONABLE EXPECTATIONS

In many cases, the leaders who expect performance without emphasizing the work of the Holy Spirit can be exposed by attitudes: arrogance, self-exultation, self-pity, dishonesty, scolding, harsh reprimands, unreasonable expectations, and accusations concerning loyalty, faithfulness, devotion, allegiance, and reliability are all designed to manipulate people into doing something.

These are ample indicators of something amiss. But the real key that leads to abuse is holding people accountable to the law and/or nonbiblical legalistic behavior for their salvation. How does one recognize the difference between someone who's trusting in the law and someone who's trusting in Christ? As Jesus said, it is by fruit (our behavior, actions) that we know ourselves and other people. (See Luke 6:43–44.) If there is mercy and not judgment in the midst of dealing with sin, it is Christ. If there is compassion, mercy, and truthfulness between people, it is Christ.

If it is anger, judgment, shame, and humiliation, it is not Christ. If it is behavior motivated by fear, it is law. Thoughts such as *I must do (or not do) a particular thing to be blessed by God, I must do (or not do) this to avoid being punished by God,* or *I must do (not do) this to avoid the anger of other people* mean that we have missed the very reason for the coming of the Holy Spirit. Please note that we are sympathetic to those who are misguided and have received incorrect training. Not everyone intentionally misleads people.

Some Christians are no different than ultra-legalistic Jews. When you meet someone, anyone, who "forces" an opinion, an attitude, or a political or religious system on you, and you sense a mind-set that is difficult to digest, you are usually looking at a person who doesn't represent the heart of Christ.

As we've said, the law is needed to show us how desperately we need a relationship with God. The law, like a CAT scan or an MRI, exposes what is on the inside, shows how messed up we are, and proves that by our own efforts we could never be good enough to personally relate to God's character. The law was meant to show our guilt, but guilt left unresolved only brings fear of punishment. Heavy preaching on guilt may initially draw people who want to get rid of it, but when the guilt message continues unabated, without giving assurance of salvation through Christ, people leave. They don't see how the Good Shepherd's rod and staff are supposed to comfort. (See Psalm 23:4.)

Preaching on guilt without an emphasis on grace is especially pernicious because it plays upon a universal weakness. After Adam and Eve left the garden, the hardship of toiling the ground made it difficult to believe that God still loved mankind. Instead, the universal belief that worked itself into mankind's narrative is that the only way back to Him requires the hard work of restitution and compensation.[37] In other words, mankind has to work rigorously to make up for past sin. The disbelief in God's love became so great to future generations that restoration seemed impossible.

This is why many people groups have endeavored to appease their god's anger by sacrifices, including human sacrifices. All religions include protocols, rules, and guidelines to approach a god. The world wants many ways to god (pluralism). But no *law* can bring us into the true God's presence. And no other name of any being (see Acts 4:12) can enter our being to fulfill the law of righteousness. The Scripture tells us that Jesus is the only way to the Father. (See John 14:6.)

So, again, was the law "good," was it "just," was it "holy," and was it "righteous"? And, again, yes. It was perfect in every way. It served better than an MRI, but like an MRI it only revealed the disease, it didn't fix it. We still needed a surgeon, a Physician. We cannot personally heal the inner condition of our heart. But the Great Physician can.

SUMMARY SCRIPTURES

We were not born as non-Jewish "sinners," but as Jews. Yet we know that a person is made right with God not by following the law, but by trusting in Jesus Christ. So we, too, have put our faith in Christ Jesus, that we might be made right with God because we trusted in Christ. It is not because we followed the law, because no one can be made right with God by following the law. We Jews came to Christ, trying to be made right with God, and it became clear that we are sinners, too. Does this mean that Christ encourages sin? No! But I would really be wrong to begin teaching again those things that I gave up. It was the law that put me to death, and I died to the law so that I can now live for God. I was put to death on the cross with Christ, and I do not live anymore— it is Christ who lives in me. I still live in my body, but I live by faith in

---

37. Restitution and compensation are normal parts of the Christian life. Occasionally they are needed in the forgiveness process in order to keep unity in the body of Christ. But they were never meant to be done out of fear or condemnation. They were meant to be done in kindness and respect for Christ and fellow believers.

the Son of God who loved me and gave himself to save me. By saying these things I am not going against God's grace. Just the opposite, if the law could make us right with God, then Christ's death would be useless.   (Galatians 2:15–21 NCV)

So what was the law for? It was given to show that the wrong things people do are against God's will. And it continued until the special descendant, who had been promised, came. The law was given through angels who used Moses for a mediator to give the law to people. But a mediator is not needed when there is only one side, and God is only one. Does this mean that the law is against God's promises? Never! That would be true only if the law could make us right with God. But God did not give a law that can bring life. Instead, the Scriptures showed that the whole world is bound by sin. This was so the promise would be given through faith to people who believe in Jesus Christ. Before this faith came, we were all held prisoners by the law. We had no freedom until God showed us the way of faith that was coming. In other words, the law was our guardian leading us to Christ so that we could be made right with God through faith. Now the way of faith has come, and we no longer live under a guardian.   (Galatians 3:19–25 NCV)

A PROVERB

Listen carefully to wisdom; set your mind on understanding. Cry out for wisdom, and beg for understanding. Search for it like silver, and hunt for it like hidden treasure. Then you will understand respect for the LORD, and you will find that you know God.

(Proverbs 2:2–5 NCV)

PSALMS FOR THE WOUNDED

But, LORD, you are my shield, my wonderful God who gives me courage. I will pray to the LORD, and he will answer me from his holy mountain. Selah. I can lie down and go to sleep, and I will wake up again, because the LORD gives me strength. Thousands of troops may surround me, but I am not afraid. Lord, rise up! My God, come save me!   (Psalm 3:3–7 NCV)

Answer me when I pray to you, my God who does what is right. Make things easier for me when I am in trouble. Have mercy on me and hear my prayer.   (Psalm 4:1 NCV)

12

WHAT'S WRONG WITH THESE PEOPLE?

Bad days happen to everyone. They come more often than we think
we deserve, and they sometimes last much longer than we think we
can stand. That's the reason every disciple of Jesus needs to have
a framework for processing bad days. And God's word directs us
to one: "Let us run with endurance the race that is set before us,
looking unto Jesus, the author and finisher of our faith, who for the
joy that was set before Him endured the Cross" (Heb. 12:1–2).[38]
—*Jack Hayford*

The method of counterfeiting, if successful, will require Satan to
appropriate and incorporate in his false systems every available
principle of the true, for the deception of the counterfeit depends
wholly upon its likeness to the real. By this is revealed the reason
for calling that a lie or deception which is externally so like the
truth. Certainly there could be no greater pitfall for souls than
a system which seems to be the truth of God, and yet robs its
followers of any basis for a true hope, and it will be found that
the strongest condemnation of the Bible is uttered against such
systems and their promoters.[39]
—*Lewis Sperry Chafer*

This is Dan's story, now a veteran of the faith, remembering when he was
just a new Christian.

38. Jack Hayford, *How to Live Through A Bad Day* (Nashville, TN: Thomas Nelson, 2001), ix–x.
39. Lewis Sperry Chafer, *Satan* (Grand Rapids, MI: Zondervan, 1919), 92.

When I was about sixteen years old, I had an insatiable desire to find and know God's will. At that time I had no real understanding of how God spoke to a person and what kind of things He wanted to say. All I knew is that I wanted to know Him.

While speaking to a friend who had the same desire, she told me about a person in our church who had a unique experience. She said that God told this person if she would take off her wedding ring, He would answer her prayer. I happened to be wearing my class ring and from that day on all I could think of was that if I took off my ring, God would answer my prayer. Eventually, the thought became excessive. No matter what I did, I couldn't get rid of it. Day and night it pounded on my mind until one day I decided to take it off. When I did, I wondered if something similar would be next. Right away it was my watch and I couldn't get rid of the thought that I needed to take that off too. Today I'm in my seventies. I've had a long and healthy life both naturally and spiritually. I love the Lord today more than ever, but still wonder what all of that was about. I've come to know God in a much more personal way and His voice has never been anything like those promptings of those many years ago.

However, these events were no small thing in my life. I agonized over them. I didn't want to miss God. If I had been sure they were from God I would've acted immediately. But I was never sure. I don't like to rationalize and try to figure out things when I'm not sure about them. But it became obvious later in life that the turmoil at that time drove me hard to seek the Lord. I doubt whether I would know as much today about God if I hadn't spent so much time on trying to understand the pain I was suffering.

IMPERFECT PEOPLE IN AN IMPERFECT WORLD

It doesn't take much examination to figure out that we live in an imperfect world. Though we could wish it were otherwise, there are no perfect people, not even Christians. Although the Scriptures speak of Christ's church as a bride without spot or wrinkle, there is the unmistakable fact that it still has problems. Some maintain that the true church is hidden away far beyond human view, and that it is exempt from suffering, sorrow, and the sin of this world. Others believe the church is isolated in pockets where particular belief systems prevail. But the disciples, Peter, James, and John, and later Paul, all identified a struggling church, one in which sin and worldliness were constant problems. They saw the church anywhere and everywhere men and women accepted Christ. Their teaching and preaching often dealt with making a break from immoral lifestyles. But they also were concerned about divisions and heresies. They labored to see the church unified and whole. In short, the early church faced tremendous difficulties that the early disciples knew needed addressing.

It is no surprise that the church today continues to struggle with many of the same problems it dealt with nearly two thousand years ago. But of all the difficulties and sins we face, and you can name dozens of them, the religious spirit has perhaps struck the most powerful blow to the church's ongoing progress and is intensely damaging God's people and their ability to complete the Great Commission.

The term "religious spirit" may be confusing to some and troubling to others. But if, indeed, it is a major problem among us, then we must understand what it is and how it works. As you read, please keep several things in mind:

1. We are not on a witch hunt looking for demons. We do, however, want to understand better what we are up against, and what often keeps portions of the church divided and ineffective. Therefore, we will look carefully at what the Scripture says about how the enemy of our soul tries to work in our midst.

2. We are not looking to specifically identify certain people or groups of people who we think might be demonized. This chapter is not an attempt to separate the wheat from the chaff, or the sheep from the goats. That we will leave to God. It is, however, an attempt to expose abuse, whether or not the abuser recognizes it as such.

3. We do not want to create attitudes of suspicion, where Christians become increasingly skeptical of one another. There are far too many divisive things in the body of Christ today. We don't need another one.

4. We do not have a hidden agenda or an ax to grind. This is not an attempt to put forth some doctrinal belief or position that the church is slow, or reluctant, to accept. Rather, it is to show how all of us, at one time or another, abuse people, and to help us recognize it when we do it.

5. Our hope is that you, the reader, will become increasingly alert and aware enough to prevent some attitude or action from doing damage to Christ's body.

> Deliverance ministry ought never to be isolated, adulated or separated from all gospel ministry. Otherwise, too easily a kind of cultish or elitist group of the "initiated" will submit to a pathetic sense of superiority for having gained some small insight into this great truth. Becoming inflated with an overactive ego, such blinded ones proceed to the supposition that they have somehow gained a superiority and dimension of authority that has now negated their need to walk with that childlike simplicity that is always to characterize Kingdom people.[40]

WHAT IS A RELIGIOUS SPIRIT?

Television and movies often portray preachers as eccentric, frail, narrow-minded lunatics dressed in black and carrying the message "Repent, or go to hell." Their ranting and raving not only scare children, but also cause adults to shrink away in either fear or deep disgust. These pastors weren't always villains, but often were portrayed as ridiculous, witless, demented people whose presence made most people uncomfortable.

Although Hollywood carries some of the blame for a flawed portrayal of the ministerial office ordained by God, some of the blame for the portrayal is shared by our own religious culture. Hollywood didn't invent the description as much as they copied it. And they didn't copy it only from that fringe element that has trouble coping with reality. A spirit lurks today in pulpits all over that has a surprising similarity to the Hollywood depiction.

The apostle Paul described a kind of godliness that had only *"form"* (2 Timothy 3:5). There was the appearance of righteousness, but God's

---

40. Jack Hayford, *The Finger of God* (Jack Hayford Ministries), 28.

Spirit was not manifest in it. Not all that appears good comes from God. Religion is everywhere, and much of it has nothing to do with heaven's king. This is godless, powerless religion.

The counterfeit spirit behind godless religion is well described as a "religious spirit." Better yet we could describe it as a "deceptive, evil religious spirit." In some cases we can call it an "attitude," but it's an attitude often generated by a demon at work against a real person. Some religious people express themselves as a direct result of the influence of demons. Some of these vent themselves out of sinful passions. Still others are the consequence of over-zealous, deceived people (most of them professing Christians). However, there is a real difference between an actual demon spirit and a person with a religious spirit, or a religious attitude. A person with a religious attitude often operates as if they were the Holy Spirit directing the church. They set themselves up as the standard by which church ministry is judged; they are the thirty-six-inch yardstick that measures everything. (This is seriously illogical because how could a flawed person, a sinner in common with all other sinners, believe they have such authority?)

In both cases, we are looking at the attempts of fallen angels and fallen man to produce spiritual life outside of God. Some of the people involved know what they are doing. Most do not. An overwhelming number of the manifestations of religious spirits happen through people who are mostly unaware that something very wrong is happening in and through them.

CAN DEMONS AFFECT CHRISTIANS?

The magnitude of the wars fought during the last century is incomprehensible. One estimate of the total casualties of World War II alone is 72 million people. What an overwhelming amount of suffering and sorrow!

But there is another war currently being fought in an unseen realm that is causing far more casualties than any war ever fought on earth: *"For we do not wrestle against flesh and blood, but against principalities, against powers, against the rulers of the darkness of this age, against spiritual hosts of wickedness in the heavenly places"* (Ephesians 6:12).

Historically you don't often find the subject of spiritual warfare discussed in the church as a biblical reality. Little has been written on the subject. While some churches are more aware of spiritual warfare than others, there still remains an overall disfavor for the subject. It is looked upon by many people like the zealot standing on a street corner yelling, "Turn or Burn." The subject of war in the heavenlies seems just as crazy. But this disregard leaves worshipers short of the knowledge they need to prevent satanic influence—the kind of influence that is so often behind many of our emotional difficulties.

> One of Satan's clever strategies against us is to keep us in ignorance of his power and working. A pastor friend once stated to me his conviction that if he would just occupy himself with the gospel, the winning of souls, and the Person of the Lord Jesus Christ, he would not have to be too concerned about Satan. Such a view sounds very pious and spiritual, but it is very unbiblical and dangerous. Any believer who determines to occupy himself with the gospel, the winning of the lost, and knowing the Lord Jesus Christ is going to be a special target of Satan. To ignore the weapons of our warfare provided by the Lord against Satan and his kingdom is spiritual suicide. We will soon meet spiritual disaster if we ignore this enemy.[41]

Many insist that a born-again believer cannot be affected by a demon. However, notice Peter's words to Corinthians, *"Be sober, be vigilant; because your adversary the devil walks about like a roaring lion, seeking whom he may devour. Resist him, steadfast in the faith, knowing that the same sufferings are experienced by your brotherhood in the world"* (1 Peter 5:8–9). Look at the words of Paul who told the Corinthians that they needed to forgive, *"lest Satan should take advantage of us; for we are not ignorant of his devices"* (2 Corinthians 2:11). Don't forget James, who wrote *"Therefore submit to God. Resist the devil and he will flee from you"* (James 4:7). These verses would not be in Scripture if it were impossible for a demon to affect a Christian. And these are just a few of the Scriptures that speak to the enemy's influence over Christians. There are many more.

> It is unreasonable, therefore, for scientific and medical men to assert, as some do, that demonology is the mere figment of a diseased

---

41. Mark Bubeck, *The Adversary* (Chicago, IL: Moody Press), 68.

sensibility or magnetized brain. The Bible throughout affirms the collusion of men and demons. Our Lord made provision for His Church in future contact with them. The apostles and early teachers legislated concerning them. To deny the activity of demons is to insult the Inspirer of Holy Scripture.[42]

At the same time, notice that by submitting to God, His Holy Spirit works in us to keep anything or anyone from harming us. (See Luke 10:19.) This God in us, or more precisely, *Christ* in us by His Spirit, is the product of the born-again experience. Working with God's Spirit is the only way to fight the spiritual forces of darkness.

In view of the Scriptures above, does this mean that believers can be demon-possessed? Absolutely not! What it does mean is that even though the Holy Spirit resides in our human spirit, we still have a mind and emotions that can be influenced by things around us, including demons. Possession is not the point. The point is that our minds have been hit with worry, anxiety, temptations, fear, torment, and harassment—and usually because of the persuasion and influence of demons: *"Now the Spirit expressly says that in latter times some will depart from the faith, giving heed to deceiving spirits and doctrines of demons"* (1 Timothy 4:1).

A word of caution before we proceed: People and ministries who focus heavily on demons face the danger of deception. It is a subject that can easily occupy the mind to the point of excess. Although the topic is important, concentration must be first and foremost on God and His continual work in us through the Holy Spirit. It is not a matter of being afraid of demons, it is a matter of paying as little attention to them as possible while still maintaining a proper awareness. Remembering that through Christ's life in us, we are assured victory: *"He who is in you is greater than he who is in the world"* (1 John 4:4).

INFLUENCED BY DEMONS

The word "spirit" can be classified into three distinct types. One, the Holy Spirit. Two, the human spirit (we are made spirit, soul, and body). *"The Spirit Himself bears witness with our spirit that we are children of God"* (Romans 8:16).

---

42. Mrs. George Needham, *Angels and Demons* (Chicago, IL: Moody Press, 1935), 100.

And three, the false religious demonic spirit (and others like it), a very real being with an assignment against our souls. *"But if you have bitter envy and self-seeking in your hearts, do not boast and lie against the truth. This wisdom does not descend from above, but is earthly, sensual, demonic"* (James 3:14–15). Notice that James says that bitter envy and self-seeking are demonic. When we use the term "religious spirit," we are referring to a demonic assignment.

People with religious spirits of Christ's day expressed themselves in an arrogance that tried to dominate true spiritual leadership. These people were known as scribes and Pharisees. Their job was to know the law, and to instruct the people. They were highly regarded and held positions of prominence, but by and large they utterly failed at their job. They maintained the guise of a spiritual person, but inwardly failed to preserve the heart of the law—which is to love God and to love others.

The exterior of a man can appear godly while the interior is full of vicious and vile attitudes. Outward generosity can cover up inward selfishness. A friendly smile can easily hide racism, prejudice, and bias. What is said to one's face can be different from what's said behind one's back. Hatred can cloak itself in loveless intolerance.

It is easy to maintain a religious veneer that looks polished and slick. The "gifts of the Spirit," an "anointing," and even an emphasis on being "filled with the Spirit" contribute to an outward appearance. But Jesus cautioned that *"a tree is known by its fruit"* (Matthew 12:33). In reality, nothing much of what a person says is as important as his actions, which are motivated by inward attitudes. Does everything about us exemplify Christ? Or, at the least, is that the desire and goal we are seeking? Could it be that the cares of life, hurt feelings, discouragement, disillusionment, or even deception have worn away at our soul until our spirit has been affected, and in the process we have lost our first love? Have we contracted attitudes of negativism, bitterness, and criticism? Do we murmur and complain? Do we seek some element of control over the body of Christ that is reserved for the Holy Spirit or his designates? And have all of these things been affected by the assignment of a religious spirit?

Christianity is literally "Christ in us" (see Colossians 1:27), and the manifestation of His Spirit is always seen in *"love, joy, peace, longsuffering, kindness, goodness, faithfulness, gentleness, self-control"* (Galatians 5:22–23). Yes, He corrects, but does so as a Father. That is why there is no condemnation. (See Romans 8.) And yes, He will deal with unrepentance.

Today God is moving powerfully by His Spirit. Many want to be a part of what He is doing. Those of us who desire to be used by God, however, must understand the desired qualifications for usability. And there must always be a constant awareness of the potential for deception. Only those who are alert and awake to the possibility and danger of having a *"form of godliness, but denying its power"* (2 Timothy 3:5) will escape the subtleties of false religion manifested by a religious spirit.

TACTICS OF THE ENEMY

How does the enemy use the religious spirit to attack the church? One of his favorite tactics and devices is accusation. *"Then I heard a loud voice saying in heaven, 'Now salvation, and strength, and the kingdom of our God, and the power of His Christ have come, **for the accuser of our brethren, who accused them before our God day and night**, has been cast down'"* (Revelation 12:10). The greatest of Satan's accusations have always been directed at the church. His accusations usually contain a degree of truth—because deception is more difficult to identify if it is partly true. And it only takes a small amount of deception to get started on a path to a lie.

> The devil is at church as often as you are. And he stands outside your closet door and listens to what you say to God in secret, all the while studying how he may accuse you. The rebellious spirit who dared to criticize God's rule of heaven will not hesitate to pass judgment on the way you rule your soul. He is like those who listen to sermons only to find fault so they can call the minister an offender for some misplaced word or other. Satan delights in taking your duties to pieces and so disfiguring them that they appear superficial, though they are truly zealous; pharisaical, though they are really sincere. He will not rest until he can hand in a verdict of 'Guilty!' against your soul.[43]

---

43. William Gurnall, *The Christian in Complete Armour* (Carlisle, PA: Banner of Truth Trust, 1986), 100–101.

For the most part, destructive religious attitudes are the manifestation of our attempt to get back to spiritual life lost in the garden of Eden. Something deep inside each of us cries for significance, meaning, and importance. Something within tells us that we are supposed to be something that we intuitively know we are not. Much of our feelings of guilt and condemnation come from this knowledge. The convenient facade for covering up the shortfall is a religious spirit, and its chief characteristic is arrogance. It manifests itself in attitudes all the way from "There's nothing wrong with me" to "I've arrived spiritually, let me tell you about it." The pride that led to Satan's disgrace is no less ours if we do not guard against it.

> Guilt that has never been dealt with is an open invitation to demonic powers. Before we can bind the strong man, we need to deal with the sins that have given the enemy a legal right to occupy. The devil and his principalities have been defeated by Jesus on the cross and they would not be able to stay on unless they were relying on old invitations that have never been canceled."[44]

Consider for a moment the person who has been deceived into believing that no one serves the Lord anymore, and it's up to him to do what no one else is doing. It's not uncommon to find people who feel they are under contract to blame leaders in the church for dereliction of duties. When trying to ferret out the religious spirit, too often the very person with it is the one who goes looking for it.

It is easy to get acclimated to people with a religious spirit, even to the point of never stopping to question their attitudes, actions, and motives. Then, too, some of this spirit gradually rubs off on us, and often we are oblivious to the changes in us. But visitors to the church will recognize this spirit and won't stay long. The church that should have produced so well has yielded little, even while some saints toil ardently for a crop. Negativism, bitterness, and criticism abound where negative attitudes have influence, and few recognize how deadly these mind-sets can be.

The best way to determine the validity of an accusation is to recognize the difference between condemnation and conviction. Condemnation comes from the devil and tears us down, whereas conviction comes from

44. Peter Wagner, *Breaking Strongholds in Your City* (Ventura, CA: Regal, 1993), 108–109.

the Spirit and builds us up. Condemnation is accusatory, highly critical, and offers no hope, while conviction points out the difference between right and wrong and offers hope and help to accomplish that which is right. (See Philippians 2:13.) It also implies God's desire for reconciliation.

In many churches, those with a religious spirit are, for a while, hidden and disguised behind an air of love and concern. They can sympathize with others who are hurting, and are able to comfort them with kind words, but are doing it with an attitude that sows seeds of discord. They push their own agenda. They rope in anyone who will listen to them while at the same time undermining legitimate spiritual authority. They might say things like, "Have you noticed lately that the pastor seems tired and out of touch?" Or, "The pastor had an interesting interpretation today; I wonder where he found it!" Or, "I'm not saying anybody is doing anything wrong, but I feel very neglected as a member of this church." *"The first one to plead his cause seems right, until his neighbor comes and examines him"* (Proverbs 18:17).

One of our purposes in exposing attitudes and dispositions that are contrary to God's Word, and damaging His people, is to help the reader examine his or her own life and faith, so as not to latch onto some destructive, lifeless spiritual element. The clichés and confusing statements revealed in chapter 14 might be a good place to start a period of self-examination.

PURPOSES OF RELIGIOUS EVIL SPIRITS

Religious spirits are commissioned to:

+ Promote spiritual arrogance

+ Promote self-reliance

+ Promote human reasoning

+ Promote false religion by way of ritual, tradition, and formula

+ Promote hyper-spiritualism

+ Promote "works" and "religion" as a way to God

+ Promote the "god of self"

+ Promote disobedience

+ Promote passivity

- Promote nationalism and conspiracy theories
- Promote escapism
- Promote self-glorification
- Promote the destruction of spiritual truth
- Promote the destruction of the joy and peace in Jesus

ASSIGNMENTS OF RELIGIOUS EVIL SPIRITS

Religious spirits are assigned to cause:

- Strife
- Divisions
- Confusion
- Anxiety and worry
- Scorn
- Hatred of correction and instruction
- Murmuring
- Fear
- Wrong attitudes
- Impetuousness

WORKINGS OF RELIGIOUS EVIL SPIRITS

Religious evil spirits work to:

- Twist the truth into new religions
- Overemphasize holiness
- Foster false guilt and false condemnation
- Minimize sin
- Stir up hatred through offenses
- Confuse godly sorrow with true repentance
- Conceal the truth through misinterpretation of the Scriptures

- ♦ Attack the body of Christ
- ♦ Speak into the human mind to confuse
- ♦ Deceive and keep a person from hearing the true Word of God

RELIGIOUS ACTIVISTS

Well-intentioned believers often see deep and glaring issues that need to be dealt with in the church. The danger is becoming an activist apart from the Holy Spirit's plans to make things right. The "activist" easily gives into self-righteousness and aggression in their desire for reform, often leaving hurt people in their wake.

No doubt activists have been around since the beginning of time. Allow us this tongue-in-cheek example:

The first time Eve burned the toast, Adam became an activist. He knew that if he didn't create a small calamity, Eve wouldn't listen to him—which was one of his primary complaints, anyway. Eve reacted, wondering why Adam had to be so demanding.

Adam shot back, "Because God made me the head of the house."

"What's that supposed to mean?"

"You know exactly what that means," Adam retorted.

"No, tell me."

"You just don't get it do you? God made me just a little lower than the angels, but He made you a lot lower."

"I thought he made us equal," she countered.

"Well He sort of did, but somebody had to be the boss."

With that he stormed out of the room. That night Adam slept on the sofa in the living room.

Eventually Eve told her friends what had happened.

Adam considered that a violation of their trust.

Eve asked, "What trust?"

Adam got angry and stormed out of the room again.

When Adam came back home, there was a note on the table. It read, "I'm shopping, there's leftover meatloaf in the refrigerator."

Adam was furious, he shouted, "What's wrong with women? They're all the same—stupid!"

Later they kissed and made up.

But eventually, they didn't kiss and they didn't make up.

Soon, Eve joined a women's rights group and became an activist.

Adam began drinking.

Moral of the story: Whatever you do, don't burn the toast.

Cain and Abel fared even worse. Every war ever fought has been the product of someone protesting against discrimination and prejudice, and especially oppression, greed, persecution, and hunger. Activism has two basic forms; those who want reform, but insist on using nonviolent actions, and those who want a voice and change, but don't much care who gets hurt in the process. Our use of the word activist should not suggest that it is a negative word only. However, we would rather use the word "reformer" for those who truly want change and accomplish it without hurting others.

Throughout history, activists were needed to bring about reform. In fifteenth-century Europe, Martin Luther, among many others, strongly disapproved of certain abuses within the Catholic Church of which he was a part. He was able to articulate ninety-five different situations he believed were in error within the church. In the beginning he and others only wanted reform, but when that didn't happen, the Protestant movement was formed. Yet these were men hoping for a peaceful solution. They had no desire to take up arms and fight.

When black American activist Martin Luther King Jr. appeared in the 1960s to contest racial injustice, he was eventually hailed as a hero throughout much of the United States and the world. Unlike most others, he controlled his speech and in the process controlled the crowds. Today he stands high on the list of reformers who changed the world. But why him more than others? Certainly there were more men and women who went down in history for their positive participation and contributions to the civil rights movement and many of them are still well-known. But there were also many visible leaders whom history has forgotten because they promoted division over reconciliation. They weren't interested in the truth as much as they were interested in retaliation and vengeance.

Retaliatory groups increase already-existing hatred and division. Their words are inflammatory, not reconciliatory. They fire up crowds, knowing well that their rhetoric could lead to further hostility. It doesn't matter that antagonism and the fierce venting of anger only increases the conflict, as long as their human ego is satisfied. The man who opens his mouth and shouts the loudest at injustice, may in truth be correct, but will accomplish nothing because of bitterness. Anger, hatred, and hostility offer no solutions. You can suffer loss in a court of law, even though your case is justifiable and appropriate, if your presentation is heavily laced with vengeance and retaliation.

It's a reality. The more you press on people, especially with force, the more they press back. Agitation makes a difficult situation worse and increases wounds. Pause for a moment and think about some of the above statements. Did you become more than a little uneasy wondering where we're going? Did you start to take sides over an issue that has caused division for hundreds of years: racial inequality and discrimination? Were you looking for us to lean to one side more than the other? If you did, you are quite normal. All of us do these things because it's our nature. Bigotry and bias become increasingly difficult to deal with as the issues become more visceral and emotions accelerate. Ever since the civil rights movement and the ensuing uprisings over racial issues, we can only hope for men and women with a plan, a "dream," who would tenaciously pursue it with level heads and gracious hearts.

And may it be so in the church as well.

ACTIVISM IS ALIVE TODAY

We've used the above illustrations to paint a picture of how human beings respond to conflict. Now let's relate them to the Christian church today. Down through history many reformers have brought positive changes and a new direction when the church began to stray. They were men and women who stood up to those who would have eventually done great damage to the church if not confronted. In many ways their challenge was similar to that of Martin Luther King Jr. They avoided reactionary statements and worked instead within a framework of reconciliation. With the help of the Holy Spirit, they moved forward, mindful that the church needed some drastic changes, but at the same time knowing that positive change would never happen through people with a negative spirit. These were people who knew the church belonged to Jesus and not to them.

We are aware that the ego-laced actions of many of the reformers detracted from the goal and slowed the process of reconciliation. But the bright side was, and still is, that many others labored under ethical and unselfish principles, wanting the best possible unity that could be obtained.

Here are some things that we can learn from them and apply to the struggles of today, especially within the church:

1. Wrestle with your anger to keep it restrained. You lose influence the moment it is out of control.

2. Listen at least twice as much as you speak. It tricks people into believing you are wise.

3. Avoid interrupting the opposition. It's called "talking over."

4. Don't appear to be upset. Emotional speakers eventually lose trust.

5. Dogmatism will make you an instant enemy.

6. Keep in mind that often others don't see things the way you do because they haven't had your experiences. To become angry with someone because their background is different from yours is insulting to them.

7. Be aware that many people are much smarter than you, and can make you look silly in a hurry. Far too many people have lost respect and the right to give their testimony by not having the knowledge to carry on a debate properly.

8. You will always face opposition by unprincipled people. Better, however, to back off if you are in opposition to principled people.

9. Recognize that all of your opinions, ideas, and beliefs will help no one if the Holy Spirit is not with you.

10. Know that a misplaced word in any confrontation can turn to anger and antagonism.

11. Don't forget that integrity is one of the most powerful forces at hand.

12. Always attempt to move toward unity. If you fail to do so, it will result in discord. And if you choose discord, you will always lose.

13. Consider that you can be right in principle but be highly unprincipled in your actions and attitudes.

14. Challenging someone's actions is far different from assaulting his character. Point out an error and you may preserve peace. Call a person a liar and you challenge his character. Saying "you're a liar," is much different from, "That's not accurate and borders on a lie."

15. Avoid blanket statements such as, "I heard the Lord say that the church is grieving His Spirit." It may be true that some are grieving His Spirit, but then the Spirit Himself will usually be the one to convict and correct. Wouldn't it be wiser to first pray and ask God to bring conviction where it's needed, rather than taking matters into your own hands? You could end up being the one who grieves the Holy Spirit if you don't handle it correctly.

16. Don't use "weasel words": "They say…"; "It is said…"; "I've heard…." Weasel words are intended to persuade people to a particular way of thinking without backing it up with facts.

17. The moment you lose your temper or begin a verbal attack, you lose respect.

18. Always consider that another person may have a different perspective and will have trouble grasping yours.

19. It's tiring to listen to people who believe they have knowledge about everything. *"Don't make friends with quick-tempered people or spend time with those who have bad tempers. If you do, you will be like them. Then you will be in real danger"* (Proverbs 22:24–25 NCV).

You might want to pray the following prayer, keeping in mind that we *pray* to God, but *declare* to the enemy. In the following paragraphs the first part is a prayer to God. The second part is a *declaration* to the enemy. The last part is a *prayer* concerning the Holy Spirit.

Heavenly Father, I recognize that I have fallen prey to a religious spirit. I repent of all attitudes and actions that in any way have offended You and hurt others.

I now declare to you, religious spirit, that I renounce all words and actions that have given you any authority to operate in my life, and in the name of Jesus I break your power and authority over my life. I command you to get out of my life in the name of Jesus.

Father, I welcome the Holy Spirit to guide and teach me in the ways of Jesus.

CASUALTIES OF THE UNSEEN WAR

Who are the casualties of this unseen war between heavenly forces where Satan acts as the everlasting accuser? Those who were condemned by an authority figure and learned to believe that they were no good. Those who had been abused by a sexual predator and came to believe it was their fault. Those in whom the power of rejection never leaves no matter how hard they try to get rid of it. Those who live in constant anxiety because their nervous systems have been damaged.

The casualties are everywhere, and sometimes they are us.

Our deep desire is that the local church be fully equipped to bring all believers into the freedom for which Christ paid the price.

The thought of a church full of people who are equipped and functioning in such a manner can be scary for many pastors, especially when viewing it through the lens of the past, when wrong teachings, attitudes and behaviors too often prevailed. Many are apprehensive to allow people to lay hands on others to pray for them, let alone to cast out demons. For these hesitant leaders, it is not a hard stretch to imagine a chaotic mess that gives their churches the reputation of being the weirdest churches in town. But what if it were done decently and in order? What if it could be established scripturally and maturely?"[45]

---

45. Chris Hayward, *God's Cleansing Stream* (Ventura, CA: Regal Books, 2005), 28.

It is our belief that instead of a few disciples having some "secret" understanding of spiritual warfare and casting out demons, every disciple should be filled and anointed by the Holy Spirit to continue doing what Jesus was anointed to do: *"To preach the gospel to the poor;...to heal the brokenhearted, to proclaim liberty to the captives and recovery of sight to the blind, to set at liberty those who are oppressed; to proclaim the acceptable year of the Lord"* (Luke 4:18–19).

A PROVERB

Doing right brings freedom to honest people, but those who are not trustworthy will be caught by their own desires. (Proverbs 11:6 NCV)

PSALMS FOR THE WOUNDED

If the LORD had not helped me, I would have died in a minute. I said, "I am about to fall," but, LORD, your love kept me safe. I was very worried, but you comforted me and made me happy.
(Psalm 94:17–19 NCV)

In their misery they cried out to the LORD, and he saved them from their troubles. He led them on a straight road to a city where they could live. Let them give thanks to the LORD for his love and for the miracles he does for people. He satisfies the thirsty and fills up the hungry.
(Psalm 107:6–9 NCV)

I love the LORD, because he listens to my prayers for help. He paid attention to me, so I will call to him for help as long as I live. The ropes of death bound me, and the fear of the grave took hold of me. I was troubled and sad. Then I called out the name of the LORD. I said, "Please, LORD, save me!" The LORD is kind and does what is right; our God is merciful.
(Psalm 116:1–5 NCV)

13

I JUST NEED TO BE PERFECT

America's present need is not heroics but healing; not nostrums
but normalcy; not revolution but restoration.
—*President Warren G. Harding*

There was a woman who was a true *Better Homes and Gardens* wife. Her house was immaculate, everything spotless and in its place. Her lawn looked lovely, green, and always fresh-cut. But she was driving her husband of twenty-five years crazy. He was an easygoing and compliant man, but he had reached his limit with her constant care. If he dropped a sock, sirens went off and she was after him with a vengeance.

One day in women's Bible study, the other women noticed the constant criticism this lady directed at her husband. When they asked her why she was so angry at him all the time, she answered, "You'd be angry too if you lived with him!" Caring for her as they did, the women began to ask her questions about how she grew up. They soon learned that her mother and father were both alcoholics. Their house was always a mess, and her father was abusive to her when he was drinking. As a child, this woman made an inner vow that she would someday keep her home spotless and marry a very compliant man, one she could control, and one who would not try to control her.

But all these years later, her compliant husband was ready to get a divorce. As she verbalized her past and the vow she made as a little girl, this woman's eyes were opened to the lie that she'd been living inside—that everything had to be perfect. She began the painful process of rejecting her lie and accepting the truth that life isn't perfect and that she didn't need to live a perfect life to have a perfect marriage. Finally, she asked forgiveness from her husband, from God, and from others for being such a difficult person to live with. Change doesn't necessarily happen overnight, but in her case, it began the process of healing—and saved her marriage.

WHAT IS A PERFECTIONIST?

Perfectionism is the most common religion of man. It is "natural religion," that is, Adam's religion after he fell. If you look carefully, everyone is a perfectionist to some degree or another. You find perfectionism in sports, politics, business, and sadly in church. It manifests itself as extremely strong feelings about personal preferences, establishing them as ultimate certainties. It isn't just about having a strict orderly life. It's an identity. It is the foundation of who people are and what they believe. In reality, perfectionism is just another form of pride, and that is why it is so destructive. Perfectionism is saying, "my way is the right way," and this idea is in the heart of every person and stalks our every step. We are delving into the subject of perfectionism because it is often at the root of mean-spirited behavior that causes huge amounts of pain in the church.

Generally speaking, perfectionism is a fanatical belief that anything short of flawlessness is unacceptable. A perfectionist is often thought of as a person who needs to put everything in perfect order, who can't adjust to lack of organization, who fixates over the need for harmony and arrangement. Perfectionists often set high standards and goals for themselves and are determined to achieve them. Categorization, symmetry, classification, uniformity, regulation, neatness, tidiness, and regulation all rule a perfectionist's life.

There are, however, distinctions over the intensity of perfectionism. In the seventies, a psychologist named Donald E. Hamachek made a distinction that is still commonly used: "Psychologists today differentiate between positive perfectionism, which is adaptive and healthy, and negative perfectionism, which is maladaptive and neurotic."[46] Adaptive perfectionists are usually socially adjusted, emotionally balanced, team players, cordial, and friendly. Maladaptive perfectionists set irrational and excessive

---

46. Tal Ben-Shahar, *The Pursuit of Perfect* (New York: McGraw-Hill Education, 2009), xx.

performance standards, unattainable goals, and demand disproportionate objectives for themselves and others. Failure to them is a sign of insignificance and worthlessness. Self-worth is measured by accomplishment. Besides being harsh, they are often negative, bitter, critical, compulsive, obsessive, and arrogant.

For an example, consider two people who would both be considered perfectionists: one who keeps everything in their life under their control and an athlete who regulates everything in order to achieve a competitive goal. The person who can't stand to see a picture hanging crooked on the wall and can't rest until it is straight is admittedly a different kind of perfectionist than a sports person who is determined to bench a certain number of pounds or run a certain number of miles. We want to tell the person with the picture problem not to be so picky, and then praise the athlete for her determination to excel. But both people are driven. Both are consumed.

However, let's say the athlete wins. She is confident, relieved, excited. She is done. But the hyper-perfectionist can never rest. There is always one more picture that needs straightening, one more paperclip that needs to find its place, and one more closet to arrange so that everything hangs in an orderly fashion. This person's perfectionism has become a bondage, ruining peace of mind and good judgment. Instead of ruling it, this person's perfectionism rules them. Some days, they are overwhelmed with the conviction that they have failed at life. The significant difference between the two is motivation: whereas one often feels forced by fear, the other feels excited by the challenge.

Perfectionists fear imperfection and feel that other people will like them only if they are perfect. Perfectionism is not the same thing as striving for excellence. Those who strive for excellence can take mistakes (imperfections) as incentive to work harder, but "unhealthy perfectionists consider their mistakes a sign of personal defects. For these people, anxiety about potential failure is the reason perfectionism is felt as a burden."[47]

Adaptive perfectionists pursue perfection without compromising their self-esteem, and derive pleasure from their efforts. Maladaptive perfectionists strive for unrealistic goals and consistently feel dissatisfied when they

---

47. Wikipedia, "Perfectionism: Definition," https://en.wikipedia.org/wiki/Perfectionism_ (psychology)#cite_ref-5, accessed October 24, 2016.

cannot reach them. (Now, we are not trying to say athletes cannot be maladaptive or the housekeeper adaptive! Quite the contrary!)

It is on the maladaptive, the negative side, of perfectionism we will spend most of our time, not only looking at more traits of negative perfectionism, but also why it exists from a biblical worldview. From this point, by "perfectionist" we mean "maladaptive perfectionist."

SYMPTOMS OF A PERFECTIONIST:

+ Obsesses over faultlessness, meticulousness, and exactness. Everything has to be precisely as they see it.

+ Driven to unreasonable lengths to achieve a goal, will do almost anything to reach an objective, including "walking" on other people.

+ Overly detailed.

+ At times exhibits extremely low self-esteem.

+ Strict with others he or she considers to be imperfect.

+ Unreasonably high values.

+ Wants attention and will work to get it.

+ Tries to display a perfect demeanor.

+ Stingy with possessions.

+ Fear of rejection if they fail to meet a standard.

+ Procrastinates and will not begin a job if it cannot be completed perfectly.

TWO MIND-SETS

Nothing destroys the human race and especially God's church more than perfectionism, which is a component of a religious spirit.

That is a strong statement! Can it really be true?

Consider what we have discussed previously. Much of the preaching and teaching in our churches is based on an understanding of how God views mankind. One mind-set sees Him as angry and upset, with little patience for people, a divine Being who's looking for anything He can find in order to tell us how to straighten up our lives. This mind-set sees God as a Person who is always offended and looking for someone to blame for messing up His wonderful world. Out of this mind-set comes these types of statements: "Suffering is God's way to get your attention." "Suffering pleases God because it is a way of showing humility." "Happiness is not a part of this life and shows an insincere spiritual life."

Who can stand very long under this kind of condemnation? But many do. And sadly, they pass it on to their children, who pass it on to their children. Eventually, people walk away from God, wondering why He is so cruel and mean-spirited. Those who stay must figure out how to avoid the brutality of a "mean Jesus." Some stay in churches who have this mentality because they lack even a basic understanding of salvation, believing they must do something in order to appease an angry God. All, and all means all, of us hate to admit that we can be deceived, and even more that we can be gullible.

The second mind-set trusts that God is good, kind, and merciful. That He wishes the best for His creation, both now and in eternity. That although sin stands between us and God, Jesus has opened the way to come to God without payment. This mind-set does not rest upon, "Get your life cleaned up and God will accept you." It rests upon, "Come just as you are no matter the extent of your sin."

God has been locked out of human life and wants back in. But we sense that something in us hinders us from believing that God individually wants us back. And of course that something is sin. Once the sin question is taken care of through Jesus by way of the cross, the "new life" that we so often talk about begins with the gentle Holy Spirit doing a work in us, *because God is working in you to help you want to do and be able to do what pleases him*" (Philippians 2:13 NCV). We come to a great truth when we realize it isn't about our faithfulness, our accomplishments, or our successes, but about His goodness, kindness, and love. Only then do we quit striving and learn to live in Him.

PERFECTIONISTS AND THE CHURCH

The church-oriented perfectionist believes that he or she is personally responsible for attaining the highest standards of service, of moral good, and of moral character on their own. When taken to its extreme, they believe in "sinless perfectionism," which constitutes coming to a place of sinlessness while here on earth. That means they can personally arrive at the place they are striving for by refraining from anything and everything that has any appearance of worldliness or the flesh.

Church perfectionism can be looked at in two primary categories: external and internal. The external manifestation of church perfectionism is harsh and graceless treatment of anybody in a position in church—from ordinary members all the way up to the pastor. To the perfectionist, anyone in an official church role must be perfect and are open to criticism if they are not. The internal manifestation is the dangerous yet often unspoken attitudes of "we have arrived," "we are above sin," and "most other believers are wrong."

Of course both manifestations are clever deceits from the devil. People are driven near crazy by such church perfectionism because they are not allowed to have any weakness or flaw in their acts of service. The church perfectionist impatiently dismisses the imperfect person as irrelevant, often demanding they be replaced with someone more competent, and often wounding the offender to the point that they never serve in the church again. Church perfectionism elevates spiritual pride and rejects criticism in any form, even that which comes from well-meaning people. *After all,* the pervasive, unstated attitude of a church perfectionist seems to be, *how can we be corrected if we have reached perfection?*

Perfectionism, by Donald T. Kauffman's definition, is the "theological term for belief in the necessity and possibility of sinless perfection for the Christian believer in this life. It is often associated with the baptism of the Holy Spirit."[48] It's also often tied together with an understanding of the end times: many Christian perfectionists believe that Jesus is coming back to earth to receive a sinless people. Therefore, Jesus cannot come until there is a perfect people ready to meet Him.

There are numerous problems with this kind of thinking:

*   God sees us as if we had never sinned because we are "in" Jesus, not because of what we have achieved. On earth we still wrestle with sin

---

48. Donald T. Kauffman, *The Dictionary of Religious Terms* (Westwood, NJ: Fleming H. Revell Company, 1967), 351.

and will always be tempted. *"If we say that we have no sin, we deceive ourselves, and the truth is not in us. If we confess our sins, He is faithful and just to forgive us our sins and to cleanse us from all unrighteousness. If we say that we have not sinned, we make Him a liar, and His word is not in us"* (1 John 1:8–10).

+ How will a person ever know if he or she has been perfected? What is the standard? Is there a person they can point to who has reached a perfected state here on earth?

+ God has set the day and the time for Jesus' return. Nothing in the Bible says that the day of His return is determined by anything we do or anything we become.

+ Perfectionism neglects the Holy Spirit's role of leading and guiding the church. It does not recognize the Scripture that says, *"Without Me [Jesus] you can do nothing"* (John 15:5). Various other Scriptures make it plain that only by the indwelling Christ are we able to do anything good. (See, for example, Colossians 1:27 and Galatians 2:20).

+ If a person attained sinless perfection, whose efforts were at work? If it was theirs, then it was by the works of the law which Scripture condemns: *"A man is not justified by the works of the law but by faith in Jesus Christ…for by the works of the law no flesh shall be justified"* (Galatians 2:16). If it wasn't theirs, why do they boast?

+ Righteousness has nothing to do with performance, but with who we become.

+ If you want to do well and be good, but God's divine nature isn't in you, forget it. (Don't miss this, God's divine nature is offered to *everyone*. God added to Christ the human nature that we might have the divine nature added to us.)

+ A performance mentality will constantly keep you wondering how well you are doing. There is no peace for the person who fails to recognize the indwelling Holy Spirit and His power to lead us and guide us.

♦ We don't believe that Christians have to be repenting every second of their lives, unless they are convicted by the Holy Spirit of a particular sin. The Lord does not want us to be "sin-focused" but rather "Christ-focused": "*...fixing our eyes on Jesus, the author and finisher of our faith*" (Hebrews 12:2).

THE ROOTS: PRIDE AND FEAR

Perfectionism is rooted, we believe, in a combination of pride and fear. The desire to always appear perfect incorporates the essence of pride, while at the same time displaying irrational fear. Pride says, "I know the standard better than anyone else," while fear sends shockwaves through a person who feels he is about to be found out for being less than what he considers the standard.

Of the numerous places where we find perfectionism, the church is high on the list. (To be fair it must be noted that other religions such as Buddhism and Hinduism are also known for high degrees of perfectionism.) The suggestion here is not to examine a failure only Christians have, but rather to recognize the difficulty of explaining to any person how grace works to destroy sin. These two realities, sin and grace, are the crux of the practical Christian life. If you move toward grace without recognizing the consequences of sin, you are in risk of forgetting that we must always be putting off the old man and putting on the new and not sinning more that grace may abound. (See Ephesians 4:24 and Romans 6:1.) Failing to address evil gives it an opportunity to expand. However, if you focus on sin without recognizing the power of grace, you risk thinking that it's your job to defeat sin, when in reality it is Christ and Christ alone who can accomplish that.

Numerous Christians seem to fall into one or the other of these two camps. Either they dismiss sin as something they can't control and assume God's grace will cover it, or they live in irrational fear that if they do not attain to perfection, they will miss heaven. The fear compounds itself as one failure after another sneaks into a life. They haven't prayed enough, witnessed enough, or stayed away from the world enough.

Perfectionism is the result of focusing on sin. It gains credibility among those who look at God as an angry, demanding scorekeeper whose intolerance toward sin will rain down the vengeance of a fiery eternity. With that picture of God, who wouldn't want to try to become a perfectionist? At the same time, the effort of reaching high standards without God's personal help, tends to keep many in a religious bondage that denies the good things God has for them. The perfectionist fails to remember that "*for God so loved the world*" (John 3:16) and the further declaration that "I [Jesus] *did not come to judge the world but to save the world.*" The "works" involved in perfectionism shouts loud and clear, "I can and must save myself by the good things I do."

Those who hold unrealistically high standards project those same heavy weights on others, burdening them with ridiculous ideals. They can't live without the need to tell others what they believe is right and wrong from an obsessive, hairsplitting standpoint. They are filled with a pride that God hates. They are not practically, daily relying on the Lord's grace and Spirit; they are relying on themselves. They convince their listeners that they have the sole responsibility to make the world, and especially everyone around them, right. Such arrogance quickly becomes a headache and heartache to the local church.

Among the multiple tragedies surrounding perfectionism is the damage done to themselves and to others by unreasonable and unbiblical requirements. We have a list of such requirements in chapter 15. The people who impose these requirements are usually sincere people who truly believe they are doing right. Don't miss the point. We are not referring to the careful pastor who, in carrying out his duties, reminds people of the problem of sin. No, we're talking about those who have missed the gospel and have taken on the personal responsibility of not only preaching righteousness, but also of preaching adherence to their extrabiblical requirements. These are the people who damage the church so appallingly.

In a casual conversation, a pastor mentioned that wine had never touched his lips. Why did he say anything about his past, especially when Christ's blood cleanses our past? What do newly saved Christians, or anyone for that matter, think when their pastor makes statements like that? This pastor opened the door to the misconception that he is "better" than others, that his remarkable past makes him more fit for ministry than others.

ATTITUDES AND ACTIONS

Here are four attitudes and actions that often mark a church perfectionist:

- Hyper-religion and judgmentalism.

- Gets discouraged easily and gives up. "I'll never make it." Goes back into the world.

- Upon hearing the true gospel, turns on the group who influenced the perfectionism, thus continuing in anger.

- Usually eventually buys into the liberal gospel where Christianity is more of a social activity, rather than a relationship with a Person, and is comprised of "good works."

UNIQUE ROLES

Here are some personas that church perfectionists often adopt:

- The Martyr: Easily identified by such statements as, "Nobody cares about anything around here except me. I work harder than all of them put together. If it wasn't for me this place would fall apart."

- The Innuendo Complainant: Never direct, they use of subtle criticism to their advantage. "Obviously the pastor didn't prepare well for his sermon today." Or, "I noticed that the pastor's wife doesn't attend all the meetings."

- The Bottom Liner/the Perfectionist Boss: Holds staff to unreasonably high standards to avoid criticism coming to him or the church.

- The Authority Figure: Obsessively needs to be in authority in order to control others' behavior. Gets itchy when others want to lead certain events or initiatives. Is convinced that it must be their way or the highway, because their wisdom and knowledge exceeds that of most others.

- The False Justifier: Denies there is anything selfish about them because they have a righteous cause.

- The "God Told Me" Persona: Perfectionists use "God told me" as a tool to get others to do what they want, because if God really told them something, then who can argue against Him?

(Keep in mind that God does speak to people, but they are never to manipulate others with the information. The Bible says we have the mind of Christ. No one single person has the mind of Christ by themselves. This is why 1 Corinthians 2:16 tells us that God has given different gifts to different people.)

DOING GOOD WITHOUT TRYING TO BE PERFECT

The mind-set in a leader that wounded and broken people are that way because of sin in their lives often has the terrible result of convincing the leader that their job is to keep people holy and in line by the law: *If I don't require holiness out of my people they will die in their sins,* they think. That may seem correct and admirable to some, but it is by no means the message of the gospel. The message of the New Testament is a message of a God who is willing to help us in all aspects of life. If it were a message of how to live well and obey God, we would not need the New Testament—the Old would suffice. God doesn't want us to just "be good," He wants us to know Him, and through that process be transformed by Him.

Over and over again, God said in His Word that we are unable to help ourselves and that He wants to work in us to produce true righteousness through relationship with Him. In other words, all of our personal righteousness cannot produce a righteous person. (See Isaiah 64:6.)

We already know that a common feature of anyone who tries a subjective approach to fulfilling God's laws is the manifestation of pride. You can see it in the deceptive attitude that says, "I know God's ways and if you will listen to me I will show them to you." We may accept the statement when it comes from a sincere person who simply wants to help. Far too often, however, it carries the attitude of "my help is what you really need." But "my help" is invalid when it fails to point directly to God's help. It is also invalid if it summarizes a list of things to do to stay on good terms with God.

It's not enough to tell a person to "do the right thing," he or she must also understand the Person who is in charge of personal development. Nobody takes on another person's history of faith. Each one of us must build it for ourselves. If you're a leader, the goal is never to make other believers in your image, having the same convictions and standards. The goal is always to help others become like Jesus. By pointing them to Christ, you allow the Holy Spirit to minister personally, bringing conviction, revelation, and good ethics and morality.

Paul wrote to Timothy a list of things necessary for spiritual growth:

But stay away from the evil desires of youth. Try hard to live right and to have faith, love, and peace, together with those who trust in the Lord from pure hearts. Stay away from foolish and stupid arguments, because you know they grow into quarrels. And a servant of the Lord must not quarrel but must be kind to everyone, a good teacher, and patient. The Lord's servant must gently teach those who disagree.

(2 Timothy 2:22–25)

We doubt that Timothy grabbed parchment and quill and sat down to add these things to list of what he must do to get into heaven. Timothy knew that these were not suggestions, but he also knew that Paul wasn't dictating a new list of rules and regulations to achieve salvation. Paul was an encourager knowing that wisdom, knowledge, and understanding would flow into Timothy's heart because of the indwelling Holy Spirit. Whether or not Timothy already knew these things and needed reminding, or they were new to him and Paul was now teaching them to him, we don't know. What we do know is that Paul never taught salvation from a list of ethical and moral standards. His hope was that now having the Holy Spirit, values would flow to Timothy's heart, according to God's promises:

"This is the covenant that I will make with them after those days, says the LORD: I will put My laws into their hearts, and in their minds I will write them," then He adds, "Their sins and their lawless deeds I will remember no more."   (Hebrews 10:16–17)

….clearly you are an epistle of Christ, ministered by us, written not with ink but by the Spirit of the living God, not on tablets of stone but on tablets of flesh, that is, of the heart.   (2 Corinthians 3:3)

In any discussion on perfectionism, it should be understood that following the commands of Scripture is neither a sign of perfectionism nor an optional part of the faith. All Christians have a responsibility for living righteous lives, but only because of the inner working and enabling of a loving God.

A PROVERB

A friend loves you all the time, and a brother helps in time of trouble.
(Proverbs 17:17 NCV)

PSALMS FOR THE WOUNDED

Troubles have surrounded me; there are too many to count. My sins have caught me so that I cannot see a way to escape. I have more sins than hairs on my head, and I have lost my courage. Please, LORD, save me. Hurry, LORD, to help me. (Psalm 40:12–13 NCV)

God is our protection and our strength. He always helps in times of trouble. So we will not be afraid even if the earth shakes, or the mountains fall into the sea. (Psalm 46:1–2 NCV)

God, we come into your Temple to think about your love.
(Psalm 48:9 NCV)

14

THE CHURCH DOESN'T SEEM TO CARE

> God may be saddened over what you do, but He's never disappointed in you as His unique creation. God is not disillusioned with you because He had no illusions about you to begin with.[49]
> —*Francis Anfuso*

A woman reported that she went for a walk with another Christian woman in order to develop a friendship. She recounted,

> As part of the conversation, I revealed an issue I was struggling with. My friend's response was, "Well, Jesus just wants to grind you to powder." I was very surprised, but I assumed she just didn't understand what I said, so I said it differently. She repeated, "Jesus just wants to grind you to powder." We continued our slow walk together. I said I could understand Jesus wanting to mold me into His image and it may feel like being ground, but He has never treated me like "grinding me to powder," like into oblivion. She repeated, "Jesus just wants to grind you to powder. I'm sorry if that hurts, but I don't have a filter over my mouth. That's just how God made me."

We don't have the luxury of deciding that we can say things any which way we like. We are not just responsible for the words that leave our lips, but also for *how* we say those words. Another woman reported, "I once heard a megachurch pastor say, as he was condemning a sect of Christian

---

49. Francis Anfuso, *A City That Looks Like Heaven* (Roseville, CA: Self-published, 2014), 34.

brothers and sisters from the pulpit, that 'It doesn't matter how I say the truth, the fact that I say the truth at all is love.' This is so far from the heart of God. God wants us to know the truth, but He also wants us to hear it in a way that we are able to respond to it, and to Him." We agree!

The disciples were famous for saying things that were inappropriate:

> *From that time Jesus began to show to His disciples that He must go to Jerusalem and suffer many things from the elders and chief priests and scribes, and be killed, and be raised the third day. Then Peter took Him aside and began to rebuke Him, saying, "Far be it from You, Lord; this shall not happen to You!" But He turned and said to Peter, "Get behind Me, Satan! You are an offense to Me, for you are not mindful of the things of God, but the things of men."* (Matthew 16:21–23)

The blind man in the street pleaded, *"Jesus, son of David, have mercy on me!"* (Mark 10:47). But the disciples wanted him to shut up and stop interfering with spiritual work. Then there were the children who wanted to be close to Jesus, but the disciples tried to chase them away. And then when Jesus paid attention to a woman of bad reputation, the disciples questioned why He would do such a thing.[50] These were the disciples before the advent of the Holy Spirit.

We today still say things that we haven't thought through or that are incorrect assumptions. Even worse, all of us are more likely to repeat what we've heard from someone else than to puzzle out what we actually think. In some cases we might call them clichés, but whatever they are, they can be devastating. Many of them may be true or at least have a degree of truth in them, but when given in a matter-of-fact way they take on a negative meaning and damage spiritual life.

We are including three lists of clichés and hasty assumptions, and our intention is twofold: 1) We hope that by reading these clichés and thoughts, you will gain a greater understanding of how easily words can wound, regardless of the good intentions, and 2) we hope that if you have believed any of the following, you will find freedom from them.

---

50. See Matthew 19:13 and Luke 7:36–50.

BRUTAL CLICHÉS

Cliché #1: *"If you were really serving God you wouldn't be in such a mess."*

But why do you judge your brother? Or why do you show contempt for your brother? For we shall all stand before the judgment seat of Christ. (Romans 14:10)

Those who are at ease have contempt for misfortune. (Job 12:5 NIV)

Just because a person is able to avoid trials doesn't mean they're righteous. Remember the lives of Joseph, Daniel, and Paul? How do we explain why Joseph had to be thrown into a pit by his brothers and left for dead or why he had to endure prison falsely accused, if he was such a spiritual man? Or Daniel—why did he have to endure the lion's den if he was such a mature man of God? Or why did Paul have to suffer shipwrecks and undergo beatings, scourgings, and mistreatment in prison, if he was such a man of faith? Surely a life of ease does not equal right standing with God, and a life of hardship does not equal God's displeasure.

Cliché #2: *"You have problems because you need to learn your lesson. God is trying to teach you something."*

Therefore if there is any consolation in Christ, if any comfort of love, if any fellowship of the Spirit, if any affection and mercy, fulfill my joy by being like-minded, having the same love, being of one accord, of one mind. Let nothing be done through selfish ambition or conceit, but in lowliness of mind let each esteem others better than himself. Let each of you look out not only for his own interests, but also for the interests of others. (Philippians 2:1–4)

Therefore comfort each other and edify one another, just as you also are doing.... Now we exhort you, brethren, warn those who are unruly, comfort the fainthearted, uphold the weak, be patient with all. See that no one renders evil for evil to anyone, but always pursue what is good both for yourselves and for all. (1 Thessalonians 5:11, 14–15)

It's important to examine the motives behind the things that we do. Are we trying to encourage or do we hope to just prove a point to make ourselves look good? What we say and how we say it is of vital importance. It means the difference between placing more burdens on someone and taking burdens off of someone. People who are going through various trials need consolation, comfort, affection, and mercy. The Bible describes God as a good Father, one who knows how to give good gifts to His children. (See Luke 11:13.) If we truly believe this, then why do some of us attribute trials and pain in our lives to God trying to teach us something we are reluctant to learn? We would never wish sickness on our children or break their legs because we wanted to teach them something.

Cliché #3: "If you want something too much, God won't give it to you. You have no right to ask for things for yourself."

If you then, being evil, know how to give good gifts to your children, how much more will your Father who is in heaven give good things to those who ask Him!   (Matthew 7:11)

Because a loving father always wants to give good things to His children, we are "allowed" to desire good things from God—and He desires to give them to us! *"Do not be deceived, my beloved brethren. Every good gift and every perfect gift is from above, and comes down from the Father of lights, with whom there is no variation or shadow of turning"* (James 1:16–17). Not only is the cliché false, the Bible tells us to expect the exact opposite. And as if we needed any more proof, Hebrews 4:16 tells us, *"Let us therefore come boldly to the throne of grace, that we may obtain mercy and find grace to help in time of need."*

Cliché #4: "If you ask for one thing, God will probably give you another to keep you from being selfish."

Or what man is there among you who, if his son asks for bread, will give him a stone? Or if he asks for a fish, will he give him a serpent?
                                      (Matthew 7:9–10)

The perception and lie behind this cliché is that God is not kind, loving, or deeply interested in our personal, physical lives here on earth, and furthermore that wanting anything beyond our needs is corrupt. Lack of understanding of God's character often goes back to our own personal experiences with our earthly father. This is true of the preacher as well as the congregation. If a preacher has a twisted concept of the Father, it will negatively affect the lives of others. It can stem from a spirit of discontent, as well: Christians who are bitter at their lot in life hold it against God and begin to believe that He is tightfisted and mean rather than wise and gracious.

Cliché #5: *"If I am right, it doesn't matter how I say it. I'm just God's messenger. Don't shoot the messenger."*

> *The Lord* GOD *gave me the ability to teach so that I know what to say to make the weak strong. Every morning he wakes me. He teaches me to listen like a student.* (Isaiah 50:4 NCV)

> *...but, speaking the truth in love, [that we] may grow up in all things into Him who is the head—Christ.* (Ephesians 4:15)

Heartless and thoughtless people turn others away from wanting to pursue truth in Jesus. Their obvious, blatant disrespect for anyone who doesn't agree with them pollutes the conversation and makes a way for contention.

Cliché #6: *"You're too damaged to serve the Lord."*

> *For you see your calling, brethren, that not many wise according to the flesh, not many mighty, not many noble, are called. But God has chosen the foolish things of the world to put to shame the wise, and God has chosen the weak things of the world to put to shame the things which are mighty; and the base things of the world and the things which are despised God has chosen, and the things which are not, to bring to nothing the things that are....* (1 Corinthians 1:26–28)

> *And He said to me, "My grace is sufficient for you, for My strength is made perfect in weakness." Therefore most gladly I will rather boast in my infirmities, that the power of Christ may rest upon me. Therefore I take pleasure in infirmities, in reproaches, in needs, in persecutions, in*

distresses, for Christ's sake. For when I am weak, then I am strong.
(2 Corinthians 12:9–10)

It seems that if we are to hear God correctly a key qualification for service is our very weakness! It doesn't mean that we make ourselves weak in order to be used by God; it means that God can strengthen us outside of ourselves to further His kingdom. Many who minister will say when used in powerful ways, "That wasn't me!" They can tell when something happens in them beyond their personal ability.

Cliché #7: "*If you only had faith, God would answer your prayers.*"

When trials come, some presume that the afflicted person must be guilty of a lack of faith or an unconfessed sin. This is the kind of judging the Bible condemns! Saying this to someone who is having emotional difficulties or who is momentarily discouraged adds more pain to existing wounds. It certainly isn't an encouragement.

Many have sought God desperately to see if they were failing to walk in truth or if they have an ounce of unbelief, and have yet to find the comfort they are seeking. Their faith is still growing. But when someone comes and makes the statement that all one needs is more faith, it furthers discouragement. Browbeating with the use of Scripture concerning faith or any other subject is abusive.

It's especially acute in the area of healing. If someone's prayer for healing isn't answered and one implies that the reason is a lack of faith, then the ill person now carries the burden of feeling deficient both physically *and* spiritually! If you have found yourself in a similar situation, a good question to ask is: "What is faith's purpose? To connect oneself to God or to magically determine the outcome of one's circumstances?"

Abuse begins when we arbitrarily assume that because a person has problems, he or she is lacking in faith, as if we humans are the source of faith. But no, faith is a gift from God! It's not a commodity that we can summon by just thinking really hard about it. All of it comes from God: "*So then faith comes by hearing, and hearing by the word of God*" (Romans 10:17). Or again, "*For I say, through the grace given to me, to everyone who is among you, not to think of himself more highly than he ought to think, but to think soberly, as God has dealt to each one a measure of faith*" (Romans 12:3). Notice that God is the One dealing to each their faith. And finally, "*...looking unto Jesus, the author and finisher of our faith*" (Hebrews 12:2). Again, Jesus is the author, or the source, of all faith. If you don't have it now, just wait, it will come.

Cliché #8: "*There must be 'sin in the camp' or we wouldn't be experiencing so much trouble.*"

A Christian group fell on hard financial times. Some people wanted to know where the "sin in the camp" was that was causing the problem. They really believed that sin was the primary reason for the reduction in their provisions. Not finding the sin, they should have concluded that there was another reason, or maybe some reason that God didn't want to share. But that wasn't a good enough answer for the accusers. In some Christian circles, one is guilty until they prove their innocence. They seemed to have the idea that if God was pleased, there would always be plenty of everything, including money.

Cliché #9: "*We must not make God angry!*"

This is another form of the "all-seeing eye" attributed to God. The concept is really demonic because it characterizes God as a vindictive taskmaster only interested in humanity walking the straight and narrow. Certainly God watches over us and is concerned about good and bad, but that does not suggest that He is constantly looking for failure. In reality, no one has to tell us that we must not make God angry. We know that because of the conviction of the Holy Spirit. It doesn't need to be rubbed in—and it especially doesn't need to be a constant reminder. It is good to recognize from the Scriptures that He is slow to anger: "*The LORD is merciful and gracious, slow to anger, and abounding in mercy*" (Psalm 103:8).

Cliché #10: "*God tests us to see if we can make it.*"

Listen to the person who came under this kind of teaching:

I was told that if something looked impossible or was intimidating and painful, it was probably God's will, and that God was testing my faith. On that basis, I tried a lot of things. I failed at a lot of things, and didn't get to where I thought it was "guaranteed" that

I would if I obeyed God. Instead, it got a whole lot worse than bumps and bruises. Where was God? Didn't He know I was trying to do His will? Is He the kind of God that pulls wings off flies for fun? Well, I knew it isn't right to ask those questions because I was told, "who are you to question God your Maker?" So I thought, *My failure must be my fault. God tested me to see if I was strong enough, and it's obvious I am not. My best efforts are unacceptable. I must be unacceptable. And God's going to let me rot in it. He has passed me by. I am lucky to just be allowed in church. I will never be used by God because I have proven myself unworthy. I should never try again, or God will have had enough of my failures and be angrier at me.*

The idea that God tests us to see how well we will do in difficult situations questions God's sovereignty. If God knows our heart, He also knows what we will do in complex situations. Consider instead these two biblical reasons for the existence of trials and why God allows them to come.

First, trials toughen us to the realities of life. Many will say that although the trial or testing was difficult, in the end it was helpful. God doesn't need to know how well we will do. He knows our nature, capabilities, and motives. It is we who need to know how we will do under pressure in order to trust Him for His strength. As James says, *"My brethren, count it all joy when you fall into various trials, knowing that the testing of your faith produces patience. But let patience have its perfect work, that you may be perfect and complete, lacking nothing"* (James 1:2–4).

Second, if it were true that God continually tests His people, our constant state of mind would be confusion and condemnation, always wondering when the next test will come. It would make us suspicious of God's character. From this perspective, trials must be lived through without the understanding and experiencing of God's love and comfort. But in reality, trials are meant to bring us closer to God!

The Lord *does* allow times of difficulty to enter the lives of believers. (No matter how perfect their lives may look, we promise: each Christian has difficult times!) *"The LORD tests those who do right, but he hates the wicked and those who love to hurt others"* (Psalm 11:5 NCV). This kind of testing is far from God trying to find out exactly what you will do in a situation. He is not trying to find our breaking point. It is God showing us to ourselves. When you learn that you can accomplish a lot by ignoring fear, you have a great treasure. You don't learn it by not risking. If you don't risk, you will always be trapped with what you have. It is God's conviction through the Holy Spirit that helps us to see the nature of our own hearts. This is God evaluating who we are in personal righteousness and letting us see what He sees.

Cliché #11: "I just preach God's word and let things fall where they may."

"*But the wisdom that is from above is first pure, then peaceable, gentle, willing to yield, full of mercy and good fruits, without partiality and without hypocrisy. Now the fruit of righteousness is sown in peace by those who make peace*" (James 3:17–18). The idea that we don't have to take responsibility for everything and anything we say, or for how we say it is preposterous and unbiblical. We are held accountable for every word that comes out of our mouth. (See also Matthew 12:36.)

Cliché #12: "If you are having emotional problems, you haven't forgiven someone."

If there is pain, it may not be because of unforgiveness. It is absurd to assume that all suffering and sorrow has roots in unforgiveness. That is a reckless assumption and only compounds the problems of those who God wants to mend.

Here is a sad story of a person seeking God who left frustrated, thanks to this cliché:

> I was afraid to go up for prayer, but I felt I had to try to trust. I told the person at the altar I was in pain, and they said, "You know that if you are in pain then you have unforgiveness toward someone. You need to forgive them." I almost physically collapsed. Surrounded by "ministering people" who made any escape impossible, I said I truly and completely agreed about the necessity of forgiveness. The minister hesitated, then started to pray, her hand on my forehead, pushing hard. I braced myself, not feeling anything but fear.

As we have seen in the chapters thus far, the causes of emotional pain are vast. To pin everything on unforgiveness is naïve—and can be an expensive mistake.

Cliché #13: *"You need to get your 'spiritual resume' up to par."*

God doesn't love the future version of you, He loves the *now* version. Will He love you more when you have accomplished great things for Him? Would you be closer to Him both now and in heaven if you had never sinned? This is not said to condone an ounce of sin. God hates sin and wants the person He loves, who is associated with it, to be separated from it. But what happens when a person insists there is sin in your life, sin you're not aware of, even after seeking God to make sure all is right between you and Him?

This happened to a friend of ours, who wrote: "I asked for prayer in a Bible study. The leader would not pray for me until I confessed my drug use, which she said the Lord had shown her was my problem. So I confessed that I used caffeine tablets and coffee. It was an insufficient response. She demanded that I confess my illegal drug use. Since I had not used illegal drugs, I refused to confess it. I was told my rebellion eliminated my right to receive prayer, and I had to leave the meeting."

As much as we need to try, we will never have a good enough spiritual resumes for some people. Be careful, "getting it right" can be a false goal especially if we are trying to please people. Getting it right and keeping it right with *Jesus* is the true goal.

Cliché #14: *"You will never feel or sense God until you change your ways."*

"I can't feel God" is not necessarily a reliable indicator of what is happening in a person's life. All believers experience this from time to time. In its severity we might call it the "dark night of the soul." Most of us have felt God-forsaken at times, but we must encourage each to keep going. Feelings can be very disruptive to the soul. Most often they are not reliable. Many people don't get much emotion in their Christian experience, but they do have, or are coming to the point of having, an inner confidence that God will never leave them nor forsake them. To say that a person must change his ways for any reason, and *not* to say that God will help him, is to misrepresent God. Who has ever changed his ways without God's help?

Cliché #15: *"If you ask God for something more than once, He won't hear you because it's obvious you didn't have faith the first time."*

It never ceases to amaze us that some believe they have the right to tell people what God is going to do even when Scripture does not support what they're saying. It is certainly true that some have prayed just once and received an answer. But it's much more common to keep putting forth a request until it is obvious that He has spoken—not just that He has heard. One of the common answers He gives is, "I've heard you. Just leave it in My hands." Luke 11:9 says, *"So I say to you, ask, and it will be given to you; seek, and you will find; knock, and it will be opened to you."* The Greek words for *ask, seek,* and *knock* are actually best translated, *keep asking, keep seeking, keep knocking.* Jesus instructs us to be persistent; He is not intimidated by our asking.

Cliché #16: *"If you challenge my authority, you're challenging God."*

This is probably one of the most dangerous statements that can be made from a church leader. The person uttering it has placed himself or herself in a position that does not allow for correction or comment. They place themselves above all accountability. If they have this attitude there is reason to question them. It is true that no one should question that God has given humanity the authority to act on His behalf, but if that authority is abusing its power, then we are under no obligation to obey. Anytime an authority figure equates himself or herself with God, they are terribly overestimating human ability.

Cliché #17: *"Sometimes Jesus has to hit you with a 2 x 4 piece of wood to get your attention."*

Who would really want to serve the Lord if God acted that way? How can we ever call God a good God if He treated us like this? There's no better way to defame God than to claim His character is something which it is not. There is certainly something about the way we see God that affects how we see ourselves. If He is unloving, wouldn't that give us permission to be unloving?

Cliché #18: *"If you have any kind of fear at all it means you're not trusting God."*

Fear not [there is nothing to fear], for I am with you; do not look around you in terror and be dismayed, for I am your God. I will strengthen and harden you to difficulties, yes I will help you; yes, I will hold you up and retain you with my [victorious] right hand of rightness and justice. (Isaiah 41:10 AMP)

Fear is one of our largest and most loud-mouthed opponents. Trials give us opportunity to put fear under our feet. Without the trials, we do not learn the important truth that because of His power in our life and our position in Him, we are above fear. Trials show us His strength, and His willingness to give it to us. Trials show us His loyalty to us. We can trust Him to make us endurable *without* self-pity or vengeance, *with* rightness and justice. We cannot be an overcomer without overcoming. Even Jesus had to overcome, as the good Pioneer and Captain of our faith.

INCOMPLETE AND CONFUSING STATEMENTS FROM OTHERS

Another problem we have noted more times than we care to count is the failure to explain personal experiences well. Too many well-intentioned people share their spiritual story or personal experience as if it's the only way to live, when in reality God works differently in the lives of different people. The following are some statements we hear often that offer only half of the story or are based only on personal experience, not on biblical teaching, and as such can be confusing to anybody listening who takes it for gospel truth!

#1. "God told me to turn to such and such a place in the Bible, and when I did, I found the answer I needed."

We do believe that such things happen and are valid, but they are not a biblical rule that can be counted on. Most of us never undergo this kind of experience with God. In the multiple ways that God makes things known to His people, this one is not necessarily common. If someone hears their Christian friends always saying things like this, they might erroneously think that they are not measuring up to spiritual standards because it doesn't happen to them. And when they do think God is speaking to them about a verse and don't find the answer they need when they turn there, they often become confused and frustrated. One person we know received a strong impression: "Go to James chapter 7." Look it up yourself to get the point.

#2. "We preach the whole Bible in our church."

We are not sure exactly what that means. How do we know that other churches may be preaching only 70 percent, or 50 percent, or 30 percent? Who evaluates these things? Then too, the statement sounds overwhelmingly arrogant. Far too many churches with this brand often appear condescending. When someone says, we are a "whole Bible" church, it really doesn't say anything to anyone who doesn't understand that some churches are not biblically oriented.

#3. "I would rather burn out for Jesus than rust out."

Besides being a statement that seems somewhat arrogant, the declaration certainly suggests that hard work is the measure of a good Christian. It carries no ability to speak life into another person. After all, what does "burnout" mean? Certainly hard work is necessary in kingdom living. However, keep in mind that with God's strength, *no one* burns out.

#4. "We need to go to God, seek Him, and wait for Him."

This statement is not invalid, but it's incomplete. It is Scriptural in every sense, but said this way, it can easily sound pious and even trite. To some it sets the stage for the belief that God must be "begged" in order for His presence to appear. It suggests He won't come until we have worn ourselves out with pleading. It is the misconception that God is on His throne observing our life rather than an active and engaged partner in it. Who can stand under this kind of pressure? Who can trust a God who is vague and distant? God has already come to us in the Holy Spirit. Our role is not to call God down from heaven, but to let Him clear things out of the way so that we can hear Him speak.

Always keep in mind that God dwells equally in heaven and on earth. He doesn't live up there and visit earth just on the weekends. He may feel far away to us because Adam and Eve's sin resulted in a broken relationship with Him. But He has been here from the beginning of creation. When God sent Jesus, it didn't mean that He abandoned earth and left it up to the little baby in the manger. James 4:8 says, *"Draw near to God and He will draw near to you"* (ESV). This verse describes God as responsive to those who desire Him. With this promise, we can be encouraged to get away and spend some time alone with Him.

#5. "Just turn it over to God."

This might be an excellent beginning, but it needs to be followed up with an understanding of how to turn it over to God or it seems like an empty command. A good place to begin is in Philippians 4:4–8. A few words of explanation can turn a spiritual cliché into a meaningful insight:

> *Rejoice in the Lord always. Again I will say, rejoice! Let your gentleness be known to all men. The Lord is at hand. Be anxious for nothing, but in everything by prayer and supplication, with thanksgiving, let your requests be made known to God; and the peace of God, which surpasses all understanding, will guard your hearts and minds through Christ Jesus. Finally, brethren, whatever things are true, whatever things are noble, whatever things are just, whatever things are pure, whatever things are lovely, whatever things are of good report, if there is any virtue and if there is anything praiseworthy—meditate on these things.*

Some say, "You should never make a plan. Just turn your life over to God and wait for Him to reveal His ways." It is further said that to make our own plans is presumptive and even arrogant. Such thinking invalidates God's design for humanity to "rule over the earth." Its most damaging effect is that it creates passivity, a condition that destroys relationships with both God and man. There's an old saying, "A car can't be steered if it isn't moving." Proverbs 16:9 says, *"A man's heart plans his way, but the LORD directs His steps."* Life in the Lord is a partnership. Make your plans, but surrender them to the leading and direction of the Holy Spirit.

#6. "Just trust God."

Or another favorite: "Just surrender to Jesus." They both imply, "You must not have surrendered if you have problems or if you are hurting." But how does another person know that you *haven't* surrendered to Jesus?

Certainly, there are fathers and mothers in the church who can see one's need for a deeper relationship with God, but their spiritually mature method is to tenderly suggest where and how the surrender begins and then walk through it with the suffering person.

Although this speech is similar to number 6, in reality it is quite different. A man struggled for years trying to understand the concept of faith. When people told him, "just trust God," he interpreted it to mean that if he just trusted God hard enough, God would answer all his prayers. What he was really doing was placing his trust in the sign of answered prayer. That hindered him from the real matter of trusting God. The light turned on for a moment, but he still had trouble with separating *trusting God* from *trusting a sign*. This is a common mistake. Trusting what God can do only comes after trusting God. If a girlfriend is convinced that her boyfriend is cheating on her, no amount of denials or protestations of love—of "signs"— will convince her otherwise. But eventually, as the reality of his constancy sinks in, she will begin to trust him. With God, as with any relationship, trust takes time and hard work. Most authentic *Christian trust* comes after seeing His constancy day after day.

> *God wanted to prove that his promise was true to those who would get what he promised. And he wanted them to understand clearly that his purposes never change, so he made an oath. These two things cannot change: God cannot lie when he makes a promise, and he cannot lie when he makes an oath. These things encourage us who came to God for safety. They give us strength to hold on to the hope we have been given.* (Hebrews 6:17–18 NCV)

#7. "If you want success in your spiritual life, you need to 'die' to self."

This is another case in which the idea behind the statement is true, but often inaccurate in the way that it is presented. First, the "you need to" suggests a struggle that belongs to the person alone. Much of this book has emphasized that any accomplishment in a Christian's life has to be done in partnership with Jesus. Working alone to overcome sin is disastrous. Careful consideration must be given to any words that suggest that we must muscle up and by sheer willpower accomplish the task because as it says in Zechariah 4:6, "*Not by might, nor by power, but by my Spirit, says the* LORD *of hosts*" (ESV).

Does "dying to self" mean that we become passive, inert, and lifeless? No! An easy way to understand dying to self is to connect "self" with the attributes it usually precedes: self-centered, self-pity, self-indulgence, self-seeking, self-absorption, self-importance, self-loving, and just plain selfishness. The word *self* also suggests, egotistical, conceited, insensitive, narcissistic, and vain attitudes of people. If the word is to have meaning in the biblical concept of its original intention, it must be seen as a ruination of the soul through pity, egotism, selfishness, conceit, arrogant, narcissism, and any other action or attitude that brings pain and suffering to other people. Those actions and attitudes are what need to die!

Someone put it this way:

1. When you are forgotten, or neglected, or purposely set at naught, and with God's help, you don't sting and hurt with the insult or the oversight, but rather your heart is happy that it is counted worthy to suffer for Christ...that is dying to self.

2. When your good is evil spoken of, when your wishes are crossed, your advice disregarded, your opinions ridiculed, and with God's help you refuse to let anger rise in your heart, or even needlessly defend yourself, but take it in all in patient, loving silence...that is dying to self.

3. With God's help when you are content with any food, any suffering, any climate, any society, any clothing, any interruption by the will of God...that is dying to self.

4. When, with God's help, you never care to refer to yourself in conversation, or to record your own good works, or itch after commendations, when you can truly love to be unknown...that is dying to self.

5. When you can see your brother prospering and having his needs met and, with God's help, you can honestly rejoice with him in spirit and feel no envy, nor question God, while your own needs

are far greater and your circumstances less fortunate…that is dying to self.

6. When, with God's help, you can receive correction and reproof from one of less stature than yourself and can humbly submit inwardly as well as outwardly, finding no rebellion or resentment rising up within your heart…that is dying to self. —*Anonymous*

There's another thing that goes somewhat hand-in-hand with dying to self: an over-emphasis on submission. Leaders who constantly preach on the need to be submitted to become responsible for two major problems in a believer's life. First, hearing something over and over again tends to diminish its significance. The Bible contains guidance and wisdom on many topics, and by limiting sermons to just a few topics, it increases the chance of a believer saying yes and amen every time they're preached, but do absolutely nothing when they walk out of church. Second, for the listener who does earnestly seek to be submissive in all situations where appropriate, it stunts their growth with the frustration of trying to figure out why a person has to be told so many times something they have already done so many times before.

Finally: Do not assume that you won't "feel" offended when true offenses do come. That would deny that we are still living in earthly bodies and would open the door to frustration and confusion. We can't deny feelings but those deep feelings can be sent directly to the Court of Heaven where we ask God to help us deal with them.

#8. "If you talk about Satan and his demons, you give glory to the enemy."

It is quite true that some people are more demon-conscious than they are God-conscious. But that doesn't negate the need for instruction in spiritual matters that pertain to the enemy, "*for we are not ignorant of his devices*" (2 Corinthians 2:11). In other words, we study the Scriptures to understand how and why Satan works the way he does. By knowing his goals and motives we know how to deal with him. Make no mistake, there is a very real Satan with some very real demons.

The commonest question is whether I really "believe in the Devil." Now, if by "the Devil" you mean a power opposite to God and,

The Church Doesn't Seem to Care 201

like God, self-existent from all eternity, the answer is certainly No. There is no uncreated being except God. God has no opposite. No being could attain a "perfect badness" opposite to the perfect goodness of God; for when you have taken away every kind of good thing (intelligence, will, memory, energy, and existence itself) there would be none of him left.[51] —C. S. Lewis

#9. "Have you given your all to Jesus?"

For young believers, especially, you can't expect maturity overnight. A completely consecrated life is a product of the Holy Spirit's work in a person over time. Once again, notice the emphasis on whether a person has brought personal perfection into his or her own life. This is not a helpful attitude!

#10. "You're no good."

This statement implies that God thinks we are worthless, and that is not biblical. God sees us as intrinsically valuable because of the way He initially created us (see Psalm 8), but as fallen in terms of our righteousness (see Isaiah 64:6). If you confuse the two you will often feel that God doesn't love you. But the Scripture tells us that God loves us unequivocally. John 3:16 and a host of other Scriptures that make this claim. It is critically important to make this distinction between our inherent value as made in the image of God and our inability to save ourselves as fallen people. One of the greatest deceptions of the evil one is the idea that man is basically good and can somehow measure up to God's expectations in terms of righteousness. It lies right at the heart of people's denial of the need for salvation. They think that because they have value, they also have righteousness. On the other hand, when Christians hear *"There is none righteous, no, not one"* (Romans 3:10) as the end of the story, they think that because we are without righteousness outside of Christ, we also have no value as humans. That, too, is false.

#11. "You're worthless."

This is similar to the one above. After giving mankind the earth, *"Then God saw everything that He had made, and indeed it was very*

---

51. C. S. Lewis, *The Screwtape Letters* (New York: MacMillan Publishing, 1961), vii.

good" (Genesis 1:31). If God is a good God, then He cannot create anything bad. We have become flawed because of the fall. We are corrupt in our desires, but the gospel message states that we can become good, not in the sense of saving ourselves by the good things we do, but because our final entrance into God's presence comes about by the righteousness that is given to us in Jesus:

> *But what things were gain to me, these I have counted loss for Christ. Yet indeed I also count all things loss for the excellence of the knowledge of Christ Jesus my Lord, for whom I have suffered the loss of all things, and count them as rubbish, that I may gain Christ and be found in Him, not having my own righteousness, which is from the law, but that which is through faith in Christ, the righteousness which is from God by faith; that I may know Him and the power of His resurrection, and the fellowship of His sufferings, being conformed to His death, if, by any means, I may attain to the resurrection from the dead.*
>
> (Philippians 3:7–11)

Even Lucifer was created good, although by free will he did not remain that way. God's restoration plan in Jesus is to restore us to our original status. This is one of the reasons why Christ bestowed His righteousness on us.

#12. "You're too weak to make it on your own, that's why you use God as a crutch."

God is not a crutch, He's a healer of wounds. Blind men see, the deaf hear, and the lame walk. You and God are partners. You and the Accuser are not. Don't let him run your business.

#13. "If you would get rid of your sin, things would go better for you."

How much more discouraging can you get? This statement may sound good, but notice where it puts the burden of action: on us. Can we really just make a statement to get rid of our sin and abracadabra it's gone? Only Jesus can deliver us from sin, we have only to cooperate. Such a statement condemns, it does not convict.

INCOMPLETE AND CONFUSING STATEMENTS FROM YOUR OWN MIND

Sometimes, the most hurtful statements don't come from others, but from our mind. Usually, these are internalizations of what we've heard either directly or indirectly, and then applied to ourselves. They are dangerous as well!

#1. "I don't have a right to expect anything from God because of my past sin."

If that were true no one could expect anything from God—especially not salvation. We do not want to minimize anyone's pain over the past, but this guilt will not help you out! In previous parts of this book we've shown that our relationship with God through Jesus wipes out the past. It is the warfare from demonic spirits that continues to bring past sins into remembrance. When sin is taken care of through Christ's blood, heaven never speaks of it again. That is why God has given us the right to resist lying demon spirits.

#2. "I've tried so hard to let God know I'm sorry for my sin, but I really don't know if He has heard me."

Similarly to the one above, this person is struggling with believing God and should not be condemned. He or she needs to be led gently into the Scriptures which affirm God's presence and His love, such as: *"Whoever confesses that Jesus is the Son of God, God abides in him, and he in God"* (1 John 4:15). Soaking in God's Word opens the door for the Holy Spirit to use those same Scriptures to break the shackles of doubt.

We must never assume the memory of a sin means that the sin is still there. Sin can leave long-term effects in our lives, but the bondage from that sin is broken by Christ's blood. It is important to remember that when Jesus justifies us, the penalty for our sin was laid on Him and we are free, and as a consequence we are a new creation without condemnation. The justification is *instantaneous*, although of course we have the rest of our lives to learn and grow in the Spirit.

#3. "I've sinned so much that God won't save me."

Paul wrote, *"This is a faithful saying and worthy of all acceptance, that Christ Jesus came into the world to save sinners, of whom I am chief"* (1 Timothy 1:15).

If Paul was such a great sinner who was yet forgiven, then there is certainly a great deal of grace and forgiveness for you! Also notice, *"The Lord is not slack concerning His promise, as some count slackness, but is longsuffering toward us, not willing that any should perish but that all should come to repentance"* (2 Peter 3:9).

#4. "I'll never amount to anything."

What does "amount to anything" mean, other than a deception that there is some worldly standard that God wants us to live up to—or that we gain God's acceptance through our hard work. Both ideas are false! We rest upon grace alone!

#5. "Nobody likes me."

It may be correct that some people don't like you, but you wouldn't have to look far to find those who genuinely care about you and love you. Don't fall for Satan's lie that nobody loves you just because you feel you are unlovable. You are certainly more loved and liked then you realize.

If we rely on clichés and confusing statements we can quite possibly cause pain. They may appear cute and clever, but they fail to produce the fruit we would hope for. Learning how to build each other up and encourage one another is so vital if we are to avoid wounding in the church.

A PROVERB

> Pride leads to destruction; a proud attitude brings ruin.
>
> (Proverbs 16:18 NCV)

PSALMS FOR THE WOUNDED

> Save me from those who hate me and from the deep water. Do not let the flood drown me or the deep water swallow me or the grave close its mouth over me. LORD, answer me because your love is so good. Because of your great kindness, turn to me. Do not hide from me, your servant. I am in trouble. Hurry to help me! (Psalm 69:16–17 NCV)

> I will praise God in a song and will honor him by giving thanks.
>
> (Psalm 69:30 NCV)

LORD, teach me what you want me to do, and I will live by your truth. Teach me to respect you completely. LORD, my God, I will praise you with all my heart, and I will honor your name forever. You have great love for me. You have saved me from death.   (Psalm 86:11–13 NCV)

15

HOW DO I FIND A GOOD CHURCH?

Friendship is born at that moment when one man says to
another: "What! You too? I thought it was only me."
—C. S. Lewis

Awoman wrote a letter to Michael Dye, a friend of ours, that we want
to share:

Dear Mr. Dye,

I was sexually abused by my grandfather when I was eight years
old and by my minister when I was twelve years old. I had no memory of either. Then, when I was seventeen years old, another minister sexually abused me.

I married at twenty-one years old and had four children. It was
not until I was thirty-six that I could not keep things together anymore. I went forward in a church service because I absolutely hated
my husband, and I felt that everything was my fault. Instead of
the pastor shaking my hand and praying over me, he asked to talk
with me after the service. He gave me a Taylor/Johnson Temperament Analysis and had me fill it out during the afternoon. I had
a lot of anxiety around pastors, but I decided to take a chance,
since I didn't get a sexual vibe from him. I met with him the next
week. He talked for a long time and I could not figure out where he
was going with the conversation. Eventually he said, "I can tell you

from the assessment that you have had some abuse in your life." I thought, "Who hasn't?" But he went on.

At this point, I carried a huge guilt around for what seemed to be my immorality for have relations with my second pastor. But I had no memory of the first two abuses.

During that weekend, I began to remember the memories about my grandfather. Now, at this point, I barely left my house. I avoided people and shopping if at all possible because I had panic attacks just standing in the checkout lines. My pastor would call me faithfully twice a week. He would just talk about anything. It wasn't counseling. Looking back, I knew he was really working hard at helping me stay with reality. I began to believe he really cared about me without wanting something in return.

I found a lady counselor at a rescue mission. She took me as a client for free because we did not have insurance to cover counseling. She directed me to a loyal recovery group. Those people were great. At first, I would just come in and stand at the back because my emotions were so great. When they broke up for small group, I would leave. No one crowded me or pushed me—they just let me be, and slowly I was able to join in, staying for the break-out groups. They accepted me in spite of how I felt about myself. I eventually led a group myself, which was a big part of my healing. It was not one church that help me with my recovery, but several. I thank God for His healing and how He had the right safe people, at the right place, and at the right time in my recovery. It all started by one person really caring. Thank you for letting me share this with you.

—*Jane*

A SHEPHERD WHO CARES: LOOKING AT PSALM 23

Jane eventually found both a good shepherd and the Good Shepherd. We would like to challenge the people who think, "A Christian who *cares*? What a novel idea!" But we do agree that the idea of "Christian care" doesn't seem to be what it should be. Christian care should look like a tender shepherd's care for his sheep, showing concern and responsibility. Psalm 23 has long served as a caring message from a loving shepherd. It should also serve as a message to under-shepherds that this is the mind-set of the Chief Shepherd Himself. As you look for a good church, look for an under-shepherd with these characteristics.

"*The* LORD *is my shepherd; I shall not want*" (verse 1). A clear sign of a good shepherd is when the sheep are not edgy or anxious but have put their trust in an earthly shepherd who is concerned about their needs.

"*He makes me to lie down in green pastures*" (verse 2). The good shepherd is always looking for good food to feed the sheep. Sometimes years of preparation go into planting new fields where grass will grow and the sheep will be led to eat. It is one of the rules of pastors to ensure that the flock is being fed the nutritious food of the Word. But here is some wise advice about God's Word and the need for His presence: "Sound Bible exposition is an imperative must in the church of the living God. Without it no church can be a New Testament church in any strict meaning of that term. But exposition may be carried on in such a way as to leave the hearers devoid of any true spiritual nourishment whatever. For it is not mere words that nourish the soul, but God Himself, and unless and until the hearers find God in personal experience they are not the better for having heard the truth."[52]

"*He leads me beside the still waters*" (verse 2). Notice the waters are not turbulent. If at the moment they are high and foreboding, He is intent on dealing with the situation and calming the sea.

"*He restores my soul*" (verse 3). One of the roles of a good shepherd is to build up, not tear down. To restore means to bring back to the position of good health. This requires knowing the sheep and understanding their individual needs.

"*He leads me in paths of righteousness for His name's sake*" (verse 3). The idea here is that there are "right" paths. The reputation of the shepherd is at stake. If he is found to be a good shepherd it is because he leads his sheep rightly along safe paths.

---

52. A. W. Tozer, *The Pursuit of God* (Harrisburg, PA: Christian Publications, Inc.), 10.

"Yea, though I walk through the valley of the shadow of death, I will fear no evil" (verse 4). Everyone will, at times, go through very difficult circumstances. The role of the shepherd is to offer words of life, truth, and comfort in order to dispel fear.

"For You are with me; Your rod and Your staff, they comfort me" (verse 4). The staff, with its curled end, can rescue a sheep when it is caught or in a precarious place. The straight rod is used gently to number the sheep and ungently to hurl at predators. The good shepherd knows and understands each of his flock, and is prepared to defend them against the wolves. He will lay down his life for them if necessary.

"You prepare a table before me in the presence of my enemies; You anoint my head with oil; my cup runs over" (verse 6). The good shepherd believes in you and supports you when no one else will. He picks you up when others let you down. He comes to your aid when everyone else walks away.

Whether you are a sheep or a shepherd, this psalm is relevant to you. As a sheep you are only safe in the hands of your Good Shepherd, the Lord Jesus Christ. And the more your leader looks like the Good Shepherd, the more you should rejoice! If you are a shepherd caring for sheep, you have already probably come to realize that the only way that you can fulfill this role is total reliance on the Good Shepherd.

JESUS'S RADICAL LEADERSHIP: LOOKING AT THE GOSPELS

Picture Jerusalem 2000 years ago. It wasn't much different from our world today. Bias, bigotry, racism, prejudice, intolerance, unfairness, and a host of other abuses were present everywhere. It was into this world that Jesus positioned Himself and began looking for people to heal. Everywhere He walked, He looked after those who needed help. When He went away, He commissioned others to take His place and to do the things He had done. We are going to look at Jesus' radical leadership and His followers in order to gain a better idea of what followers of Jesus look like today.

THE PROBLEM OF PHARISEES

As Jesus's ministry began to grow and flourish, the Pharisees worried that He would gain a following that would jeopardize their influence. Instead,

Jesus exposed the Pharisees for who and what they were, not people who cared for other people, but people who enjoyed the limelight. This was the first time in the history of the world that lifeless and stale religion would be forced to collide with Truth. (See Isaiah 1:10–17 and Malachi 1:6–10.) The sound of that clash can still be heard today in the words of men and women who openly seek to destroy the message of hope, healing, and restoration.

One of the reasons Jesus could not and would not blend in with the Pharisees and other religious leaders of the day was His nature and character. He was in sweeping contrast to their religion and attitudes. They had substituted rules for knowing God's personality. They appeared righteous by their fastings, and holy by their cleanliness. Jesus was from a different kingdom, another world, and one that has always been challenged by the kingdoms on earth. Jesus revealed His Father's character, respecting and caring for people. He took time to demonstrate God's love. He acknowledged how important people were by giving them His attention.

Jewish religious leaders carried considerable power in and around Jerusalem in the midst of Roman rule. They represented a lineage that was traceable to ancient times. For the Jew, the Hebrew religion was the only religion. They understood it as part of their inheritance. They firmly believed that God had given it to them personally. They believed they were a chosen people, destined always to represent God on earth. However, they failed to obey Him and to follow Him time and again.

Among many failures, the Pharisees had broken one of the most critical of God's laws by disrespecting people and becoming masters of pride and arrogance. They had placed a massive division between themselves and the common people. It's hard to believe how long it takes some of us to recognize how attitudes of exclusivism creep into our lives. Discrimination causes withdrawal where people become walled cities within themselves. The loss starts with a lack of information, wisdom, and understanding. How can a shepherd lead people they know little about?

JESUS' NEW RECRUITS

It was with the early disciples that Jesus began the training needed to bring the message of salvation to all mankind. Jesus began the process by singling out many of His disciples. These He powerfully guided, through the Holy Spirit, in order to leave a message that would last forever. God wanted us to see His work among the disciples in order to show the conflict of kingdoms. Jesus had come to earth as an invader, an army of one. His intent was to make warriors out of pacifists, extremists, diehards, hypocrites, dogmatists, and even chauvinists. Christ was far less a teacher than the teachers of other religions of the world. He was a liberator, an invader, a force from heaven to change the world. *"For the oppression of the poor, for the sighing of the needy, Now I will arise,' says the* LORD; 'I will set him in the *safety for which he yearns'"* (Psalm 12:5).

When the new recruits were assembled, they began to follow Jesus while he ministered. The lessons He taught them still remain amazing to us today. He taught on blessing, anger, sexual sin, divorce, making agreements, retribution, caring for people, giving, prayer, worship, money, judging others, the importance of right living, and that was just the beginning. He found time, a lot of time, to demonstrate God's love. He healed an army officer's servant, He healed a man with a skin disease, He healed Peter's mother-in-law, He healed men with demons, He healed a paralyzed man, and in Matthew chapters 8–9, the list continues. On His day off, He walked on water and calmed a raging storm.

Then He confronted the religious leaders and condemned them for the vice and corruption they endorsed. What he demonstrated in caring for people should have been the norm. But caring for people had been greatly deteriorated by the Jewish religion of the day.

When back in the classroom with the twelve present, He used stories and illustrations to help them understand a world much different than their own. He talked about planting seeds, about growing wheat, about treasure and a pearl, about a fishing net. He carefully told them about His Father. He prophesied of events yet to come, including His death, return to earth, and the end of the world as we know it. He talked about spiritual warfare, His power over demons, and the days ahead in which they would be persecuted and suffer because of their faith in Him. Jesus did not dominate the conversation. He was prone to ask questions and then answer them according to the dynamics of His own kingdom. People listened carefully to His teaching, knowing that it was different from anything they'd ever heard.

RELEASED TO SERVE

Then came the day of deputization. Jesus gave his disciples the authority to do the things He had done. Seemingly, they had finished the course, they were done with their training for now. When they went out, they found they could heal the sick, raise the dead, and cast out demons. It looked as if they had graduated! But not quite. Jesus needed to make a few things clearer. They needed to understand that although God's power would flow through them for the purpose of Christ's coming kingdom, they themselves were weak with weaknesses that could only be strengthened by the Holy Spirit.

It is at this point of understanding that Christians today often fall apart and wound people. They fail to see that true ministry never works unless it is directed, inspired, and carried out with the help of the Holy Spirit.

These men eventually took on a new identity. They forgot their old ego and were willing to be called Christ's disciples. If the disciples had not continued to recognize their weaknesses who knows how much pride would have developed in them. The church then and the church today continues to acknowledge the unique alliance between God and men by emphasizing the message of "Christ in us the hope of glory." That we, as individuals, could become the temple of God should forever change our thinking about developing a righteous standing before God on our own.

The next five incidents in Christ's life show in part how different our responses are from God's. When Jesus passed by someone, He looked at the person's inner pain and not just the results of the pain on the outside. This has been one of the goals of this book—to look at the inside, not just the outside. Can you see your leader (or yourself!) similarly looking at the inside and not just the outside?

"HAVE MERCY ON US"

Now as they went out of Jericho, a great multitude followed Him. And behold, two blind men sitting by the road, when they heard that Jesus was passing by, cried out, saying, "Have mercy on us, O Lord, Son of David!" Then the multitude warned them that they should be quiet;

but they cried out all the more, saying, "Have mercy on us, O Lord, Son of David!" So Jesus stood still and called them, and said, "What do you want Me to do for you?" They said to Him, "Lord, that our eyes may be opened." So Jesus had compassion and touched their eyes. And immediately their eyes received sight, and they followed Him"
(Matthew 20:29–34)

Since we the authors don't always see spiritual "lessons" in everything in life, we will simply note what happened here. Jesus had compassion while others around Him did not.

One day a burly biker who once was in a well-known motorcycle gang visited a church. He had recently come to the Lord and he and his wife showed up at the church in the middle of a service. He was dressed in leather, chains, tattoos, and riding a Harley. A shockwave went through the church as this 400-pound man with silver hair down his back walked in and sat down. At that point the pastor had one of two choices; reach out and love this couple or to outright reject them, hoping they would go away and make no sound. Even though there were some in the congregation who were afraid of them, the pastor chose to lead by example and welcome them. Other couples in the church caught the vision. Food, shelter, and friendship were given to them. They found out that these bikers were two people who had just had a miraculous conversion, and now needed a place to fellowship and time to grow in Jesus.

THE LITTLE CHILDREN

Then little children were brought to Him that He might put His hands on them and pray, but the disciples rebuked them. But Jesus said, "Let the little children come to Me, and do not forbid them; for of such is the kingdom of heaven." And He laid His hands on them and departed from there."
(Matthew 19:13–15)

How do we evaluate such an event? Notice that Jesus did not look down on children, as the passage suggests that others did. A baby cries in the middle of the service and the pastor might yell "Get that child out of here, you're interrupting the flow of the Holy Spirit," or at the least display a recognizable irritation that is obvious to all. Yet Jesus showed no such irritation.

FIRE FROM HEAVEN

And as they went [the disciples to Jerusalem], *they entered a village of the Samaritans, to prepare for Him. But they did not receive Him, because His face was set for the journey to Jerusalem. And when His disciples James and John saw this, they said, "Lord, do You want us to command fire to come down from heaven and consume them, just as Elijah did?" But He turned and rebuked them, and said, "You do not know what manner of spirit you are of. For the Son of Man did not come to destroy men's lives but to save them."* (Luke 9:52–56)

John is the disciple who is known for his love for people. It doesn't seem to be on his resume at this point. Revenge seems to be the order of the day.

WANTING PREEMINENCE

Then James and John, the sons of Zebedee, came to Him, saying, "Teacher, we want You to do for us whatever we ask." And He said to them, "What do you want Me to do for you?" They said to Him, "Grant us that we may sit, one on Your right hand and the other on Your left, in Your glory." But Jesus said to them, "You do not know what you ask. Are you able to drink the cup that I drink, and be baptized with the baptism that I am baptized with?" They said to Him, "We are able."

So Jesus said to them, "You will indeed drink the cup that I drink, and with the baptism I am baptized with you will be baptized; but to sit on My right hand and on My left is not Mine to give, but it is for those for whom it is prepared." And when the ten heard it, they began to be greatly displeased with James and John. But Jesus called them to Himself and said to them, "...whoever desires to become great among you shall be your servant. And whoever of you desires to be first shall be slave of all. For even the Son of Man did not come to be served, but to serve, and to give His life a ransom for many." (Mark 20:35–45)

If we are not careful we too can become jealous of one another, seeking to be greatest.

PETER'S FEET

Jesus…rose from supper and laid aside His garments, took a towel and girded Himself. After that, He poured water into a basin and began to wash the disciples' feet, and to wipe them with the towel with which He was girded. Then He came to Simon Peter. And Peter said to Him, "Lord, are You washing my feet?" Jesus answered and said to him, "What I am doing you do not understand now, but you will know after this." (John 13:3–7)

Peter's hesitancy in having Jesus wash his feet was no doubt a matter of false humility, "Why are you embarrassing us by doing what we should be doing to you?" Peter evidently didn't know how to receive honor without appearing to take it away from someone else.

WHAT TO LOOK FOR IN A CHURCH

Jesus's radical leadership and his disciples' reactions are telling guides to us of how to act today. But for those who desire more specific guidelines, we put together a brief how-to for anyone who may be looking for a safe place to worship God. Remember that no church is perfect!

+ If you're looking for truth, you need a Bible-based church. It's good to look over "statements of faith" and any other material that will give you an idea if what is taught and preached is biblical. You want to do this to avoid getting into an organization that is primarily based on one person's interpretation of the Scriptures. The most common error is denying the deity of Jesus Christ, i.e. God in human form. (See section on page , "What Doctrines Should I Believe?")

+ Look for leaders whom you genuinely believe care for people. Congregations are sometimes too big for a pastor to meet and counsel with everyone. But most of the time you can identify a shepherd's voice by its concern, attention, and sensitivity. Listen for this caring spirit during the service.

+ If a church is not Christ-centered and Jesus is not the constant focus, it probably isn't worth your time to stay there. Friendly people may be fun, but if they are not focused on the gospel, spiritual life won't happen.

+ Find people who genuinely respect other people.

+ Look for a sense of personal hope and quiet confidence in most adults, an air of peace in the gathered group.

+ Notice leaders who are aware of the existence and tactics of the enemy and who educate others for overcoming and not for fear and failure.

+ Look for teachers who are open to questions, discussion, and clarification.

+ Look for leaders who cultivate good relationships with other leaders in other churches (local to global), validating their ministries and looking for ways to be a blessing to each other. Look for leadership that networks with other churches and groups in the area, state, nation, and perhaps abroad. There should always be an attitude of inclusivity toward others in the Christ's body no matter where or who they are. Good leadership must understand that the body is global, not exclusive.

+ Look for people who meet you with a meaningful "glad to see you," or "how are you doing?" conveying that they are open to conversation. It might mean that you have found family.

+ Look for heart-honesty and thoughtfulness. Caring people won't gasp or stiffen when you say something they didn't expect, or if you say you were hurt by church. You might even get a kind look. You have a good thing if they are consistently kind (somewhat like our Father), if they can handle questions without punishing you for asking, if they get you some resources and information for growth or become that resource. The best is when you find people who want you involved with them in fellowship.

+ Look for people who encourage and build up those who are hurting and need help. The heart of a true leader is sensed in others by his or her humility. To sense kindness in a trustworthy person is a powerful and lasting experience.

+ When you go home after meeting with the assembly, ask yourself, "Does my heart feel stronger, more confident?" "Did the verbal and nonverbal messages give me tools to build myself up in Christ, or at least give some rest and peace?" "Can I see more hope?"

RED FLAGS IN CHURCH

Here are a few beliefs and attitudes that are red flags in a church:

+ Exclusiveness: A defensive stance toward churches and people who are thought to be a danger to the homegrown thinking inside their own church.

+ Humanism: A system of thinking that people are basically good and that with time they will continue to get better without religion.

+ Pluralism: A belief that all religions lead to God. One of the most popular tactics to counter Christianity is to claim that all belief systems that teach good living will get you to heaven, such as Buddhism, Taoism, Shintoism, etc.

+ Conspiracy theories: The idea that many world events are the plans of those who scheme to deceive the public, often including the assassination of John F. Kennedy, the 9/11 cover-up, the military's Area 51 and aliens, secret societies who control the world, the Holocaust, and fake moon landings, etc. These are often a sign of a paranoid and off-base church.

+ Doomsday preaching: It's called *doomsday* because of the way biblical end-time events are described, especially from the book of Revelation. Where the teaching should provide hope and encouragement, some make it into a horrible, grisly "end of the world" scenario that threatens to include Christians if they don't get their act together.

✦ Harshness: Some believe that the only way to get a point across is to use severe, unsympathetic, critical, and even calloused words in their preaching and teaching. They lead us to believe that sensitivity and genuine concern for people are not a part of their character.

✦ Unbiblical doctrines: Most of us pick up some pretty severe doctrinal headaches at times. We've never come across a person who hasn't wrestled with points of Scripture. For example, where do we go after we die? Or, does a person who has never heard the gospel go to hell? Certainly, doctrinal issues are important and must be dealt with throughout our Christian lives. But it could easily take volumes of books just to get a good start on the subject. So instead of another book, here's a few tasty morsels to keep on track. Jesus said, "if you seek Me, you will find me." (See Jeremiah 29:13.) God is in the process of constantly leading every man woman and child out of darkness into light, if that is what that person wants. The second thing to remember is that He has said He will never leave us nor forsake us. (See Deuteronomy 31:6.) The key is to want the truth that is found in Jesus. To find that truth, take a journey with Jesus for a while and find out what happens. We think a good place to start is a short prayer that simply says, "Show me what is real and what is true."

✦ Scare tactics: A method of motivation that always ends in disaster. Human nature refuses to be forced into anything. Play games with a person's will—and someone always gets hurt.

✦ Grace *or* law instead of grace *and* law: Some hold on to the law so tightly that they lose sight of grace and become arrogant and loveless, as we've discussed. Others hold on to grace so tightly they believe that God's goodness gives them permission to live any kind of lifestyle they wish. This problem is right at the top of the list of things that has caused much of the division in the church.

✦ Tackiness: A church will not offend the Holy Spirit by making things spiffy. A church where people pay attention to details is generally a place with people who can be counted on for integrity, honesty, and reliability—traits that God wants in those who lead in His kingdom. Keeping the place clean, tidy, and orderly is a must if newcomers are to stay.

+ Obvious lack of preparation: Preparation for fulfilling any obligation is not an option, it's a mandate. When leaders and others make excuses for an obvious lack of preparation and where urgency seems to reign instead of thoughtfulness, you can know that other priorities are likely out of line, too.

GREAT ATTITUDES TO TAKE TO CHURCH

Getting right with God also means getting right with people, often people who don't see things exactly like you do. Part of finding the right church is attitude. "What can I do to bless these people" is just as important as, "What can these people do for me?" It is wise to ask God to stir up the gifts He has given you so that you might be someone to contribute as well as to receive.

+ Don't naively bare *all* your heart at first, and even then, not to everyone. Some hurts will be re-injured if not kept confidential. Trust is to be earned, not scattered to all untested persons. Test the spirits but not with an attitude of suspicion.

+ Reduce the expectation that all people will "understand you." Be satisfied if three or four seem open to deepening relationships. Be elated if they ask you (not "tell you") what they can do for you.

+ Be aware that if you look like you are in pain when you enter a new group, you will often attract people who are "fixers." Most churches have "fixers," so don't let this detract from further investigation. Be cautious about letting the words of over-zealous people into your heart at first. Avoid their salesmanship when they say they know how to make the pain go away "if you will just do it their way." Do *not* explain your hesitancy, because there is no need to justify it. Be kind, but go slow until you are sure that attitudes and ideas are trustworthy.

+ Be careful in evaluating. Many times people judge a place by first appearances. But even if a church is biblically based, it usually takes more than one visit to determine its true character.

+ Be on guard that you do not assign yourself the job of church inspector. There is great danger in becoming an "examiner" in Christ's body. These are recommendations in order to help you find a safe haven church, they are not justifications for acting as judge and jury to every church that you visit.

WHICH DOCTRINES SHOULD I BELIEVE?

According to a biblical worldview, we were born with the ability to deceive and be deceived. (See Psalm 58:3; Romans 3:23; Romans 5:12; and Ecclesiastes 7:20, all ESV). Adam and Eve declined to believe God and instead accepted a lie from the enemy. Humanity is still in the process of watching God reverse this original deception by presenting Jesus as the truth. But there is still something deceptive in believing that truth is found in what appears to be undeniable facts. This is one reason why the Bible points to a Person, Jesus, as "truth," instead of a logical syllogism or a dictionary of statements. Facts aren't always what they seem to be. In many instances we are never quite sure what is true and what is false. But if Jesus is truth and will make His reality known to us by His Spirit, then we have something much more reliable than our five senses. *"Jesus said to him, 'I am the way, the truth, and the life. No one comes to the Father except through Me'"* (John 14:6).

We've mentioned several times in this chapter the necessity of finding a biblical church. Here are some deceived statements that strongly indicate the church is not biblical:

+ If you belong to any other church you will not make it to heaven.

+ If you don't completely obey leadership, you're out of God's will.

+ If you have sickness or emotional pain, you lack faith or you are living in sin.

+ Just do what the Word says, and your problems will go away.

+ The reason you're poor is because you're not sowing seed as God's Word declares.

+ Experience alone is valid for determining the leading of the Holy Spirit, we don't always need the Bible.

+ The leading of the Holy Spirit can be determined apart from, and even in contradiction to, the Scripture.

One helpful way to avoid being deceived about matters essential to salvation, to find a biblical church, and to stand firm in the truth, is to recognize the distinction between "essential theology" and "peripheral theology." Essential theology involves those doctrines which almost all Christians have historically believed to be accurate and indispensable—since the time of Christ! (Contrary to what some scholars believe, the central tenets of Christianity have been preserved essentially unchanged since Christ died.) Peripheral theology is that about which Christians have often differed, while still remaining faithful to Christ.

We're not saying peripheral theology is unimportant—sometimes you and your family have to make big decisions based on matters of peripheral theology, such as baptism or worship style. However, we are saying that matters of peripheral theology should never be reasons to condemn, to look down on others, or to think, *Are they even believers?*

Essential theology:

+ The Godhead: the Father, the Son, and the Holy Spirit.
+ The deity of Jesus.
+ The virgin birth.
+ Justification by faith in Jesus and not by works.
+ The crucifixion, death, and bodily resurrection of Jesus.
+ The centrality and infallibility of the Scriptures.
+ The return of Jesus.
+ The resurrection of the dead.
+ Atonement through the blood of Jesus.
+ Jesus being the only way to salvation.
+ The existence of eternity.

Peripheral theology:

+ When to take and who should take Communion.

+ The gifts of the Spirit.

+ Tithing.

+ Head coverings.

+ Dress codes.

+ Worship style.

+ Music in the church.

+ Discipline and education of children.

+ Political affiliation.

+ How to keep Sunday—the Lord's Day.

+ Church government.

The Apostle's Creed has long been considered the classic summation of essential theology:

I believe in God, the Father Almighty,
Maker of heaven and earth.
And in Jesus Christ, His only Son, our Lord,
who was conceived by the Holy Spirit,
born of the virgin Mary,
suffered under Pontius Pilate,
was crucified, died and was buried.
He descended into hell.
On the third day He rose again from the dead.
He ascended into heaven
and sits at the right hand of God the Father Almighty.
From thence He will come to judge the living and the dead.
I believe in the Holy Spirit,
the holy Christian Church,
the communion of saints,
the forgiveness of sins,
the resurrection of the body,
and the life everlasting. Amen.[53]

---

53. From the *Lutheran Service Book*.

Also, the Five Solas of the Reformation give good understanding of essential theology:

1. *Sola Scriptura* ("Scripture alone"): The Bible alone is our highest authority.

2. *Sola Fide* ("Faith alone"): We are saved through faith alone in Jesus Christ.

3. *Sola Gratia* ("Grace alone"): We are saved by the grace of God alone.

4. *Solus Christus* ("Christ alone"): Jesus Christ alone is our Lord, Savior, and King.

5. *Soli Deo Gloria* ("To the glory of God alone"): We live for the glory of God alone.

Isn't that beautiful?

A PROVERB

It takes wisdom to have a good family, and it takes understanding to make it strong. (Proverbs 24:3 NCV)

PSALMS FOR THE WOUNDED

LORD, I call to you. Come quickly. Listen to me when I call to you. Let my prayer be like incense placed before you, and my praise like the evening sacrifice. LORD, help me control my tongue; help me be careful about what I say. Take away my desire to do evil or to join others in doing wrong. (Psalm 141:1–4 NCV)

Tell me in the morning about your love, because I trust you. Show me what I should do, because my prayers go up to you. (Psalm 143:8 NCV)

Your kingdom will go on and on, and you will rule forever. The LORD will keep all his promises; he is loyal to all he has made. The LORD helps those who have been defeated and takes care of those who are in trouble. (Psalm 145:13–14 NCV)

16

HOPE BEYOND THE PAIN

Religion is religion and can be used to justify just about anything....Safe churches aren't afraid of or threatened by what others believe.
—*Michael Dye*

Friendship means understanding, not agreement.
It means forgiveness, not forgetting. It means the memories last, even if contact is lost.
—*Anonymous*

A new commandment I give to you, that you love one another; as I have loved you, that you also love one another. By this all will know that you are My disciples, if you have love for one another.
(John 13:34–35)

Our friend Michael Dye received another letter from a woman in intense pain:

When I was thirty-two, I was in an abusive marriage and seeking help. I was lost and desperate. I didn't believe much in God but decided to try going to church. I didn't believe a word I heard for months. And for months, the pastor listened to my questions (more like *accusations*), never once flinching. He never once judged

224

me about my current lifestyle. He said those changes were in God's department. He and a few of the people I saw at church seemed to have a joy that appealed to me. It was something deeper than happiness. The pastor always showed grace to everyone. He had the gift of acceptance. I expected to be judged and rejected when the church found out some of the stuff I had done and was still doing. I was looking for rejection but kept running into acceptance.

Once I became a Christian (much to my shock), a woman mentored me and included me in the woman's group she led. Her wisdom and grace still affects me now some fifteen years later. Both the pastor and my mentor helped me to heal from the abortion I had when I was eighteen and the life I led afterwards. I knew I was forgiven and the years of secret shame were lifted. They also both encourage me in youth ministry, a calling I felt from the beginning of my Christian life. Now I run a ministry for teenage mothers and pregnant girls. This first church experience of acceptance is the foundation of my ministry.

Thankful for grace,
Kathy

WELCOMING THE COMFORTER

As much as we felt we needed to write a book that dealt with the lack of unity in the church and the resulting woundedness, still in the back of our minds we knew without doubt that there are churches everywhere constantly and continuously experiencing God's blessing and presence.

From what we have written so far you can tell that we have met a lot of people who have suffered at the hands of other Christians. Now we want to tell the story of literally millions of people today who can't *wait* to have fellowship with others who have come to know the Christ. These are people who have experienced the Holy Spirit in a deeper and more vibrant way.

Countless numbers of people over the centuries lived a far better, far more peaceful, existence, because they gave their lives over to Christ. That doesn't mean they didn't have unexpected troubles and trials. It wasn't that they didn't get discouraged, especially looking at a world that is so dark.

Many of them questioned how a good God could allow such pain and suffering. But they didn't become weakened and offset by what they saw. The reason? God had sent His Holy Spirit to them as a Comforter. And one of the things He brought to them was the joy of the Lord, something so profound, so beyond human imagination, and so satisfying that they would welcome God's presence any time.

For all the preaching and teaching that Jesus did when He was here, there is no evidence that anyone could keep His instructions. Look at James and John who caused division among the rest of the disciples. Look at Thomas, who after all of the things that Jesus did, still couldn't believe that He had risen. Then there is Peter. When he should have been the most stalwart and dedicated to the man he knew was the Messiah, he failed miserably. Peter seems to have been an impetuous, rough, and undisciplined man. Even until the end he was in denial of his relationship with Jesus. When Jesus sent the Holy Spirit, God's plan for the world was revealed with stunning clarity. A new day had arrived which brought a new kind of relationship, especially for people who had tried so diligently to serve God but always fell short. After the day of Pentecost, all of these disciples were so completely changed that they were no longer recognizable. They had something new inside of them, a Something—Some*one*—that gave them wisdom, knowledge, and understanding. Everywhere they went, miracles happened and people came to Christ.

We must not forget that Jesus sent the Holy Spirit to come and live within a believer to give him or her the ability to do that which cannot be done by self-determination alone. Please don't miss this. Before Pentecost there was only the law, which, no matter how hard a person tried to follow it, was never fulfilled. But now, after Jesus preached to them the truth which, again, they were still unable to do, He did what He promised to do before He left this earth. He sent the Holy Spirit to not only walk with them, but to mysteriously live within them. Who can understand this, especially when humanity, from the beginning of the Fall, saw God as always angry and needing to be appeased?

Nobody before Pentecost could truly believe in grace. It took the Holy Spirit to show us God's love and how grace worked within that love. In the process, He would also reveal God's plan from the beginning of time which was the love of the Father and His grace toward us:

> *Father, I desire that they also whom You gave Me may be with Me where I am, that they may behold My glory which You have given Me; for You loved Me before the foundation of the world. O righteous Father! The world has not known You, but I have known You; and these have known that You sent Me. And I have declared to them Your name, and will declare it, that the love with which You loved Me may be in them, and I in them.* (John 17:24–26)

What Jesus did on earth was live out and fulfill the principles of the law in a very understandable way, something that the disciples could never do on their own. You can almost see Him smiling, knowing that what He was about to reveal concerning the Holy Spirit would shake them to the core and begin a new love relationship with God. Behind the scenes He had a plan like nothing one could imagine. That plan was to take weak, sinful, and rebellious people and place His Spirit in them in order to do what was needed to have fellowship with both people and God. But how could that happen? *It doesn't make sense, God living in me*, we think. So He explained it, and in the process called it a mystery, wanting us to know that this is certainly beyond anything we could imagine, that God would be so gracious and merciful to a dying world, and that He was so much more ready to help them than to simply tell them what to do. *"To them God willed to make known what are the riches of the glory of this mystery among the Gentiles: which is Christ in you, the hope of glory"* (Colossians 1:27). The point we're trying to make is that you cannot live out the Christian life joyfully and effectively without the person of the Holy Spirit in you. And you cannot find unity without the help of the Holy Spirit.

The message of the gospel began to change the world. Those who wanted to change but couldn't do it themselves, found such profound love in Christ as He worked in them. It made obedience so much easier. Those who had experienced the heavy weight of trying to please God may have seemed almost giddy from the Holy Spirit's presence. Now God was truly pleased that we would allow Him to help. Sadly, that would become terribly hard for some people who refused to lay down their pride and arrogance to accept this better way. There are always people who stubbornly insist that the things they do will earn God's favor and make themselves acceptable. In standing back and looking at the world since we first believed, it is unfathomable to us that anyone could for one moment resist the gift of the Holy Spirit!

THE UTTER NECESSITY OF UNITY

"For all have sinned and fallen short of the glory of God." This verse used to drive me nuts. The sinful state of all mankind was a no-brainer. Just look at the world, at me. I would ask, "What's the glory of God?" Nobody knew. Jesus said He had given us His glory for our unity. (See John 17:22.) This glory must be something other-worldly, like the new creation. And if we are that, we no longer have to compete with each other, for anything. Or be defensive, or afraid of each other. But we are in the world. A pain-filled, blind, enraged, self-crumbling and controlling world. And because it assaults the glory of God, it assaults us. Intentionally. Keep the Father's pleasure as the Apple of your eye. We only love because He loved.[54]

From the very beginning, Jesus taught that there was a kingdom on earth that was all around them, but was unseen. It was a kingdom like no other. It contained those who had agreed to an allegiance with Christ by receiving His Spirit. Unfortunately, this kingdom was at war with the kingdoms of this world. God's people would have to be taught and instructed on how this war was to be fought. Two items of instructions were of top priority. The first was that nothing was to be done for the kingdom outside of the directions given by the Holy Spirit. This was a war that, in some ways, is very much like the natural wars fought here on earth. There needed to be leadership. No man was to take on responsibilities that were not delegated to him personally, which now the Holy Spirit could impart from within. From within He could also impart such things as strength, power, authority, wisdom, knowledge, and understanding. The second item of instruction would be so important that if it was disobeyed it could cost the

---

54. Jean DeHaven, personal writings.

kingdom dearly. That's why it is one of the main themes throughout the Scriptures: the utter necessity for *unity derived from love.*

The evidence that we have received the Holy Spirit is the manner by which we love—that is care for, treat, honor, respect, and do good to—people. This should be obvious considering the natural realm; sports, war, and a host of other things all take unity to get the job done. *"A new commandment I give to you, that you love one another; as I have loved you, that you also love one another. By this all will know that you are My disciples, if you have love for one another"* (John 13:34–35).

You have no doubt noticed that in natural disasters and other catastrophes, people who in under other circumstances would not talk to each other suddenly work hand-in-hand to help someone in need. It's amazing how this act of unity gets things done in times when it's desperately needed. Many of the rescuers experienced an adrenaline high that often put these new relationships together forever. When people suffer together, they're not inclined to part ways afterwards.

We know that most of you have a pretty clear understanding of how unity works in the church, or should work. And to our great joy, we see this unity creating tremendous blessings not only amongst yourselves, but in missionary efforts to help other people outside of our own circles.

Many of us when we were younger used to see documentaries about suffering people in Africa. The sights of malnourished and dying children hurt deeply. However, many started to contribute willingly and joyfully to help those in need. No one has done more than the unified church in helping these people. Houses and hospitals were built, wells were drilled, education became a priority, selfish rebellions were put down, and people experienced life as never before. But not one of these things would have happened if there were not unity in the church.

You can actually become an adrenaline junkie yourself when you see personally how God used you and others in unity to change lives. There is exquisite joy and happiness when you are a part of making someone else's life better. It's why some very wealthy people have gone off to other countries, leaving riches and comfort behind, to live a life of service in unity.

SATAN AND DISUNITY

Most of us wouldn't think of going off to war by ourselves. It would be sheer idiocy! However, there are times in the Christian walk when we find ourselves alone and attacked by our adversary, the devil and his angels. In those moments we can draw upon the tools that God has given us; His Word, His Spirit, and His name, and have great results. And sometimes circumstances call for our joining together with other brothers and sisters to engage the enemy. This is a wonderful reality if we are going to get on with life.

That inner rage and hostility, that fire that sometimes blazes like a volcano toward others, are things God wants to help us with. You would think He wanted to condemn us, but His Word makes it clear that He actually wants to heal us. There are moments of despair, despondency, and hopelessness which pound away at our emotions until we think we're going to die. But here is where unity comes in again. We cannot and must not try to fight the enemy by ourselves. And we must not think that a single *person* is our enemy. The only way to freedom is through the Holy Spirit and God's kingdom people. Forsake the body and you stand alone, up against something so powerful that it often takes the force of many people praying and using their gifts in order to win. "*...lest Satan should take advantage of us; for we are not ignorant of his devices*" (2 Corinthians 2:11).

It's a different and indescribable path, walking with and getting to know Him. You could say it's difficult, due to the trials and tribulations. But the alternative requires no energy at all. Only capitulation, acquiescence, silently not protesting. But we serve a God who will not let us rest in trials and tribulations. He says, Speak! For that is why you have a voice! Language is not for the unskilled! And so we walk with Him, feeling His strength, and wondering at the greatness and awesomeness of what we have gotten ourselves into. Lean into the yoke, for only then will you feel His strength. A resting yoke is a burden to be carried.... I work with people that angrily say, "Well, the Holy Spirit just better give me...." I wonder if He would like a little kindness, a little trust in quietly walking in peace with Him. He bought it, after all. Yes, we take ours and others' needs to Him, but He is the greater prize. He is so attractive! What the King can do is not Who the King is. Knowing Him is the greatest treasure. It is He that made and makes us, and is our fulfillment of joy. There is no other like Him.[55]

LOVE TRANSFORMING

So what do we hope that the reading of this book will accomplish? It has been our attempt to make clear the obvious difficulties that exist within many if not most churches. We are expecting that you will be able to identify with what has been written. It is also our hope that some of the solutions that we have presented, such as dealing with unforgiveness or how to assess a good church, have all been helpful. But the overriding theme of this book is the recognition that without love inspired by the Spirit none of us can move forward. That's what we want you to take away.

It was fitting that the last story we are going to share with you came to us at the end of the writing of this book. Dr. Holmes shared this story with us and it seemed to exemplify everything we've been trying to say: our great need is for inspiration from the Holy Spirit mixed with a healthy dose of conviction resulting in a kind of love that can only come from God.

I am a chiropractor, also trained in Traditional Chinese Medicine. In the mid-1980s, the first cases of immune system failure in homosexual men was spotlighted, not only in the media but in medical and chiropractic practices as well. At a seminar for Traditional Chinese Medicine, there were presentations pertaining to wasting diseases. They proposed as a solution the traditional Chinese herbs, which had been used for the treatment of such diseases for more than eighteen hundred years.

At the time of the seminar, probably 1986 or thereabouts, there was little medical help given to homosexual men, or anybody else for that matter, with immune system failure. The diagnosis was a virtual death sentence.

---

55. Jean DeHaven, personal writings.

After the seminar, my practice began treating many homosexual men who had the diagnosis of acquired immune deficiency disease or AIDS with traditional Chinese herbs. They worked, and patients with AIDS were beginning to recover and improve, not to the extent that they were HIV negative, but to the extent that they regained their health and a degree of vitality and no longer felt that the diagnosis was a death sentence. Over the course of the next eight or nine years, we treated hundreds of HIV-positive patients. The Chinese herbs and the spark-plug stimulating effect of chiropractic treatment were demonstrating a profound and life-changing result.

To say the least, the Christian community was not terribly loving toward gay men with a death sentence, and notwithstanding the fact that I was treating hundreds of these patients, I, too, was not particularly loving or compassionate. I was rather generous in the description of my own attitudes.

Approximately two years after I began treating AIDS patients, I was abruptly awakened at two o'clock. As clear as I can hear my own voice, I heard the question in my mind, "How would you sentence a whole segment of society to hell?" The answer was just as clear and immediate, "By having Christians be unloving and hateful toward them."

I felt immediately convicted in my own attitude, realizing that by now I was helping thousands of gay men to recover their health while my attitude was anything but loving, embracing, or compassionate.

The next day at my office, I asked several gay patients, "Do you feel that I have a heart of love toward you?" I continued asking my gay patients this over the course of the next several weeks. I got a lot of weird and unusual reactions, but one stands out as literally profound. This man, Brian (not his real name), said that he wondered what church I went to. He knew that I must be a true Christian in order for him to feel such a sense of love and acceptance from me.

I am not sure that I was the true Christian he had in mind, but I was happy that he felt a sense of love, compassion, and acceptance. My own personal journey of having God's love transform me was much longer and very rocky. Notwithstanding, Brian and his partner became Christians. However, Brian eventually succumbed to the insidious effects of HIV. On the evening that he lay dying in a hospital, he asked me to come and talk with him and be there at his bedside. Over the course of fifteen minutes and through labored breathing, Brian thanked me for introducing him to the love and compassion that Jesus' love for us truly represents. Brian died about two hours later. Unbeknownst to me, in a conference room in the same wing of the hospital, dozens of Brian's friends gathered; twenty-five of whom came to the Lord as a result of Brian's life and testimony.

Is love transforming? Is love the healer? Absolutely!

—*Dr. Bruce WS Holmes DC, QME*

There is no way that we, the authors, can talk you into going back to church if you have left. What we do realize, however, is that if you still believe, there will be a point in time in which you are willing to risk again and be in some way associated with others of God's people. That is an easy thing to say, but for you who have been wounded, there might not be anything easy about it.

Recently, Jean DeHaven, whom we have acknowledged in this book numerous times, said something amazing about staying on the healthy path:

My pastor says we humans were created with the need to love. Yet we are in a world that seems to support the idea that loving other humans is hazardous to one's health. Burned over and over, many turn to animals, or hoarding, or anything else that can't hurt like people do. I don't want to admit my pastor is right, for it makes me frustrated that I can't find this "need to love" in the church. But is that true in all cases? There are individuals that have proved themselves to be of a loving nature. Yet will I accept their proof? Or, will

I apply the rule of universal rejection for self-protection? That's even lonelier. And God doesn't back that. Why put myself in such a position of self-destruction? Forward. Attack the fear. Demand it yield. Trust God to catch me in all cases.

Jean has decided not to allow the fear of rejection to overwhelm or defeat her. She has chosen to fight against fear and those things that would hinder her from going forward as a Christian.

If you are a believer in Jesus Christ, the most natural thing is to love with your heart. His love is inside you and your great joy is allowing that love to be felt by others. But if you have been wounded deeply, you might be more than reluctant to put yourself out toward people. The subtitle of this book is "Hope Beyond the Pain." To have hope beyond the pain, there must involve a determination to move forward at any risk. It is quite possible that even though you find a very caring and loving church, there will be someone in that church that gives a passing remark or suggestion that turns your stomach and reminds you of all the pain of previous experiences. But if you are to go forward in life and not become a hermit, you must yet again make the decision to take a risk. To love. To forgive. To be unified. It is our hope that through prayer and correct evaluation you will be willing to step beyond the threshold of fear because moving toward, and eventually associating with God's great army allows for protection and healing that can't be found in a solitary existence.

So, in this last chapter, we want to encourage you in every way possible to experience this hope. But simultaneously, we know that it will require boldness; you have to be willing to fight for some of your freedom and growth. This is why we turn again and again to the Holy Spirit. You are not alone in your fight. He is in you, He is your companion, He is the one who will walk with you and give you the courage and weapons to fight with. Let Him fight for you. Let Him pour out His love in your heart and make you brave once again. Don't allow all that God has given you to be wasted or set aside because of the wounds in your life. Be healed by the grace of the Spirit.

ONE LAST WORD

A final word from Jesus.

But now I come to You, and these things I speak in the world, that they may have My joy fulfilled in themselves. I have given them Your word; and the world has hated them because they are not of the world, just as I am not of the world. I do not pray that You should take them out of the world, but that You should keep them from the evil one. They are not of the world, just as I am not of the world. Sanctify them by Your truth. Your word is truth. As You sent Me into the world, I also have sent them into the world. And for their sakes I sanctify Myself, that they also may be sanctified by the truth.

I do not pray for these alone, but also for those who will believe in Me through their word; that they all may be one, as You, Father, are in Me, and I in You; that they also may be one in Us, that the world may believe that You sent Me. And the glory which You gave Me I have given them, that they may be one just as We are one: I in them, and You in Me; that they may be made perfect in one, and that the world may know that You have sent Me, and have loved them as You have loved Me.

APPENDIX A

DEMONIC LIES AND DOCTRINES

Now the Spirit expressly says that in latter times some will depart from the faith, giving heed to deceiving spirits and doctrines of demons.

(1 Timothy 4:1)

In this appendix, we pinpoint some of the lies that Satan uses so cleverly to slander God and slander what it means to be a follower of God. In a way, it's an extension of the clichés in chapter 14. Some of these lies may be painfully familiar to you! Our hope is to provide an easy reference for you to combat Satan's lies with the truth of Scripture. When Jesus was tempted in the wilderness, He used Scripture to refute Satan. We should do the same! Let us not be deceived.

LIES OFTEN DIRECTED AT THE DOUBTING MIND

"Everybody is a child of God."

Not everyone who says to Me, "Lord, Lord," shall enter the kingdom of heaven, but he who does the will of My Father in heaven.

(Matthew 7:21)

You are of your father the devil, and the desires of your father you want to do. He was a murderer from the beginning, and does not stand in the truth, because there is no truth in him. When he speaks a lie, he speaks

from his own resources, for he is a liar and the father of it.
(John 8:44)

"If God is a good God, He wouldn't send anyone to hell."

Then He will also say to those on the left hand, "Depart from Me, you cursed, into the everlasting fire prepared for the devil and his angels."
(Matthew 25:41)

He who keeps your soul, does He not know it? And will He not render to each man according to his deeds? (Proverbs 24:10–13)

"All God expects is for us to lead a good life and do the best we can."

Knowing that a man is not justified by the works of the law but by faith in Jesus Christ, even we have believed in Christ Jesus, that we might be justified by faith in Christ and not by the works of the law; for by the works of the law no flesh shall be justified. (Galatians 2:16)

For by grace you have been saved through faith, and that not of yourselves; it is the gift of God, not of works, lest anyone should boast.
(Ephesians 2:8–9)

"God only helps those who help themselves."

I am the vine, you are the branches. He who abides in Me, and I in him, bears much fruit; for without Me you can do nothing.
(John 15:5)

"Christians use God as a crutch because they can't make it on their own."

...casting all your care upon Him, for He cares for you. (1 Peter 5:7)

"You have to give up too much to be saved."

Every good gift and every perfect gift is from above, and comes down from the Father of lights, with whom there is no variation or shadow of turning. (James 1:17)

"It is too hard to serve God."

You are of God, little children, and have overcome [evil spirits], because He who is in you is greater than he who is in the world. (1 John 4:4)

"Jesus is not the only way to heaven."

Nor is there salvation in any other, for there is no other name under heaven given among men by which we must be saved. (Acts 4:12)

"I'm too weak to serve God."

Yet in all these things we are more than conquerors through Him who loved us. (Romans 8:37)

"Christianity is not for everyone."

Do not marvel that I said to you, "You must be born again." (John 3:7)

All that the Father gives Me will come to Me, and the one who comes to Me I will by no means cast out. (John 6:37)

"Churches have too many hypocrites."

Not forsaking the assembling of ourselves together, as is the manner of some, but exhorting one another, and so much the more as you see the Day approaching. (Hebrews 10:25)

"The Bible is too hard to understand."

But even if our gospel is veiled, it is veiled to those who are perishing. (2 Corinthians 4:3)

However, when He, the Spirit of truth, has come, He will guide you into all truth; for He will not speak on His own authority, but whatever He hears He will speak; and He will tell you things to come. (John 16:13)

"The Bible is full of errors."

Knowing this first, that no prophecy of Scripture is of any private inter-pretation, for prophecy never came by the will of man, but holy men of God spoke as they were moved by the Holy Spirit. (2 Peter 1:20–21)

"There are too many religions. How can you know which is right?"

Jesus said to him, "I am the way, the truth, and the life. No one comes to the Father except through Me." (John 14:6)

"All the church ever does is ask for money."

Give, and it will be given to you: good measure, pressed down, shaken together, and running over will be put into your bosom. For with the same measure that you use, it will be measured back to you.

(Luke 6:38)

"I'll worry about heaven when I get there."

Some men's sins are clearly evident, preceding them to judgment, but those of some men follow later. (1 Timothy 5:24)

"I believe that when I die, that's it."

And as it is appointed for men to die once, but after this the judg-ment. (Hebrews 9:27)

"As long as you are sincere and moral, that's all that counts."

Not by works of righteousness which we have done, but according to His mercy He saved us, through the washing of regeneration and re-newing of the Holy Spirit. (Titus 3:5)

"There might be a God, but it does not need to affect my life."

You believe that there is one God. You do well. Even the demons be-lieve—and tremble! (James 2:19)

"I don't believe in a God."

The fool has said in his heart, "There is no God." (Psalm 14:1)

"I'm as good as anybody."

As it is written: "There is none righteous, no, not one."
(Romans 3:10)

"I have my beliefs and you have yours. It doesn't matter what you believe just as long as you believe."

So they said, "Believe on the Lord Jesus Christ, and you will be saved, you and your household." (Acts 16:31)

"As soon as I get my life cleaned up I'll serve God."

"Come now, and let us reason together," says the LORD, *"Though your sins are like scarlet, they shall be as white as snow; though they are red like crimson, they shall be as wool."* (Isaiah 1:18)

Come to Me, all you who labor and are heavy laden, and I will give you rest. (Matthew 11:28)

"If I go to hell, I'll just look up all my friends."

And do not fear those who kill the body but cannot kill the soul. But rather fear Him who is able to destroy both soul and body in hell.
(Matthew 10:28)

"God doesn't see what we do."

So then each of us shall give account of himself to God.
(Romans 14:12)

And there is no creature hidden from His sight, but all things are naked and open to the eyes of Him to whom we must give account.
(Hebrews 4:13)

"God wants me happy, therefore I've got to do what I've got to do to be happy."

Beloved, do not think it strange concerning the fiery trial which is to try you, as though some strange thing happened to you; but rejoice to the extent that you partake of Christ's sufferings, that when His glory is revealed, you may also be glad with exceeding joy. (1 Peter 4:12–13)

"It doesn't matter what I do, just so long as I don't hurt anybody else."

They will give an account to Him who is ready to judge the living and the dead. (1 Peter 4:5)

"It would be better for everyone if I were dead."

You are not the only one that has said this (see 1 Kings 19:4), and God is acutely aware of the mercy you need (see 1 Kings 19:5). Identity is not based on what everyone else wants. If God wanted you dead, you would be dead. Remember that a man's enemies may be those of his own household. (See Matthew 10:21.) If they want you dead, that may not be a sign of their righteousness. This may be a calling, an opportunity to ask Him what your real identity is, and not accept what others have labeled you. (See Matthew 10:37; 19:29.) You may have to leave the people you value behind, but not by killing yourself. Leave them behind by following the One who is acutely aware of the love and mercy you need.

LIES OFTEN DIRECTED AT THE COMPLACENT MIND

"I don't go for all this shouting and praising the Lord stuff. God expects us to be reverent."

But let all those rejoice who put their trust in You; let them ever shout for joy, because You defend them; let those also who love Your name be joyful in You. (Psalm 5:11)

Be glad in the LORD and rejoice, you righteous; and shout for joy, all you upright in heart! (Psalm 32:11)

"I don't believe we should talk about demons, we need to take responsibility for the way we live our own lives."

Lest Satan should take advantage of us; for we are not ignorant of his devices. (2 Corinthians 2:11)

For we do not wrestle against flesh and blood, but against principalities, against powers, against the rulers of the darkness of this age, against spiritual hosts of wickedness in the heavenly places. (Ephesians 6:12)

"God has called me to be the watchdog over this church."

Christ is head of the church; and He is the Savior of the body. (Ephesians 5:23)

"God has placed me in this church to keep the pastor humble. I needle him periodically to keep him on his toes."

Obey those who rule over you, and be submissive, for they watch out for your souls, as those who must give account. Let them do so with joy and not with grief, for that would be unprofitable for you. (Hebrews 13:17)

"I have a prophetic ministry and when God speaks to me, even the pastor had better listen."

Obey those who rule over you, and be submissive, for they watch out for your souls, as those who must give account. Let them do so with joy and not with grief, for that would be unprofitable for you. (Hebrews 13:17)

"This is our church; we built it and it belongs to us."

Christ is the head of the church; and He is the Savior of the body. (Ephesians 5:23)

"I don't like all that loud music in church."

Sing to Him a new song; play skillfully with a shout of joy.
(Psalm 33:3)

Endeavor...to keep the unity of the Spirit in the bond of peace.
(Ephesians 4:3.)

"Drums don't belong in church."

Praise Him with the sound of the trumpet; praise Him with the lute and harp! Praise Him with the timbrel and dance; praise Him with stringed instruments and flutes! Praise Him with loud cymbals; praise Him with clashing cymbals! Let everything that has breath praise the Lord. Praise the LORD!
(Psalm 150:3–6)

"Tithing is not for us today."

Give, and it will be given to you: good measure, pressed down, shaken together, and running over will be put into your bosom. For with the same measure that you use, it will be measured back to you.
(Luke 6:38)

So let each one give as he purposes in his heart, not grudgingly or of necessity; for God loves a cheerful giver.
(2 Corinthians 9:7)

"I could probably preach a whole lot better than my pastor."

But now God has set the members, each one of them, in the body just as He pleased.
(1 Corinthians 12:18)

And He Himself gave some to be apostles, some prophets, some evangelists, and some pastors and teachers.
(Ephesians 4:11)

"If the pastor can't say everything he needs to say in twenty to thirty minutes, he doesn't have anything important to say."

Now on the first day of the week, when the disciples came together to break bread, Paul, ready to depart the next day, spoke to them and continued his message until midnight. (Acts 20:7)

"Nobody cares about the old people around here anymore."

Looking carefully lest anyone fall short of the grace of God; lest any root of bitterness springing up cause trouble, and by this many become defiled. (Hebrews 12:15)

"I've sinned after becoming a Christian, and God won't take me back."

If we confess our sins, He is faithful and just to forgive us our sins and to cleanse us from all unrighteousness. (1 John 1:9)

"I can date an unbeliever just as long as we don't talk about marriage."

Therefore "Come out from among them and be separate, says the Lord." (2 Corinthians 6:17)

"I'll get my boyfriend/girlfriend saved before we get married."

Do not be unequally yoked together with unbelievers. For what fellowship has righteousness with lawlessness? And what communion has light with darkness? (2 Corinthians 6:14)

"If you are going to sin, you might as well go all the way."

He who sins is of the devil, for the devil has sinned from the beginning. For this purpose the Son of God was manifested, that He might destroy the works of the devil. (1 John 3:8)

"You make your mistakes, and I'll make mine."

Therefore, to him who knows to do good and does not do it, to him it is sin.   (James 4:17)

"We might as well have sex now, we're going to get married anyway."

Now the works of the flesh are evident, which are: adultery, fornication, uncleanness, lewdness.   (Galatians 5:19)

"Once a person does something wrong it becomes a part of their character and they can't change."

If we confess our sins, He is faithful and just to forgive us our sins and to cleanse us from all unrighteousness.   (1 John 1:9)

"That person did me wrong. Now I have a right to do them wrong."

For if you forgive men their trespasses, your heavenly Father will also forgive you. But if you do not forgive men their trespasses, neither will your Father forgive your trespasses.   (Matthew 6:14–15)

APPENDIX B

101 PRINCIPLES FOR LIVING IN THE KINGDOM OF LIGHT

He has delivered us from the power of darkness and conveyed us into the kingdom of the Son of His love. (Colossians 1:13)

Moving from the kingdom of darkness to the kingdom of light is a most wonderful experience. However, we quickly discover the principles that helped us survive in our old kingdom don't work in the new one, and we have brought a lot of that old thinking with us in the move. We can quickly become frustrated if we try to make things work that were not meant to work. The solution is to discover and adhere to the new principles of our new kingdom.

Here are some important principles succinctly stated that we have learned the hard way and that have guided us. We do not offer explanations of our principles here; however, if you want to talk about them further, we'd love to hear from you! Please send us an email at info@cleansingstream.org.

1. Stand guard over your victories.

2. When you fall, get up immediately.

3. Set your mind on things above.

4. Avoid the appearance of evil.

5. Be content with what you have.

6. Learn to fulfill your God-given need to give.

7. Learn to receive so that others are able to give.

8. Keep on praying with the belief that prayer changes things, even if in small degrees.

9. Look for ways to serve that utilize your strongest gifts and talents.

10. Avoid comparisons.

11. Consider how much is enough.

12. Rejoice always.

13. Do all things without murmuring or complaining.

14. Bless others.

15. Be alert to powerful temptation coming right after blessing and anointing.

16. Guard against a negative spirit.

17. Avoid a critical spirit.

18. Refuse a religious spirit.

19. Be anxious for nothing.

20. Avoid presumptions.

21. Recognize loneliness as a deadly enemy.

22. Overcome rejection.

23. Guard against tiredness.

24. Reject isolationism.

25. Know the sources of fear.

26. Contend for the truth that is in Jesus.

27. Control anger.

28. Refuse to allow your mind to become passive.

29. Control thoughts that lead to an overactive mind.

30. Reject stubbornness.

31. Guard against discouragement.

32. Don't let others be the brunt of a foolish joke or unkind word.

33. Remember that what is spoken in secret will be broadcast from the housetops. (See Luke 12:3.)

34. Learn to bring thoughts into captivity.

35. Overcome laziness.

36. Guard against self-pity.

37. Avoid sarcasm.

38. Be careful with idle words.

39. Allow yourself to laugh.

40. Avoid busyness.

41. Refuse to be cynical.

42. Contend with forgetfulness and strive to be thoughtful.

43. Learn to think properly. (See Philippians 4:8.)

44. Remember that your body is the temple of the Holy Spirit.

45. Attend to your affairs.

46. Pray always.

47. Work to overcome procrastination.

48. Adjust responsibilities so that the load is bearable.

49. Learn to be a listener.

50. Recognize love as an action.

51. Avoid a persecution complex.

52. Seek good counsel.

53. Dress modestly and appropriately.

54. Learn to sing.

55. Avoid a conspiracy mentality.

56. Present a positive demeanor.

57. Keep your conscience from being seared.

58. Avoid dominating the conversation.

59. Learn to make decisions.

60. Admit mistakes.

61. Learn to abide.

62. Avoid manipulating or controlling other people.

63. Learn to rest.

64. Determine to speak with accuracy.

65. Avoid the blame game.

66. Practice loyalty.

67. Determine to be dependable.

68. Establish yourself as trustworthy

69. Learn to wait.

70. Practice unity.

71. Be prepared.

72. Organize your life.

73. Envy no one.

74. Love righteousness.

75. Stand against apathy.

76. Avoid developing an argumentative spirit.

77. Be open to change.

78. Guard against jealousy.

79. Avoid factions.

80. Shun moodiness.

81. Guard against greed.

82. Make restitution.

83. Practice kindness.

84. Avoid worldliness.

85. Rejoice in small things.

86. Be thankful.

87. Become a worshiper.

88. Avoid the desire to get even.

89. Keep yourself from the center of conversation.

90. Avoid wordy conversations.

91. Seek wisdom above all.

92. Do not despise correction that comes from God.

93. Learn to hate sin without hating the sinner.

94. Avoid proclaiming your own goodness.

95. Open your ears to the cry of the poor.

96. Don't meddle in quarrels that are not your own.

97. Be careful to whom you vent your feelings.

98. Be angry without sinning.

99. Avoid flattery.

100. Know the source of guilt.

101. When God seems distant, continue on anyway.

WHERE DO WE GO FROM HERE?

It is our hope that in your life, you will not only discover your identity in Christ but that you will also discover that you have a voice worth hearing. You don't have to become the product of someone else's opinion or be controlled or manipulated in order to become accepted. You have worth and value just as you are. You have a loving Father who will bless you and teach you and guide you the remainder of your life.

It is also our hope that along the way, the hurts you have received will be healed. Perhaps this book has helped a little in that process. And, as you are being healed, it would be our great joy to know that you have found a group of fellow travelers, believers who you can identify with and who are safe. Keep in mind that there will always be a few dangerous people in every group. You just don't have to go along with their ways. Our prayer is that you truly discover your identity, begin to move in the direction of your destiny, and become fully fulfilled within the body of Christ.

> *We have troubles all around us, but we are not defeated. We do not know what to do, but we do not give up the hope of living. We are persecuted, but God does not leave us. We are hurt sometimes, but we are not destroyed. We carry the death of Jesus in our own bodies so that the life of Jesus can also be seen in our bodies. We are alive, but for Jesus we are always in danger of death so that the life of Jesus can be seen in our bodies that die.*   (2 Corinthians 4:8–11 NCV)

ABOUT THE AUTHORS

Chris Hayward has been the president of Cleansing Stream Ministries (CSM) for over eighteen years. CSM is an organization dedicated to equipping local churches for biblically balanced, sound and effective healing and deliverance ministry. Before his time with CSM, Chris was the founding pastor at Christian Fellowship Church in Mount Vernon, IL for over twelve years, and has served in pastoral ministry for over thirty-five years. Previous to that, he served as VP Marketing for Word Publishing, and Executive VP of Vision House Publishing. He is also the author of *God's Cleansing Stream* and *The End of Rejection*. He currently makes his home in Santa Clarita, CA, with his wife, Karen. They have three children and four grandchildren.

Ray Beeson is the director of Overcomers Ministries, a teaching ministry with a special emphasis on spiritual warfare and prayer. Ray was a junior high and senior high school mathematics teacher until joining the International Prayer corps with Dick Eastman. When Dick joined World Literature Crusade, Ray went with him teaching seminars called "The Change the World School of Prayer." In 1983 Ray and four others established Overcomers Ministries, where he remains today. Ray has authored numerous books including *Signed in His Blood* (Charisma House, 2014) and co-authored *The Hidden Price of Greatness* (Tyndale House, 1991). He lives with his wife, Linda, in Ventura, CA, their home for over thirty-five years. They have four grown children.

CLEANSING STREAM INTERNATIONAL

equipping, restoring, sustaining

For more information, contact us at:
info@cleansingstream.org

www.cleansingstream.org

cleansingstream

Welcome to Our House!

We Have a Special Gift for You

It is our privilege and pleasure to share in your love of Christian books. We are committed to bringing you authors and books that feed, challenge, and enrich your faith.

To show our appreciation, we invite you to sign up to receive a specially selected **Reader Appreciation Gift**, with our compliments. Just go to the Web address at the bottom of this page.

God bless you as you seek a deeper walk with Him!

WHITAKER
HOUSE